ATLANTIC OCEAN

●osua

●La Vega   ●Samaná
         SAMANÁ BAY

REPUBLIC

San Santo Domingo La Romana
Cristóbal●
Bani ●
                                    PUERTO
                                    RICO

HISPANIC

Miles

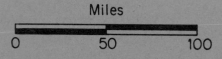
0   50   100

THE UNITED STATES AND
THE TRUJILLO REGIME

THE UNITED STATES
AND THE
TRUJILLO REGIME

by
G. Pope Atkins
and
Larman C. Wilson

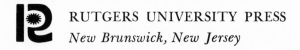
RUTGERS UNIVERSITY PRESS
New Brunswick, New Jersey

Copyright © 1972 by Rutgers University, the State University of
New Jersey
Library of Congress Catalog Card Number: 79-163956
ISBN: 0-8135-0714-6
Manufactured in the United States of America

TABLE OF CONTENTS

PREFACE

The Latin American policy of the United States has always suffered severe and extensive criticism. One perplexing and continually troublesome aspect of this policy has been the official United States attitude toward dictatorship and militarism in other American republics. Examining the problem in a specific political setting like the Dominican Republic may help answer some of the charges that have been made. For the record of official relations with the Dominican Republic's dictatorial regime of Rafael Leonidas Trujillo Molina from 1930 to 1961 provides excellent material for a case study of the inconsistencies of United States policy toward dictatorship in Latin America.

United States relations with Trujillo were significant and controversial for several reasons. First, though there was little doubt among Latin Americans and North Americans alike that Trujillo was an oppressive leader, the United States maintained friendly relations with him until the latter part of his rule. Second, the Caribbean region, as distinguished from the South American continent, traditionally has been of special concern to the United States. Third, United States policies toward Trujillo, because of the lengthy tenure of his dictatorship, spanned a dynamic period of United States action and policy-making in Latin America, during which time the Dominican Republic was an important object of policy. Finally, the Organization of American States, and the United States operating through it, devoted considerable attention to the problems of inter-American conflict in which the Dominican Republic was deeply involved.

Philosophically, we as authors could better satisfy our personal value preferences if we concluded that the United States has had a major role to play in furthering democracy in Latin America and has played it successfully. But evidence in the Trujillo case forces us to conclude that operationally, no matter how dedicated the United States might be, its influence on political development in Latin America is highly limited. The United States experience with the Trujillo dictatorship, in all its tragicomic aspects, illustrates the limits of politics: The United States is not omnipotent, not even in the Caribbean area.

To our knowledge, this is the first study to cover the entire span of United States relations with Trujillo from the specific viewpoint of his having been a dictator. We have consulted most of the published material on the subject, in Spanish as well as in English.

We wish to acknowledge the assistance and counsel of several of our former professors, present colleagues and friends. We are especially grateful for the advice and encouragement of Harold E. Davis. Appreciation is expressed for the aid and stimulation of Willard F. Barber, John J. Finan and Horace V. Harrison. Our thanks are also extended to Joan E. Hetzel and Catharine Ryan for aid in locating official documents of the Pan American Union and Organization of American States. The authors are solely responsible for any errors of fact or interpretation.

G.P.A.
L.C.W.

Annapolis, Maryland
Washington, D.C.
April, 1971

THE UNITED STATES AND
THE TRUJILLO REGIME

I A POLICY FRAMEWORK

A relevant and enlightening case study must be presented within a framework that makes comparison possible. The subject investigated in the present work is United States action with regard to the Trujillo dictatorship in the Dominican Republic. However, this study seeks to go beyond the unique features of the Trujillo case to help illuminate the general issue of United States policy toward other Latin American dictators and militarists.

The present chapter will establish a policy framework within which the particulars of the Dominican case can be described and analyzed. It will provide a perspective for comparing North American-Dominican relations with broad United States foreign (Latin American) policy and with actions taken toward other Latin American dictators during Trujillo's tenure. The analysis threaded throughout the entire study stems from general considerations raised in this chapter. And the lessons the Trujillo experience provides, with respect to the general policy problem, are noted in the topical context of each individual chapter.

1. POLICY ENDS AND MEANS

The fundamental issue of policy for evaluation is that of the republican form of government (representative democracy) as a goal of policy. In general terms, democracy is a system of government in which public opinion is periodically measured honestly and accurately, usually through elections, and with mechanisms making the political leadership responsible to the manifested opinion. It is usually characterized by civilian rule, political party competition, the right of dissent and a measure of individual freedom. Democracy in Latin America is illustrated by political processes in Chile, Costa Rica, Mexico and Uruguay. These four systems are mentioned as culturally more appropriate than the United States model.

Over the years there have been difficulties in arriving at satisfactory working propositions concerning how much the policymakers should be affected by the actual forms of government that exist in Latin America. Exponents of one position or another have had recourse primarily to abstract ideas and to different concepts of policy goals in Latin America. A great deal of the journalistic-writing and congressional-speaking on the subject has tested policy in ideological and unpolitical ways. Abstractions such as "democracy," "anti-dictatorship," "nonintervention" and "anti-communism" have been elevated to the status of absolute values exclusive of other considerations. Foreign policy cannot be reduced to such simplistic terms, for doctrinaire positions disregard the circumstances with which the real-world policy-maker must be concerned, overlooking the limits that exist for the foreign policy of a great power. The policy problems arising from questions of democracy and dictatorship must be viewed within the concept of the limits of politics.

Ends-means analysis provides a useful, realistic method for evaluating foreign policy. The construction of a rudimentary analytical model might be helpful in establishing an organizational and conceptual overview of the United States' Latin American policy which may be applied here. This particular mode of analysis has three basic components: policy objectives, policy instruments and techniques, and capability analysis.[1]

Objectives may be ultimate or proximate. Ultimate objectives ("the national interest") are expressed in both mythical and realistic terms. For example, the myth of America's democratic mission in the world has at times been expressed as an ultimate purpose of American foreign policy, to be achieved either by example, good works, assistance or even force, depending on the predilections of the policy-proponent. The rationalizing of decision-makers tends to be more realistic than idealistic, however. Most states seem to conclude that their ultimate national interests are self-preservation, security and well-being. Such goals are applicable to the Latin American policy of the United States, as well as to all of its foreign policy. In either case – mythical or realistic – ultimate objectives are expressed in highly generalized terms and consequently are of little help in evaluating policy action. Specific content is given to policy goals by translating the national interest into various ranges of proximate objectives designed to serve the ultimate ones.[2]

Proximate objectives act as springboards to the achievement of ultimate goals. In Latin America, the long-range proximate goals have remained relatively constant at least since the time of the war with Spain. Policy has been regularly preoccupied with three major long-range objectives: (1) to prevent and exclude as far as possible foreign influence and control, and to assure the independence and self-determination of Latin American states; (2) to insure United States leadership in the western hemisphere and domination of the Caribbean area; and (3) to maintain political stability in Latin America.[3] The United States has identified these semi-permanent ends with the ultimate promotion of its own self-preservation, security and well-being. Long-range goals in turn have been served by middle-range objectives. For example, both anti-fascism and anti-communism have been related to all three long-range goals. Variable short-range goals are also involved in the striving for various superior objectives. This idea of a hierarchy of related objectives will be used in several contexts throughout the study.

The kinds of policy selected to achieve the various objectives in Latin America have ranged the full gamut of options, both coercive and cooperative. They have included landing military forces and establishing military occupation, creating constabularies or national police forces in occupied countries, supervising elections, setting up customs receiverships, recognizing or refusing to recognize new governments, selling arms to Latin

American states or imposing arms embargoes on them, granting foreign assistance (economic, military, and technical), engaging in trade, and taking part in diplomatic negotiations and consultation. These techniques have been pursued by the United States unilaterally, bilaterally and multilaterally; they have received varied emphasis at different periods of time.

When considering the Latin American policy of the United States, distinction should be made between its official attitude toward the Caribbean region as a whole and that with respect to the more southerly continental area. Throughout the nineteenth century it was felt that the destiny of South America directly affected the security of the United States. This special concern became an intense one after the Spanish-American war greatly increased the Caribbean's strategic importance to the United States, especially when arrangements were being made for building an isthmian canal and securing its approaches. Today, with the harsher aspects of its Caribbean imperialism subdued, the United States is still willing to exert more effort and take more risks to secure its objectives there than on most of the South American continent.[4]

Promotion of democracy has been expressed as both a mythical ultimate goal and an operational proximate goal. The myth of America's democratic mission has been expressed as an ultimate purpose of American foreign policy in Latin America through the "western hemisphere idea" — the idea that all of the Americas stand in special relationship to each other, distinct from Europe, partly because of their moral superiority and superior (democratic) political institutions, in contrast to the evil, autocratic old world.[5] This nineteenth-century idea has lost much of its meaning in the twentieth, as relations with Europe and European institutions themselves have changed, and with the slowness of substantive progress in Latin America toward achieving the ideal of continental democracy. The idea does linger, however. President Kennedy's original Alliance for Progress proposal in March, 1961, referred to a "special relationship" between the American nations and posited democracy as a continuing goal of inter-American policies.

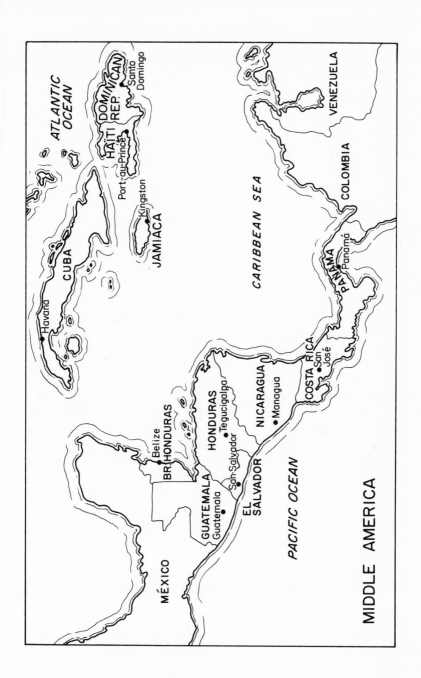

MIDDLE AMERICA

In the proximate range the promotion of democracy has received shifting emphasis, but when utilized it has in some manner been viewed as an instrumental objective aimed at achieving the three long-range proximate goals of excluding foreign influences, assuring United States leadership and promoting stability. The most recent example (the historical development of democracy as an instrument of policy will be investigated in all its aspects by this study) has been the desire to achieve democracy in Latin America under Alliance for Progress programs. It has been argued that offering a counter-ideology to communism will undercut its appeal (thus excluding "foreign" influences) and that only through a democratic system can real stability be achieved. This stability in turn will be a further deterrent to communist advances.

A state does not simply choose an objective and move toward it. Policy ends and means are inseparable; that is, successful foreign policy requires that each be calculated in terms of the other. Attempting to achieve objectives without selecting appropriate techniques results in frustration; whereas the application of policy means divorced from relevant objectives is futile at best.[6] In addition, ends-means calculations must take into consideration a state's ability to make effective use of its policy instruments and to hold realistic expectations of achieving its policy objectives. Among the most important elements of capability affecting the range of ends-means choices open to the policy-maker are the real-world settings with which the decision-maker must deal. A number of environmental and systemic factors affect a state's action.

With the obvious vast disparity in power between the United States and Latin America, it may seem ludicrous to be concerned with the capabilities of the United States vis-à-vis the other American states. Yet there is a great deal of evidence demonstrating that the United States is far from omnipotent in achieving its goals in Latin America, despite its relative preponderance of power. Formal systemic limitations on United States action are imposed by the regional inter-American organization and its laws and principles, today reflected in the Organization of American States (OAS). Informal situational factors impinging upon United States policy stem from the very state of Latin American societies: for example, the levels of social and economic development, types of political and administrative systems and their effectiveness, the resources available to Latin American states to achieve their own objectives, the actions Latin Americans themselves take in international politics.

The United States—its government and politically articulate populace—has always sympathized with democratic development in Latin America. Although the United States has maintained an ideological preference for democracy as well as formal commitments to democratic government through several inter-American conventions, conclusions concerning the appropriate magnitude and nature of United States support of democracy and the ways in which authoritarians should be dealt with require an ends-means analysis. Three related calculations should be made: first, the effectiveness of the techniques being utilized, including those associated with intervention and foreign aid; second, the extent of limitations impinging upon United States capabilities, especially those resulting from inter-American legal and organization principles and from Latin American political realities; and finally, the validity of democratic promotion as a means to achieve the goals of excluding extra-continental interference, insuring North American leadership and maintaining Latin American political stability.

2. INTERVENTION AND NONINTERVENTION

Part of the problem of analyzing policies of intervention and nonintervention is the lack of precision and agreement on the meaning of these concepts. The term "intervention" has been used to describe such a wide range of actions—in economic, diplomatic, legal, military, moral, political and strategic contexts—that it could refer to almost any form of influence a major power has over less powerful states, such as the United States vis-à-vis Latin America. In addition to these various techniques of intervention, the recipients of foreign aid sometimes consider it another form of intervention. Even negotiations and the absence of action have at times been considered to constitute intervention. Thus the term "intervention" has been broadened at times to include all forms of action and inaction that might influence another state's affairs. The members of the Organization of American States, despite many years debating the subject of intervention and using the term in inter-American conventions, including the OAS Charter, have yet to agree on a listing of the specific acts that constitute intervention.

However, to be useful as an analytic or operational concept, intervention must be defined more precisely than as a synonym for influence. While the purpose here is not to develop a doctrine or theory of intervention, a more precise interpretation is needed before the development of United States policies of intervention with reference to Latin American dictators can be traced. Professor John C. Dreier has formulated an acceptable definition that can be used to give some meaning to the concept. He states that intervention consists "of arbitrary acts of any government to impose its will on another by the use of force or other coercive measures that violate the sovereignty of the other state." According to Dreier, "the emphasis should be on the *arbitrary* and *coercive* character of the measures which are taken by *unilateral* decision." It is this intervention, he says, that has been outlawed by the inter-American community.[7]

Throughout the nineteenth century and into the twentieth, the United States dealt with the reality of Latin American dictatorship as opposed to the ideal of democracy. During this period Latin American political processes were often characterized by dictatorship, with civil liberties unrealized by large portions of Latin America's population for extended periods of time. Despite the widespread existence of dictatorship, many Latin Americans shared the North American view that constitutionalism and republicanism were desirable values and ideal goals. The initial United States response to this dictator-democracy ambivalence was the enunciation of broad policy outlines in the spirit of its recognition of the revolutionary French government in 1793. On that occasion Secretary of State Thomas Jefferson said: "We surely cannot deny to any nation that right whereon our own government is founded that everyone may govern itself under whatever form it pleases." [8] Later, as President, Jefferson applied this principle specifically to Latin America and set a policy that became a tradition.

The automatic recognition of frequent revolutions and dictatorial governments in Latin America did not consider political forms. When a new government came to power, by whatever means, recognition was accorded, in Charles Fenwick's words, "once it had demonstrated its *de facto* character and manifested its intention to abide by the rules of international law." [9] With few exceptions (such as Secretary Seward's opposition to monarchy in Mexico in 1865), this Jeffersonian tradition remained as United States policy until the Presidency of Woodrow Wilson.

Wilson came to office in 1913 and soon radically altered the traditional United States attitude toward Latin American political forms and processes. The Wilson credo reconciled the President's liberal political principles with his policy of frequent intervention in the Caribbean by considering the following: Political instability in Latin American (Caribbean) countries was a threat to North American interests; instability was caused by political immaturity; maturity was measurable by the extent of progress toward "constitutional democracy." As a policy matter Wilson assumed that democracy could be imposed by external pressure or force and that the United States, as the most politically mature (democratic) and powerful nation in the western hemisphere, was responsible for taking an active role in the political development of Latin America. [10]

Distinction should be made between Wilson's intervention by landing troops and that by using recognition power. Intervention by refusing to recognize governments that assumed power through unconstitutional means was motivated by a desire to restore constitutional government and to encourage representative democracy. Troop intervention was not employed to bring down dictatorships, nor was it immediately occasioned by any constitutional-democratic desire. However, once a military occupation was begun, local police forces were trained in the hope that they would protect future constitutional governments when the United States withdrew its forces. This practice occurred in three countries: the Dominican Republic, Haiti and Nicaragua. Two other practices developed by Wilson and utilized by his successors — Presidents Harding, Coolidge and Hoover — were the supervision of elections and arms control, either the sale of arms to the government or an embargo on arms. Supervised elections were held in Cuba, Panama, the Dominican Republic, Haiti and Nicaragua; arms sales or embargoes on arms involved Cuba, Mexico and Nicaragua.[11]

Beginning with the administration of Herbert Hoover, and given increased impetus by Franklin Roosevelt, United States policy remained oriented toward nonintervention, except for a brief episode involving Argentina at the end of World War II. Abandoning the nonrecognition of unconstitutional governments and adopting a policy of noninterference in the internal affairs of other governments meant dealing with dictators, militarists and other non-democrats on an equal, often partnership, basis, As a result, nonintervention came under attack, because it seemed to permit the continued existence of dictators and allowed despots to seize power.[12]

Initially, the United States rejected the criticism, restated its commitment to nonintervention and complained that those who deplored the effect of nonintervention on Latin American forms of government were the very ones who had deplored intervention in the first place. But toward the end of World War II, the United States briefly returned to the idea of intervention in behalf of democracy and in opposition to dictatorship.

The leading North American advocate of intervention was Assistant Secretary of State (for Inter-American Affairs) Spruille Braden. The basis of Braden's thinking was that the position and power of the United States vis-à-vis Latin America made it impossible to avoid some manner of intervention in their affairs. Intervention occurred through inaction as well as action. Braden said: "It is clear that, since we are bound to be engaged in continuous transactions and intimate contacts with our fellow American republics . . . whatever we refrain from saying and whatever we refrain from doing may constitute intervention no less than what we do or say." [13] Since intervention is inevitable, Braden concluded, the United States must use its formidable influence in a positive manner by assuming democratic leadership.

Braden was openly antagonistic toward the military regime of Argentina, of which the major figure was Juan D. Perón. With obvious reference to Argentina, Braden stated a corollary to his pro-democratic position when he said that the United States could not be true to its democratic traditions and principles, nor to its war dead, if "it did not point the finger of accusation at those governments that still serve the ideology of National Socialism." [14] In February, 1946, two weeks before a presidential election in Argentina, the United States Department of State attempted to influence the Argentine electorate against Colonel Perón by issuing the famous "Blue Book." [15] Based on captured German foreign office documents, it described in detail Argentina's wartime collaboration with the Axis powers. Perón was the main target, and his active role in forming Argentina's pro-fascist policy was emphasized, as well as his totalitarian practices and use of electoral intimidation. Perón subsequently made United States intervention a primary campaign issue and easily won the presidency.

The Argentine experience (and the fate of the Larreta proposal for collective pro-democratic intervention, to be discussed) represented a turning point in United States policy. The United States ceased advocating intervention in the name of democracy. Spruille Braden's resignation as Assistant Secretary of State in June, 1947, marked a return to strict nonintervention. The United States did not abandon interest in the development of Latin American democracy, however. In 1948 the United States government announced that it had "made known to a number of other governments of the American republics its growing concern with respect to the overthrow of popularly elected governments by military forces," and had assured them that "the United States wishes to make every legitimate effort to encourage democratic and constitutional procedures." However, nonrecognition was not considered a "suitable approach" to the problem.[16] A few months later Secretary of State Dean Acheson said that the United States was opposed to intervention, but it was not content with "blind adherence to the status quo," and recognition "need not necessarily be understood as a forerunner of a policy of intimate cooperation with the country concerned."[17]

In May, 1950, Assistant Secretary of State Edward Miller explained that maintaining diplomatic relations with nondemocratic regimes was not determined by approval of the form of government, but by whether a government could maintain civil order and also respect its international obligations. "Diplomatic recognition of a government," said Miller, "should not be used as a moral force to bring about internal reform."[18] It seemed that traditional Jeffersonian principles again formed the basis for United States recognition policy in Latin America.

Despite negative responses to proposals and actions employing anti-dictator intervention, the Latin American consensus favoring nonintervention over any other principle, and the lack of significant support for nonrecognition as an instrument for the defense of democracy, many Latin Americans expressed discontent with United States policy, sometimes in a violent manner. Critics, both Latin and North American, were outspoken toward postwar United States policies with regard to Latin American dictators. The violent treatment of then-Vice-President and Mrs. Nixon in Venezuela and Peru during a 1958 "good will" tour of South America in part reflected dissatisfaction with United States attitudes toward Latin American dictators. Nevertheless, the Eisenhower administration continued to emphasize the principle of nonintervention over all others, insistent that intervention to overthrow oppressive regimes would result in an aftermath of disorder and tension that would provide Communists with political opportunities.

On March 13, 1961, a short time after his inauguration, President Kennedy, who had been critical of the Eisenhower administration's policies toward Latin American dictators, formally proposed the Alliance for Progress. It contained a ten-year plan for economic, social and political development in Latin America. In August, 1961, the American Ministers of Economic Affairs (with the exception of Cuba) met in Punta del Este, Uruguay, and formalized the Alliance for Progress by enacting an inter-American document known as "The Charter of Punta del Este." The first of the Alliance's twelve stated goals was "to improve and strengthen democratic institutions through application of the principle of self-determination by the people." [19]

The Alliance for Progress immediately faced serious problems. From 1961 through 1963 military coups overthrew constitutionally elected governments in seven Latin American countries, which challenged the ideological (democratic) commitment and assumptions of the Alliance. The general pattern of response by the United States was to refuse recognition of the new governments, suspend diplomatic relations and terminate economic and military assistance. Several Latin American governments supported the United States, but most were reluctant to agree to any meetings of consultation, invoking the inter-American tradition of noninterference in the internal affairs of others. Latin Americans were criticized in the North American press for damning the United States when it tolerated dictatorships but refusing to cooperate in opposing them despite their espousal of the democratic goals of the Alliance for Progress. The United States eventually resumed diplomatic contacts and restored most aid programs.

President Johnson did not oppose dictators or promote democracy through intervention. Thomas C. Mann, Assistant Secretary of State for Inter-American Affairs, Alliance for Progress Coordinator, and Special Assistant to the President, expressed the administration's position in a speech delivered in June, 1964. Mann reaffirmed the American commitment to and preference for representative democracy and human rights. However, he noted the lack of support for proposals of collective action and rejected any form of unilateral intervention by the United States. He warned against the "doctrinaire straitjacket of automatic application of sanctions to every unconstitutional regime which arises in this hemisphere" and is in effect "attempting to dictate internal developments in other countries." In order to help democratic realization, Mann suggested continuous encouragement through diplomatic discussions and support for collective action in "those cases where repression, tyranny, and brutality outrage the conscience of mankind." In any event, he said, government overthrows must be appraised individually in terms of specific circumstances.[20]

The Johnson administration subsequently accepted military coups in several Latin American states including Argentina, Brazil, Peru and Panama. At this writing, President Nixon has shown no inclination to alter the pragmatic policies toward military governments and intervention that were established in the latter part of the Kennedy Presidency and continued by Lyndon Johnson.

3. NONINTERVENTION, DEMOCRACY AND THE INTER-AMERICAN SYSTEM

An important situational factor affecting United States policy is inter-American law, which has posited the principle of nonintervention as the basis for inter-American relations. In addition to the commitment to nonintervention, the American states have committed themselves to the promotion of representative democracy and the protection of human rights. Consequently, a dilemma has arisen for both the United States and the inter-American community directly relating to the problem of dictators: How can representative democracy be promoted and non-democratic regimes be opposed without violating the nonintervention principle?

Latin Americans were strongly critical of what they regarded as interventionist techniques utilized by the United States during the first third of the twentieth century. They considered United States policies an interference in their domestic affairs and a violation of their sovereign rights. Using the International Conferences of American States as a forum to attack intervention as unjust and illegal, these states attempted to persuade the United States to accept nonintervention as the legal corollary of sovereignty and to renounce its right to intervene. By stressing the principles of international law and organization, Latin American governments managed to bring a major controversy concerning the concepts of intervention and nonintervention to the forefront.

The ensuing debate reflected differing views as to what acts constituted intervention as well as the need for and meaning of nonintervention. Whereas the Latin American approach was a broad one (including diplomatic, economic and military actions), the United States had a narrow view limited to military intervention. The Latin American quest finally succeeded at the outset of the Good Neighbor Policy when, at the Seventh International Conference of the American States in 1933, the United States accepted the nonintervention concept. Since then nonintervention has been reaffirmed at subsequent conferences and incorporated into treaties, from the Additional Protocol of Non-Intervention adopted at the special Inter-American Conference for the Maintenance of Peace in 1936, to the Charter of the OAS (Articles 15 and 17) adopted by the Ninth International Conference in 1948. This process has established nonintervention as the *sine qua non* of the inter-American system.

Coincidental with the acceptance of nonintervention has been the hemisphere's commitment to representative democracy and the protection of human rights, which has also been expressed at inter-American conferences (both regular and special) and regularly reaffirmed. Consequently, two principles have come into conflict for the United States as it attempts to promote democracy in order to prevent foreign influence and maintain stability, while being legally and morally limited to noninterventionist actions. Although Article 19 of the OAS Charter provides for collective intervention — a possible way out of this dilemma — most Latin American republics are unwilling to invoke it or to compromise the rule of nonintervention in any way. For them nonintervention transcends democratic development; the majority view nonintervention as a legal obligation and their commitment to democracy as a moral obligation.

This Latin preoccupation with nonintervention directed principally at the United States has not deterred North American governments from intervening in Latin America when they felt that their own national security was involved. The United States is considered to have departed from the nonintervention principle in Argentina in 1945–1946. Guatemala in 1954, Cuba in 1961 and the Dominican Republic in 1965. But the Latin American consensus has largely, if not totally, deterred both the United States and the inter-American community from adopting anti-dictatorial policies.

In late 1945 and early 1946, while the United States was diligently applying a unilateral anti-dictator policy in Argentina, the American states considered a closely related multilateral intervention proposal. The Uruguayan foreign minister, Dr. Eduardo Rodríguez Larreta, appealed for collective (multilateral) intervention to oppose dictators and promote democracy and human rights.* Dr. Larreta's plan was implicitly directed against fascist-inclined Argentina, small Uruguay's powerful neighbor, but it had broad implications for inter-American relations. Dr. Larreta argued the parallelism between peace and democracy: "Peace is safe only where democratic principles of government prevail." He proposed that the inter-American obligation to promote democracy and human rights should transcend the principle of nonintervention: "In the case of [the violation of the basic rights of man] in any American republic, the community of nations should take collective multilateral action to restore full democracy there." [21]

The United States quickly and fully endorsed the proposal,

---

* His proposal is known in English as the Larreta Doctrine.

which was supported with some reservation by six Latin American governments. The remainder either rejected the Larreta note outright or made such serious qualifications as to be tantamount to rejection.

The Latin American governments that opposed the Larreta proposal were unwilling to permit any modification of the nonintervention principle, which they seemed to view as absolute. They regarded nonintervention as the bulwark of their defense against the United States; any weakening of it would weaken their position *vis-à-vis* the United States.

Several specific objections were made against collective intervention to promote democracy and protect human rights. First, such a relative term as "democracy" was too difficult to define in view of the disparity between its theory and practice. Second, there was no automatic or direct relationship between democracy and peace. Finally, realizing the United States preponderance of power, collective action could never be undertaken by Latin American states against the United States; it could only be taken against a Latin American state on the initiative of the United States. This view prevailed despite the American community's awareness that absolute nonintervention tended to insulate oppressive governments from community action.

After World War II inter-American judicial procedures were applied on a variety of occasions when ideological differences contributed to conflicts between dictatorial and "democratic" countries in the Caribbean. Edgar S. Furniss noted in 1950 that the problem of the OAS was that two fundamental inter-American principles had been put into opposition and the organization had to "measure the doctrine of non-intervention against the doctrine of democratic development." [22] The OAS paid special homage to the principle of nonintervention. At its meeting on April 8, 1950, the OAS Council resolved, among other things, the following:

[Considering] that both the principle of representative democracy and that of non-intervention are established in many inter-American pronouncements, and that both are basic principles of harmonious relations among the countries of America; and that there exists some confusion of ideas as to the means of harmonizing the effective execution and application of the basic principle of non-intervention and that of the exercise of democracy; [be it resolved] to reaffirm the principles of representative democracy but to declare that the aforementioned principles do not in any way and under any concept authorize any governments to violate inter-American commitments relative to the principles of non-intervention.[23]

In one case the OAS appeared to serve as an "anti-dictatorial alliance." [24] This involved the response of the OAS at the Sixth Meeting of Foreign Ministers (San José, Costa Rica) in August, 1960, to the Trujillo government's attempt to assassinate President Rómulo Betancourt of Venezuela. The Venezuelan government responded to the June assassination attempt by appealing to the OAS Council under Article 6 of the Rio Treaty. The council acted as the provisional Organ of Consultation and appointed an investigating committee. When the committee's subsequent report to the council established the Trujillo government's complicity in the plot,[25] the Sixth Meeting of Ministers moved to consider what action should be taken. At the meeting the Dominican government was condemned, and sanctions were voted for breaking diplomatic relations and imposing an arms embargo (the scope of the sanctions was later broadened).

This handling of the Dominican action was important for a number of reasons. First, contrary to past conferences and meetings, the debate did not revolve around the usual preoccupation with nonintervention. Why? Because the Trujillo regime was almost universally detested in Latin America, and the Dominican government itself, by its acts, had violated the non-intervention principle and was guilty of aggression. However, there was no desire to intervene directly to promote democracy and protect human rights, which had also been violated. In the debate United States Secretary of State Christian A. Herter opposed the application of sanctions and argued for OAS sponsorship of free elections. Since the end of the Trujillo regime in 1961, however, no similar "anti-dictatorial alliances" have been formed.

4. MUTUAL SECURITY

Foreign aid programs, especially military, may be regarded as interventionist, because they may potentially affect the recipient's internal affairs either by altering social structures or by helping to preserve the status quo. Whether constituting intervention or not in a conceptual sense, such aid is important and controversial enough to deserve special attention. The subject of military aid lies in the area of mutual security, which became a problem with the development of hemispheric defense and the approach of World War II. During the decades since 1940, the United States has been especially interested in Latin American stability and in maintaining the status quo. After World War II, within the specific context of global Cold War, this interest was reenforced by a preoccupation with Europe as evidenced by the Marshall Plan and the North Atlantic Treaty Organization. Arthur P. Whitaker pointed out then that the United States was eager to consolidate western hemispheric military cooperation in terms of worldwide Cold War concerns, even if dictatorial governments had to be included.[26]

Both the Truman and Eisenhower administrations signed mutual defense assistance pacts with several Latin American governments, including dictatorial and military regimes. In each case the granting of aid was to be determined by its value in promoting mutual security rather than by the political form of its recipient. Continuance of this policy was justified in 1958 by Dr. Milton Eisenhower, who reported to his brother, the President, that although the United States should maintain strictly formal relations with dictators and reaffirm its belief in democracy, it should not withdraw economic and military programs from countries governed by dictators. Dr. Eisenhower said that the "reasoning which caused one to feel that we should do so would lead logically to the conclusion that throughout the world we should cease cooperating with any nation in which democracy is not complete. Patently, such a policy would paralyze the conduct of all foreign relations." [27]

The major dimensions of the controversy over security and military aid as they relate to democratic government have developed essentially into two points of view. First, a number of critics of United States military assistance programs in Latin America see a causal relationship between military aid and Latin American militarism in which the former impedes democracy and development, both economic and political. As a result, these critics accept the existence of a positive correlation between military assistance and the increase in or maintenance of Latin American militarism, and they hold the United States responsible. Some supporters of the military assistance-militarism link are Edwin Lieuwen,[28] John Duncan Powell,[29] Jesus Silva Herzog,[30] Senator J. W. Fulbright and Wayne Morse.

Other observers view the military as an important part of the political-social structure and believe it plays a necessary role in the process of "modernization," which facilitates development and change. This group, therefore, does not accept the military assistance-militarism causal relationship. Some advocates of military assistance as a potential contributor to the modernization process are Charles Wolf,[31] Edward B. Glick,[32] Gino Germani and Kalman Silvert,[33] John J. Johnson [34] and Theodore Wyckoff.[35]

The official United States position moved to a version of the second point of view in 1963 during the last days of the Kennedy administration and has remained there to the present. President Kennedy's attitude toward military takeovers was illustrated by his response to a series of seven coups in 1962 and 1963. Consistent with the anti-dictator thrust of the Alliance for Progress, the pattern of American response to *golpes* by the military in Argentina, Peru, Guatemala and Honduras was official censure followed by a severing of diplomatic relations and the suspension of aid. With the Ecuadorian coup in 1963, hints of disillusionment about the effectiveness of such policies were discernible. The Ecuadorian military junta was recognized shortly after coming to power, and the Kennedy policies began to take a pragmatic turn, appearing to accommodate military governments. In a statement to the *New York Herald Tribune* published on October 6, 1963, Assistant Secretary of State for Inter-American Affairs Edward M. Martin condemned the coups but observed that some military regimes had exhibited able and responsible leadership (the Ecuadorian junta was mentioned favorably).

After the assassination of President Kennedy in November, 1963, and the succession of Vice-President Johnson, the approach to military governments continued to reflect a belief in the disutility of the former policy and the need for "realism" as well as an optimistic attitude toward the military role in economic development and social reform. It was also argued that the United States, via its military assistance programs, must work with existing military establishments even if they are corrupt, inefficient and unprofessional,[36] and try to transform them over a long period of time through training. This point of view, supported by many members of United States military missions, is illustrated by the statement of General Robert W. Porter, Commander of the Southern Command, before the House Foreign Affairs Committee on April 6, 1966:

> The primary objective of overall U.S. national policy in Latin America is to assist the economic and social development of the individual countries. . . . In pursuit of this objective, the U.S. . . . instituted the Alliance for Progress. The U.S. military programs in Latin America must . . . contribute to the success of the Alliance for Progress. It cannot be questioned that economic and social development has a priority; but many fail to recognize the corollary that such development is not attainable in the absence of law

and order . . . and [that] political stability [is] guaranteed
by military and other security forces.[37]

The Johnson administration resumed relations with the
Dominican Republic after the military coup in 1963, accepted
the overthrow by the Brazilian military of President Goulart in
April, 1964, and did not protest the military takeover in Argentina in June, 1966. The United States' primary concern, following a coup in Peru in October, 1968, was not the creation of a
military government there but rather its nationalization policies.

The Nixon administration, as evidenced by the 1969 report
on Latin America made by Governor Nelson Rockefeller of
New York, clearly accepts the idea of a "new military." Among
other things Rockefeller said:

> In short, a new type of military man is coming to the fore
> and often becoming a major force for constructive social
> change in the American republics. Motivated by increasing
> impatience with corruption, inefficiency and a stagnant
> political order, the new military man is prepared to adapt
> his authoritarian tradition to the goals of social and eco-
> nomic progress.[38]

This debate concerning the role of foreign assistance as a policy
instrument raises the larger question of how receptive developing Latin American societies are to foreign (external) attempts
to direct the outcome of the development process.

5. IS DEMOCRACY EXPORTABLE?

A final factor to be considered is the limitation to achieve
stated goals imposed upon United States capabilities by the very
nature of Latin American societies and the processes of political
development. The problem revolves around the extent to which
democracy is exportable from one society to another. No matter
how good the intentions of the "exporter" and the vigor of the

methods employed, the absorptive capacity of the "receiver" is an almost fixed factor which can only be changed slowly. Thus the policies of the state that is attempting to promote democracy in another are profoundly limited. The concern here is with ideas of political development in an "underdeveloped" or "developing" setting in most Latin American states.

The very process of economic, social and political development, as illustrated by policy experience, imposes limitations on United States capability to influence development in a direction that seems desirable. Although the proximity and power of the United States influence the affairs of the other American states, the United States itself is not all-powerful.

One integral component of Latin American political systems is the continuing reality of authoritarianism. This phenomenon has many aspects, ranging from the predominance of the executive branch in republican experiments to military dictatorship and occasional totalitarianism. If the United States is to operate successfully and constructively in Latin America, it must do so in the Latin American context. Militarism and dictatorship are phenomena to be understood in the total structure of society. They result from the same conditions that impede social and political achievement but are not major impediments themselves. The failures and debilities of political and social systems that have been the scourge of democracy and reform have also given militarists and dictators their chance. Although the three facets of development are interrelated (economic, political and social) and must proceed together, the real base of each is political.[39] This is the base that is most relevant to democracy, is most often atrophied by dictators and is the most difficult to foster as an instrument of foreign policy.

The United States has had enough experience attempting to export democracy to Latin America to enable tentative conclusions to be drawn concerning the effectiveness of such action. Despite energetic endeavors on behalf of democratic government, and later attempts to cope with a dynamically changing Latin America (emphasizing economic and social reform within a democratic framework), the record of results is poor. The failure of overt United States attempts to foster representative democracy in Latin America suggests that (1) it cannot be imposed by external force nor achieved by the mere formality of holding elections; (2) the absence of dictatorship does not in itself insure democratic progress; and (3) representative democracy requires an indigenous life so it can evolve and develop according to the social configuration of the nation.

A related problem has been the apparent conflict between the policy goals of democratic development in Latin America and the maintenance of political stability and continued prevention of foreign control. Through most of the period of inter-American relations, much of Latin America — especially the Caribbean — has been politically unstable. The goal of stability has often been achieved by dictatorial regimes with which the United States maintained regular relations. To the United States, reluctant to reform its policies toward these regimes, stability has meant the status quo, no matter how oppressive. Another policy view, implemented less often than that of tolerating non-democratic regimes, suggests that ultimate stability cannot be achieved by dictators, but only through open democratic societies and free elections in which all political groups have equal opportunity. This view, inherited from Woodrow Wilson's Latin American policy, provides part of the rationale of the Alliance for Progress as originally conceived. Questions raised by the apparent contradictions in the simultaneous goals of stability and democracy must be considered. The United States has been heavily criticized for allegedly sacrificing representative government in favor of dictators and other non-democratic elements because they seemed to assure the economic and political stability that would prevent foreign influence.

6. SOME QUESTIONS CONCERNING THE TRUJILLO CASE

In order to shed light on the broader problems of policy, and in terms of the general considerations raised in this chapter, the following chapters will consider a number of specific questions about United States-Dominican relations during the Trujillo era. Did United States military intervention and occupation of the Dominican Republic from 1916 to 1924 pave the way for Trujillo's dictatorship? Should the United States have refused to recognize the Trujillo government after it came to power via revolution against a constitutional government? Should the United States have severed diplomatic relations after certain of Trujillo's oppressive actions, such as the massacre of Haitian peasants in 1937 or the disappearance of Jesús Galíndez in 1956, or because of the general wielding of tyrannical power in the Dominican Republic?

Further, should the United States have pressured Trujillo to move toward some form of representative government in the 1930's while he was consolidating his power? Did the principle and practice of nonintervention permit the existence of Trujillo and his exemption from accountability in the hemisphere for thirty years, and should the nonintervention concept have been subordinated in some way to the ideal of representative democracy? Did the United States cynically prefer Trujillo to more democratic governments because, as a crass opportunist, he supported the United States and its major foreign policies until the late 1950's? Did United States military aid to the Dominican Republic during and after World War II tend to buttress his regime? Was the United States finally willing to turn against Trujillo, in 1960 and 1961, not out of opposition to dictatorial governments and a preference for democracy, but because of fear that communism would follow in the dictator's path? These are the questions to be answered concerning relations between the United States and the Dominican Republic during the era of Trujillo.

II INTERVENTION AND THE RISE OF TRUJILLO: UNITED STATES–DOMINICAN RELATIONS, 1904–1930

This chapter is designed to provide background for the treatment of post-1930 United States policies, which follow in subsequent chapters. It will consider allegations that the United States was responsible for the rise of Trujillo in the 1920's until he became president of the Dominican Republic in 1930.

1. PRELUDE TO THE ERA OF TRUJILLO

General Caribbean policies of the United States during the first quarter of the twentieth century developed as part of the aftermath of the Spanish-American War and the acquisition of canal rights in Panama. The major national security objectives of the United States in the Caribbean were the maintenance of political stability and the prevention of further foreign (European) influence and control.[1] Intervention became the almost inevitable culmination of these policies.

The United States intervened in six Caribbean countries, including the Dominican Republic, in pursuit of its post-Spanish-American War policies in the Caribbean area. Intervention was justified by the Roosevelt Corollary to the Monroe Doctrine, which was articulated by President Theodore Roosevelt in 1904 with reference to the Dominican political and financial situation. The rationale of the corollary was that to keep European powers out of the western hemisphere (especially the Caribbean area), the United States must correct the fiscal irresponsibility of its neighbors and maintain political order through the exercise of an international police power. According to this theory, European governments would have no legal basis to intervene if the United States assumed the task of bringing about Caribbean fiscal responsibility and political stability; that is, the United States should intervene when necessary in the other American republics in order to prevent European intervention.

One of the first instances of the application of the Roosevelt Corollary was the 1905 agreement to establish a customs receivership in the Dominican Republic. Under this form of fiscal intervention, the United States administered Dominican international finances, an action prompted by Dominican internal disorder and international financial arrears. The Dominican government's default on bonds, among other unmet obligations, nearly resulted in intervention by European powers demanding payment and threatening to use force. In order to forestall such interference, the Dominican Republic was obliged to entrust the collection of customs duties, which constituted the major source of its revenue, to United States officials. President Theodore Roosevelt maintained the customs receivership for two years as a *modus vivendi* based upon an executive agreement dated January 20, 1905.[2] The United States Senate consented to this agreement as a treaty in 1907.[3] Under terms of the Dominican Customs Treaty, a general settlement was reached with creditors; debts were paid with a loan from the United States, and the Dominican Republic's financial condition improved considerably.[4]

President Wilson took office in 1913 and assumed the direction of Caribbean and Latin American policies. The new Chief Executive believed that Caribbean political instability, dangerous to North American security, was caused by lack of progress toward "constitutional democracy." As a policy matter for the United States, Wilson assumed that democracy could be imposed by applying external pressure. Thus the United States, as the most democratic and powerful nation in the western hemisphere, had the responsibility, even the moral duty, to foster democracy in Latin America, by force if need be. Wilson applied this conviction in his relations with the Dominican Republic.

Intermittent Dominican political chaos and revolution jeopardized the collection of customs by the United States. The chaos was attributable primarily to a struggle between the two leading political groups: the *horacistas,* supporters of General Horacio Vásquez, and the *jimenistas,* followers of Don Juan Isidro Jiménez. In the wake of receivership difficulties, United States-sponsored and supervised elections were held in October, 1914. Jiménez was elected. However, the *jimenistas* and *horacistas* could not work together, and armed strife ensued. As a result, President Wilson, "with the greatest reluctance," [5] accepted Secretary of State Robert Lansing's recommendation of military intervention.[6] This decision resulted in the initial landing of United States Marines on May 5, 1916, the subsequent establishment of a military government, and a military occupation that lasted until September 18, 1924. It should be noted that troop interventions were not immediately occasioned by the desire to restore constitutional government, but rather to stabilize a chaotic political situation. However, once military occupation was begun, local police and military forces were trained by the United States in the hope that they would support and protect future constitutional governments when the foreign troops were withdrawn. United States-supervised elections also had the goal of promoting constitutional government in the Dominican Republic.

In November, 1916, the United States proclaimed its occupation and the creation of a military government.[7] Since no Dominican cabinet members and few other government officials would serve in or even cooperate with the military government, all governmental positions except the Supreme Court were filled by United States officers. This made the occupation government almost completely foreign, despite which the "essentially judicial mind" of Captain Harry S. Knapp, USN, the first military governor, tempered the impact of foreign control and inspired a

Dominican "spirit of tolerance" toward the military officials.[8] This tolerance changed rapidly to bitterness and resentment when Knapp was superseded in 1919 by Rear Admiral Thomas Snowden, who, according to Sumner Welles, established a foreign military dictatorship that boasted complete control and suppression.[9] Fortunately, the last two military governors — Rear Admiral Samuel S. Robison and General Harry Lee, USMC — had a more enlightened attitude and were more cooperative with Dominican nationals.

Two related goals of the military government were the paci-

Czama Fortress, Santo Domingo City, U.S. Marine Corps Regimental Headquarters during the first military occupation (1916–1924), later one of Trujillo's prisons and torture chambers. *Defense Dept. Photo (Marine Corps)*

fication of the country (which meant disarming the populace) and the establishment of a professional, apolitical National Guard. The pacification program proceeded well except in certain outlying areas where banditry was a continuing problem. One writer maintains that the country was not "truly pacified" until May, 1922.[10] Because of the relative inefficiency of the newly formed constabulary, especially during the first few years, the Marines assumed responsibility for combating the bandits. The military authorities perhaps exaggerated the threat of banditry in order to justify greater restrictions on the populace. This seems to be indicated by the limited number of combat casualties during a period of over eight years: five officers and ten others killed, and five officers and fifty others wounded.[11]

Disarming the populace was a difficult undertaking, especially in a country where to possess and carry firearms was not only common but also a status symbol. Nevertheless, a reported

U.S. Marines searching for civilian arms during the first military occupation. *Defense Dept. Photo (Marine Corps)*

53,000 firearms were collected during the first eighteen months of the occupation.[12] Forcible searches and seizures had to be employed until the Dominican Republic was effectively disarmed.

During the occupation period, Dominican armed forces were reorganized and trained by United States Marines in the hope that they would maintain order and protect constitutional government after the United States withdrew. In 1917 the military government began to organize a national constabulary. Progress was slow because of disagreements over the nature of the proposed constabulary among North American military authorities, over the nature of Dominican society itself and over the previous status of the Dominican armed forces. For example, Captain Knapp favored the creation of a police force as opposed to an army because he feared the latter would become the tool of future dictators; whereas Colonel Joseph H. Pendleton, Commander of the United States Marine Forces, favored the formation of an army and opposed a police force.[13]

The previous organization of the Dominican military establishment and the nature of Dominican society posed major problems. Control over the armed forces had been decentralized, divided between the president of the republic and the provincial governors. The president had been responsible for financial support of the armed services, while the governors had been commanders of the military forces in their districts as well as chiefs of the rural (provincial) police. The provincial governors had a vested interest in civil strife, for the more disorders in their provinces, the more public funds they were entitled to receive from the national government, and the more power they had to force men into military ranks for a period of four years.[14] The governors, in effect, had their own private armies, which could be utilized to support their respective political positions and maneuverings. Therefore, the provincial governors, allied with the landholding elite, opposed the establishment of a truly national police force because they feared it would undermine their power. In general, the ruling class violently opposed the United States-created constabulary and refused to permit their sons to become officers in it.

Because of this opposition, Dominican officers were drawn from the lower middle class or from the ranks—the ranks comprising the bottom strata of Dominican society. In addition, the United States Congress passed a law permitting Marines to accept appointments as constabulary officers. However, few Marine officers could be spared during the period of World War I, and few were interested in such appointments, since the Navy Department was reluctant to pay extra compensation such as was being paid in Haiti.[15] As a result, most of the Marine-supplied constabulary officers came from the ranks of the United States Marine Corps (sergeants and corporals).[16] To help solve the officer shortage and to provide professional training for Dominican nationals, the Haina Military Academy was established in the Dominican Republic in August, 1921.

No serious problem existed in recruiting Dominican enlisted men because of the greatly improved pay and fringe benefits (such as free board, bunk and medical care). Most of the recruits were illiterate, and many were former bandits and criminals. The constabulary, which had an authorized strength of 1,234 men, ranged in size from 729 officers and men in late 1917 to 590 in late 1921.[17]

By the summer of 1921 the constabulary was effectively organized along United States Marine Corps lines. (In June, 1921, its name was changed to the *Policía Nacional Dominicana*.) Now Dominicans of society's lower strata—in many cases motivated by ruling-class antipathy toward them and the *Policía Nacional* as well—could join, move up through the ranks, attend the Haina Military Academy and climb the economic and social ladder in a class-conscious, stratified society.

United States intervention and occupation had never been popular in either the Dominican Republic or the United States, and its unpopularity throughout the western hemisphere increased with passing time.[18] When Dominican intervention became an issue in the United States Presidential election of 1920, the State Department announced that the United States would withdraw. In the summer of 1921 Sumner Welles was appointed United States Commissioner to Santo Domingo to negotiate agreements for holding national elections and withdrawing the Marines. Because of persistent maneuvering among the various Dominican political groups, the elections were postponed, and a provisional government was organized in October, 1922. Considerable publicity, much of it adverse, was given the military government in both the Dominican Republic and Haiti, from the summer of 1921 to March, 1922, when the United States Senate appointed a special committee to hold hearings on the military occupations.[19]

National elections were finally held in March, 1924, directed and supervised by the United States. General Vásquez, elected to the presidency over Francisco Peynado, was inaugurated in July. A new treaty with the United States, signed in 1924, outlined the terms of the troop withdrawal and, in effect, continued the convention of 1907 with regard to the Customs Receivership.[20] The last Marine left the Dominican Republic on September 18, 1924. For the first time in eight years and four months, no United States occupation forces remained in the Dominican Republic.

The United States left the Dominican Republic with a newly elected government, a reasonably good financial position (the public debt had been reduced from RD$12 million to RD$3.5 million *) and internal stability. Considerable material progress had been made since 1916 in public school construction and teacher training, public health and sanitation, public administration, communication and roads. However, little political development accompanied the significant economic achievements. This became evident in subsequent activities of the *Policía Nacional Dominicana*, which the United States presumably had left to the new government to administer. Instead, the modern,

---

* There is disagreement about the accuracy of these official (U.S.) figures, particularly the reduction.

unified force that had been created continued to grow—on its own. By 1924, due to its own centralized power and the disarming of the Dominican populace, the constabulary had a monopoly over arms and munitions. However, as Marvin Goldwert has said:

> Viewed in retrospect, the constabulary policy represented a tragic over-simplification of the causes of Latin American instability and chronic militarism. The broad chasm between democratic forms and political and socioeconomic realities in those nations doomed the idea of the nonpartisan constabulary from the outset.[21]

The constabulary force caused a shift in the locus of political power, especially when Trujillo gained control.

2. THE RISE OF TRUJILLO AND THE REVOLUTION OF 1930

Objective analysis of Trujillo's rise to and maintenance of power, of the nature of his dictatorship and of the techniques he employed, is made difficult by the extremes of praise and condemnation showered upon him after 1930. Even when the narratives of his friends and enemies are discounted because of bias, they still resemble the fantasies of fiction more than the facts of history.[22]

Trujillo's career is a leading example of the social mobility offered by commissioned service in the constabulary. He was born in 1891 in the village of San Cristóbal, near Santo Domingo city. During the period of United States military occupation he began his rise to power. He entered the Haina Military Academy as a second lieutenant in August, 1921, and graduated in December, thereby confirming his rank. He was a major by the time United States forces withdrew in 1924. Later that year, after the Marine evacuation, he became a lieutenant colonel. Under President Vásquez he continued to receive rapid promotion and in 1928 became chief of staff and commander of the armed forces.[23]

President Vásquez had been elected to a four-year term in 1924, after which he was ineligible to succeed himself. In 1927, however, Vásquez called a constitutional convention that supported his ambition by extending his term of office to 1930 through constitutional amendment. He later announced his intention to be a candidate in the presidential elections scheduled for May 15, 1930, contrary to constitutional provision.

The opposition was disgruntled by the president's maneuverings, and on February 23, 1930, just three months before the elections, an insurgent movement against the seventy-year-old chief executive broke out in the northern city of Santiago. Little more than a week after the uprising had been initiated, the insurgents succeeded in overthrowing Vásquez. Rafael Estrella Ureña, the young lawyer who led the uprising, was named to act as provisional president pending the regularly scheduled elections. The United States Legation in Santo Domingo mediated negotiations between the government and the revolutionaries, and through its efforts an armistice was arranged and a settlement reached between the Vásquez and Estrella forces.[24]

After the Vásquez government was overthrown, the United States had to make a policy decision as to whether to recognize governments established by revolution. The official trend of thought was set early in the affair. Although the revolutionary methods that led to the appointment of Estrella Ureña as provisional president were "deplored" by and "displeasing" to the United States minister, Charles B. Curtis, and although he felt that an undesirable precedent was being established, he did not object openly to the arrangement, partly because the revolutionaries had complied with all legal constitutional provisions. The State Department concurred with Curtis' thinking and informed the legation that the United States would "continue to maintain normal friendly diplomatic relations with Señor Estrella Ureña's government." [25]

History would prove that General Trujillo's activities had been largely responsible for the success of the revolution, for he had been commander-in-chief of the national army during the planning and execution phases. Although Trujillo conspired with

Trujillo as General Commandant of the National Police, March 30, 1930, at about the time of the insurgent movement against Dominican President Vásquez. *Defense Dept. Photo* (*Marine Corps*)

the revolutionaries, he succeeded in concealing his political alignment from all outsiders until the fall of the Vásquez government had been assured. During the revolution the United States minister had been informed by General Trujillo that he and the army were loyal to President Vásquez. Later Trujillo's true role became clear. Minister Curtis reported that Trujillo had repeatedly betrayed the Vásquez government, had shipped arms to the revolutionaries in Santiago and had been in league with Estrella Ureña from the very beginning. Curtis was convinced that without Trujillo's support the revolution could not have succeeded and probably would not have broken out.[26]

While Minister Curtis had reluctantly accepted Estrella's government, the acceptance of Trujillo was another matter. Because he believed the latter had betrayed his government and made false statements to the legation, Curtis thought it "highly desirable that General Trujillo be not nominated on the list of any party" for the forthcoming elections. Curtis even informed Estrella that the legation would under no circumstances recommend the recognition of a government led by Trujillo.[27]

One provision of the agreement between Vásquez and Estrella was that in the May, 1930, elections no restrictions as to candidates would be imposed other than that neither Vásquez' Vice-President, José Dolores Alfonseca, nor General Trujillo should run. Nevertheless, Trujillo formally — and successfully — sought the presidency, to the surprise of no one, including Curtis. Estrella Ureña asked the legation to make it publicly known that the United States would not recognize a Trujillo government should he be elected president. The State Department's telegram to Curtis rejecting Estrella's request shortly before the election is significant enough to quote extensively:

> We feel that through scrupulously avoiding even the appearances of interfering in the internal affairs of the Dominican Republic our relations with Santo Domingo have been put on a very sound basis in the 6 years since the withdrawal of the military occupation. . . . Your view that it is

most unfortunate that the head of the army should use that position for his own political advancement and as a means of obtaining the Presidency is concurred in by the Department. The Department would be willing for you to talk personally, confidentially and in the most friendly manner with Trujillo, urging on him as your personal advice the damage which he will do to the political development of the Dominican Republic by being a candidate rather than by using his power to guarantee free and fair elections. . . . Any duress through a public statement would defeat the ends we are seeking. While the Department hopes that you will be able to persuade Trujillo not to be a candidate, yet it realizes the great difficulty of bringing it about and should you not succeed and Trujillo be elected it is most important that you should not impair in any way your relations with him. . . . For your strictly confidential information the Department desires you to know that it expects to recognize Trujillo or any other person coming into office as a result of the coming elections and will maintain the most friendly relations with him and his Government, and will desire to cooperate with him in every proper way.[28]

After betraying the Dominican president in the 1930 revolution, Trujillo was elected to the presidency through coercive electoral techniques and fraudulent electoral procedures. During his campaign, he had set aside his military uniform as chief of the Dominican armed forces in order to "allay the fears of those who regarded his candidacy for president as a threat of military dictatorship." [29] Nevertheless, after attaining the office, Trujillo established a regime that was to last more than three decades. Despite his eloquent verbal defense of democracy and the need to preserve its forms, Trujillo built a regime that can be classified neatly with regard to its political institutions and outlook: an authoritarian, arch-conservative, absolute Latin American military dictatorship. Dominican politics were completely dominated by the personality of the dictator; his control

over Dominican affairs was total, whether he was officially president or not. Trujillo consolidated power into the second longest-
lived dictatorship in Latin American history (exceeded in length
only by Porfirio Díaz, who ruled Mexico from 1876 to 1911).

Trujillo embellished himself with all the trappings of honor
and glory. In 1933 his Congress raised his rank to generalissimo
and later voted him the title of "Benefactor of the Nation." In
1934 he was awarded an honorary doctorate from the University of Santo Domingo, the first university to have been established in the western hemisphere. In 1936 Santo Domingo, the
oldest city in the New World and presumably the burial place
of at least part of Christopher Columbus, was renamed "Ciudad
Trujillo." The dictator was said to have held at least forty differ-

Church and State in the Dominican Republic, date unknown. *Courtesy
of the OAS*

ent official titles, including those of "Chief Protector of the Dominican Working Class," "Genius of Peace," "Father of the New Fatherland," "Liberator of the Nation," "Protector of Fine Arts and Letters" and "The First and Greatest of the Dominican Chiefs of State." This adulation increased with the passing years; one observer reported in 1960 that "at the latest count, there were 1,870 monuments to the 'Benefactor' in the ancient city of Santo Domingo; no reckoning has been made of the monuments in towns and villages. Public buildings blaze with neon signs 'God and Trujillo.' A new hospital carries the slogan 'only Trujillo cures you.'" [30]

Two caudillos, Franco and Trujillo, converse in Spain, June 11, 1954.
Courtesy of the OAS

By the end of 1931 Trujillo's own Dominican party was the only legally functioning political party, and his reelection in 1934 was uncontested. He was succeeded in 1938 by his hand-picked candidate, Jacinto Peynado. When Peynado died in 1940 Vice-President Mañuel de Jesús Troncoso became president. During this time the government continued under the aegis of General Trujillo, who unctuously declared that although he had "declined to continue in the executive position that the unanimous will of my people was offering," he nevertheless did not decline the obligation that he contracted with his "conscience in 1930 to keep a constant watch for the well-being of the Republic." [31] The generalissimo again ran successfully for reelection in 1942, unopposed.

Trujillo continued to hold absolute power after World War II. In 1947 he was elected for a fourth five-year presidential term, and when it expired in 1952, his brother, Héctor B. Trujillo, assumed the presidency. Rafael continued as commander-in-chief of the armed forces and became ambassador-at-large to the United Nations. In 1957 Héctor was again elected President unopposed, and Vice-President Joaquín Balaguer became titular head of the republic upon the president's resignation in 1960. However, Rafael Trujillo continued to guide the destiny of the Dominican Republic until his assassination on the night of May 30, 1961.

3. WAS THE UNITED STATES RESPONSIBLE FOR TRUJILLO?

Some critics of United States policy have charged that American military intervention between 1916 and 1924, which was aimed in part at preparing the Dominican Republic for democracy, had actually allowed Trujillo to establish his dictatorship.[32] One major objective of the eight-year United States military occupation, which had been a response to continued Dominican anarchy and political strife, was to create a national police force. This constabulary was to be an apolitical and professional force to maintain law and order, support constitutionally elected governments and thereby assure the country's stability. The fact that Trujillo was admitted to the United States Marine Corps-organized and commanded National Guard in 1919, and was a major in the national police force when the military government was terminated in 1924, does not make the United States responsible for the subsequent Trujillo dictatorship, however.

Certainly there was no intention that the *Policía Nacional Dominicana* be used as an instrument for overthrowing constituted government or for maintaining a military dictatorship. Even so, the United States can be criticized for failing to understand the Dominican political process and for believing that a truly apolitical, professional police force could be organized without becoming the instrument of a future faction or *caudillo*. However, the rise of Trujillo as a power-hungry strong man was consistent with the Dominican Republic's history, its legacy of strife and violence.

President Horacio Vásquez, elected in the Marine Corps-supervised elections of 1924 that preceded the withdrawal of United States troops, was responsible for bringing Major Trujillo to the capital and promoting him until he was head of the armed forces. Furthermore, in the crisis surrounding the election of 1930, which was a Dominican affair since the republic had resumed exercising its sovereignty in 1924, Trujillo manipulated a coup d'état to get himself elected president. During the crisis, precipitated by President Vásquez' attempt to violate the constitution and succeed himself, the United States minister urged Trujillo not to run and attempted to get firm pledges that he would not do so. Trujillo ran — and won — in spite of external pressure against him.

The United States was also criticized for not opposing Trujillo after the *golpe de estado* and fraudulent election of 1930, and for according his government the recognition that was invaluable to him. One such critic said that, considering Trujillo's past record and the manner in which he had attained the

presidency, the United States should never have extended diplomatic recognition to his regime.[33] The endeavors of the United
States minister, acting on his government's instructions, indicate that the United States did not want Trujillo to run in the
1930 presidential contest. Once elected however, he was recognized reluctantly and with misgivings.

It is most unlikely that a United States refusal to recognize
the Trujillo government, or a persistent bargaining for reforms,
would have had any real effect on Dominican democracy. From
a realistic viewpoint the United States had little choice, short of
intervention, but to recognize Trujillo and try to deal with him.
At the time there was no clear pattern of conduct on his part
to enable the United States to anticipate that he would inaugu-
rate an oppressive dictatorship that was to last thirty-one years.
Furthermore, it is likely that the United States would have been
criticized if it had opposed Trujillo in 1930, just as it was for
the action it did take, and that conditions in the Dominican Republic concerning the form of government would not have been
substantially different.

Certain aspects of international law were also involved in
formal relations between the two governments. The United
States as a sovereign state had the prerogative, if it so desired,
to recognize and establish relations with the Dominican government. The recognition of a *de facto* government, which the Trujillo regime became from the outset, is the choice of the recognizing state. Historically, the United States had been committed
to recognition of *de facto* governments. Recognition and the
resultant establishment of formal relations are in themselves no
expression of preference or support of a government. Recognition is merely the acceptance of an international reality, no
matter how unfortunate that reality might be. But there is always the possibility that the recognizing state might have some
impact on altering that reality through its relations with the
recognized state.

The return of the Marines and a resumption of the military

government and occupation in order to preempt Trujillo's rule was out of the question as a policy alternative; the political price would have been too high to violate Dominican sovereignty again. The United States had withdrawn in 1924 in response to the increasing unpopularity of its occupation and the realization that it was exacerbating its relations with Latin America in general.

III NONINTERVENTION, THE OAS AND TRUJILLO

The principle of nonintervention, which made illegal the interference of an American state in the affairs of others, and its positive corollary of consultation among the American republics on problems of mutual concern formed the bases for United States policy toward Trujillo during most of the dictator's tenure. From its earliest relations with Trujillo until the last days of his regime, the United States was careful to avoid any intervention in Dominican affairs such as had marked its actions for the preceding quarter-century. The consultation procedure was becoming important among its policies during the Trujillo era. Thus the United States found itself consulting about chronically bad Caribbean international politics (in which the Dominican government was intimately involved for three decades) within the framework of the developing inter-American system. While the new policies were applauded, they were also criticized by those who objected to the lack of pressure placed on dictators such as Trujillo by the United States.[1]

1. THE CUSTOMS RECEIVERSHIP

After Trujillo came to power in 1930, the most immediate continuing issue for the next ten years was the United States-administered Customs Receivership. The receivership arrangement was regulated in the 1930's by a treaty signed in 1924 that had superseded a 1907 convention.[2] An astute observer in 1936 accurately described the receivership as "both the closest link and the greatest potential source of friction" between the United States and the Dominican Republic.[3]

After 1930 the customs arrangement was "informally revised" in several respects, modifying the provisions of the 1924 treaty. Following his inauguration on August 16, 1930, Trujillo faced staggering national problems, resulting primarily from the worldwide economic depression and worsened by a hurricane that devastated the capital city of Santo Domingo on September 3. Trujillo soon devised his own "plan of refinancing" to lighten the burden of external debt; he enacted the Emergency Law of October 23, 1931.[4] Even though the law violated the 1924 convention, the United States announced that it was "not disposed at this time to take any action other than to continue to follow with close attention and care, the developments in the Dominican Republic." Eventually the Dominican financial condition improved, and the Emergency Law was repealed as of September 1, 1934. The receivership was restored to its original status.[5] Meanwhile, another readjustment of the Dominican Republic's foreign obligations was in the making.

In August, 1934, a Dominican proposal to readjust the republic's foreign obligations was approved by the State Department and the Foreign Bondholders Protective Council.[6] The agreement provided that maturities for the two outstanding bond issues were to be extended from 1942 and 1940 to 1962 and 1970, respectively. United States supervision of customs collections was to continue until 1970, and amortization payments were reduced. The United States commended the Dominican government for its "spirit of cooperation" and expressed the hope that "adjustments of a similar nature might be made with other Latin American countries that are in default on their foreign bonds."[7]

Despite these friendly accommodations, the United States and the Dominican Republic began to dispute the spending of Dominican revenues. Dominican thinking was well summed up by the United States minister in Ciudad Trujillo:

From the Dominican Government's standpoint, the real issue was not considered to be the question as to what particular proposed expenditures of the Dominican Government required the consent of the United States, but rather the necessity of consultation of the United States at all regarding any of the Dominican Government's financial matters outside the scope of the external funded debt now outstanding.[8]

Beginning in 1936 and for some four years thereafter, negotiations were held with a view toward revising the treaty.[9] During this period, the Dominican government argued that (1) the existence of the receivership conformed neither with the "new way of life" of the Dominican Republic nor with the spirit of the Good Neighbor Policy; (2) the 1924 treaty was an obstacle to the economic development of the Dominican Republic, since conditions were so different from those of the past; and (3) the arrangement was offensive to Dominican sovereignty and conflicted with the new Pan-Americanism that stressed nonintervention and was being promoted by the United States. The United States government countered that it was obligated to uphold the bondholders' interests. With assurance that the rights of bondholders would be respected, the United States announced that it would welcome the termination of the receivership in accordance with its policy of refraining from interference in the domestic concerns of other American republics.[10]

The United States minister in Ciudad Trujillo recognized that the two governments were attempting "to achieve two mutually conflicting objects" and admitted that the 1924 convention was by then "anachronistic." He could see no advantage "in keeping up the fiction" that the two governments were governed by the treaty, even though he was "well aware that the fiction remains a solace to a considerable body of informed opinion, not to mention the bondholders and floating-debt creditors of the Dominican Republic."[11] During a visit to the United States in

1939, Trujillo stated that negotiations to end the "vexing and anachronistic" Customs Receivership, which constituted intervention in the internal affairs of the Dominican Republic, had "failed in the face of an imperialistic attitude" by the United States. Nevertheless, said Trujillo, the Dominican Republic would continue "to be a good and sincere friend of the United States." [12]

The United States was beholden to the bondholders under the treaty whose provisions were binding until abrogated or revised. Nevertheless, the receivership had been established originally to prevent European intervention, and the Trujillo dictatorship had removed any occasion for intervention by displaying financial responsibility as well as achieving public order. Thus the United States found it difficult to justify its responsibility to the holders of Dominican bonds when the Good Neighbor Policy stressed absolute nonintervention.

As of August, 1940, negotiations that had been proceeding for four years in an effort to revise, replace or abrogate the 1924 convention appeared to be at a standstill. But because both sides were anxious to reach agreement, a new treaty was signed on September 24, 1940. Six months later, the Customs Receivership was officially terminated. The agreement provided for closing the Office of the General Receiver of Customs and resuming the collection of customs by Dominican authorities. New arrangements were provided for guaranteeing the servicing of bonds, arrangements which included provision for a first lien on total revenues of the Dominican nation in lieu of customs receipts; that is, redemption of the outstanding bonds and payment of the interest charges were guaranteed without reference to any particular source of revenue. The United States had the right to select the depository bank for all revenues of the Dominican government in order to assure service on bonds held by American citizens.[13]

The United States Senate consented to the treaty on February 14, 1941, with only one dissenting vote; it was proclaimed on March 17 by President Roosevelt, and on April 2, 1941, the

Customs Receivership was officially terminated. The United States had earlier suggested that a suitable "neutral agent" would be the First National City Bank of New York, as it was the only United States bank to have a branch in the Dominican Republic, a fact that might appeal to the bondholders. The branch was later designated the sole depository bank, undertaking to make no disbursements for the account of the Dominican government until payment of amortization and interest charges on the bonds had been made. Later, the Dominican Republic bought the First National City Bank branch and established its own National Bank.

Senator Theodore Francis Green (D–R.I.), recommending

Secretary of State Cordell Hull and Trujillo signing treaty in Washington, D.C., ending U.S. Customs Receivership, September 24, 1940. *United Press International Photo*

approval of the treaty by the United States Senate, said that the main purpose of the agreement "was not so much in the interest of the bondholders — although we believe it is for their interest — as to get rid of an irritating feature of the relations between the two countries." The State Department hailed the treaty as "another step in the development and coordination of the good neighbor policy based on mutual respect and confidence among the countries of the hemisphere." A Dominican diplomat was of the opinion that the new treaty was final proof that the Good Neighbor Policy had completely replaced American "intervention and aggression." [14] The Dominican Congress in 1940 gave Trujillo the title, "Restorer of the Financial Independence of the Republic."

Some years later, on July 19, 1947, the Dominican Republic delivered funds sufficient to redeem all outstanding bonds, together with all interest due, to a representative of the American bondholders; it also advertised that the 1922 and 1926 bonds would be redeemed on September 1 and October 1, 1947, respectively. The convention of 1940 provided that after redemption of the bonds the convention would automatically cease to have effect. Inasmuch as the Dominican Republic had retired the bonds in advance, an exchange of notes was signed with the United States on August 9, 1951, recognizing the termination of the 1940 convention and the fact that the Dominican Republic had redeemed in full its external debts in accordance with the bond contracts.[15]

2. THE HAITIAN AFFAIR AND THE INTER-AMERICAN SYSTEM

The idea of the peaceful settlement of disputes had always been part of the concept of Pan-Americanism, and it became an integral component of the inter-American system. Closely related to this idea was the procedure of consultation regarding problems of mutual concern to members of the system. During the Trujillo era, a number of conflicts involving the dictator's regime were discussed by representatives of the American republics within the multilateral framework of the inter-American system, beginning in 1937 with a serious dispute between the Dominican Republic and Haiti.

In October, 1937, Dominican military forces attacked and killed large numbers of Haitian peasants near the border between the two countries. Although the number of victims was never firmly established, some observers estimated that as many as 25,000 people had perished. The Haitian Legation in Washington set the number of fatalities at 12,168 in the heat of the subsequent charges and counter-charges.[16] Why the massacre took place is unclear, although little doubt exists that Trujillo was responsible for the deed, and this assumption was actively fostered by his enemies. Critical comment in sensational accounts was widespread, although nothing more than circumstantial evidence is available and only scant suggestion of Trujillo's possible motives.[17] Nevertheless, the problem was a real and serious one for the dictator, for public opinion was almost totally against him. So certain were his opponents that Trujillo was near his end that Dominican exiles in Puerto Rico, looking forward to a new regime, pledged their support to follow exile Angel Morales, then living in New York, as the next president of the republic.[18] But after a series of negotiations, Trujillo emerged well in control of his country, although with a reputation more blemished than before.

The governments of both Haiti and the Dominican Republic exercised strict censorship and succeeded for some time in keeping the news from the rest of the world. In 1936 the problem raised by the long history of border disputes between these two countries led to an agreement on peace-keeping procedure, and reportedly an investigation was proceeding under the terms of that agreement. On October 15, 1937, the Dominican Republic promised Haiti "speedy action to apprehend and punish the guilty." One week later the Dominican Legation in Washington made public a joint Dominican-Haitian statement, in reality a diplomatic facade, that "the cordial relations between Haiti and the Dominican Republic had not been impaired" as a result of "a recent border incident in which several citizens were reportedly injured." [19]

Shortly thereafter Haiti decided it did not wish to leave the determination of responsibility to the Dominican government. By then the prevailing general impression was that Haiti had a substantial case against the Dominican Republic. On November 12, 1937, dissatisfied with the "dilatoriness of the Dominican authorities," Haiti asked the governments of Cuba, Mexico and the United States to mediate the dispute. All three readily agreed to tender their good offices.[20]

The United States was concerned over the dispute not only because of its continuing interest in two Caribbean countries in which it had intervened in the past, but also because of the existence of inter-American peace treaties as well.[21] These treaties, eight of which were in effect at the time, exemplified the accelerating stress on nonintervention and the peaceful settlement of disputes. (Haiti was to invoke two of the treaties, as will be discussed.)

After the Dominican-Haitian dispute had been settled, Minister Norweb observed that Haiti's request for good offices "made the matter squarely a test of that will for peace which found concrete expression at the Buenos Aires Conference." Accordingly, he had "strongly impressed upon President Trujillo the necessity for securing a settlement of the controversy within the spirit of the American peace treaties." [22]

Haiti agreed with the mediators that a commission should be appointed to investigate and fix the terms of a settlement, but the Dominican Republic refused on the grounds that the issues were really domestic ones. The three friendly powers then concluded that the incident fulfilled the conditions described by the Buenos Aires declaration that "every act susceptible of disturbing the peace of any American republic affects each and every one of the republics." [23] Haiti then resorted to other peace treaties to which it and the Dominican government were signatories, the Gondra Treaty of 1923 and the General Convention of Inter-American Conciliation of 1929.

Under the 1923 agreement signatories pledged not to resort to war until a commission of inquiry had made an investigation and submitted a report. The 1929 pact stipulated that the commission was not only to investigate but also to submit a plan of settlement.[24] Trujillo resisted the conciliation procedures and argued that they were unnecessary,[25] but on December 18, 1937, he finally yielded and agreed to accept the form for settlement specified in the treaties.

At this time a voice of protest against the dictator and killer of Haitians was raised in the United States Congress. Representative Hamilton Fish, Jr. (R–N.Y.), delivered "a plea; a protest; a remonstrance [against] the most outrageous atrocity that has ever been perpetrated on the American continent." He called for the withdrawal of recognition by the United States "if this matter is not settled after an impartial investigation, and if apologies are not offered, if compensation is not paid, and if guarantees are not given by the Dominican Republic," which was being ruled "by one of the most autocratic and high-handed dictators alive."

Representatives James A. Shanley (D–Conn.) and John E. Rankin (D–Miss.) disagreed with the proposal. Shanley protested that Fish's recommendation constituted interference with the domestic difficulties of a republic, even if it were a dictatorship, and that there should be no interference unless the affair produced some "repercussion" in the United States. Rankin said that Fish's criticism was unfair "since the United States is carrying on the Good Neighbor Policy with Latin America." [26]

In the meantime a peace commission had gone to work and an agreement was signed on January 31, 1938, at the Pan American Union in Washington. The Dominican Republic agreed to pay the sum of $750,000 as indemnity to Haiti, to fix responsibility for the incidents and to give the results of its investigation full publicity. Both parties agreed to prevent similar recurrences, and measures were proposed for protecting nationals in the future.[27]

Minister Norweb felt that two pressures had forced the Do-

minican government into a settlement "against its will." First
was the world press, which "gave with considerable accuracy of
detail a dramatic picture of the savage murders . . . and enlisted
the sympathy of outside nations with the injured party." Second
was the "practically unanimous will among the nations of the
Western Hemisphere that international disputes should have
peaceful settlement." Although the settlement is still acclaimed
because it utilized the formal framework of the inter-American
peace structure, there is one point in this regard which has
generally been overlooked. Minister Norweb observed that "the
actual instrument of the settlement was not the Permanent Commission of the Gondra Treaty sitting in Washington nor the
American Governments invoking the various instruments for
the settlements of international difficulties, but the diplomacy of
the Vatican." [28]

Norweb was convinced that due to the considerable influence
of the Archbishop of Santo Domingo over Trujillo, and the
strong interest in the dispute of the Papal Nuncio to both countries, the Church offered a common meeting ground. Norweb
believed that once Trujillo realized some form of settlement
would have to be offered, "he found in the Legation of the
Vatican an exit which had been all along the principal object
of his government." The role of the Nuncio appeared when, on
January 11, 1938, he took a proposal from Haiti to Trujillo
setting forth the demand of the former. Trujillo was ready then
to grant most of Haiti's terms with some modifications, notably
a 50 per cent reduction of the demand for a cash settlement of
$1,500,000. But the convention finally signed was the protocol
originally drafted by the Papal Nuncio.

Neither the Dominican government nor press (or any other
government or press, for that matter) made reference to the
assistance of the Nuncio in bringing the parties together. On
the contrary, said Norweb, the settlement was "played up as an
example of Dominican fidelity to the principles of inter-American solidarity and peace."

The Haitian imbroglio may be closed on the ironic note that

in 1939 the Dominican Republic established an annual "Trujillo Peace Prize" of $50,000, designed "to rival" the Nobel Prize.[29]

3. EARLY CRITICS OF NONINTERVENTION

As a policy matter nonintervention carried with it the necessity of dealing with dictators like Trujillo. For almost three decades the United States defended itself against the criticism that nonintervention in Dominican affairs constituted support of a vicious dictator. Some critics felt that in the 1930's the United States should have pressured Trujillo to reform his government. A few years prior the United States had been criticized for intervening in the Dominican Republic, but now nonintervention was being attacked on the grounds that it permitted the continued existence of Trujillo. Therefore a policy of noninterference was "as bad as our former one of ultra-intervention."[30]

During the early 1930's Trujillo was quietly consolidating his power, and the real nature of his regime had not yet manifested itself. Furthermore, the United States, in response to increasing Latin and North American opposition to its intervention in other American states, was moving toward accepting the principle of nonintervention as a basis for policy. The United States pledged adherence to nonintervention, with some reservations, at the Montevideo conference in 1933; the principle's acceptance was reiterated with no reservations at the Buenos Aires conference in 1936. Thus the United States had no legal basis to intervene with Trujillo — politically, economically or militarily — to voice objections to his governmental policies or practices. The intervention principle was the *sine qua non* for intervention operation.

As the 1930's, with the principle of nonintervention established as a cornerstone of the inter-American system, the United States became increasingly concerned over both the situation in Europe and security in the hemisphere. The question of inter-American cooperation for defense became a major concern. During World War II the Dominican Republic was of great strategic importance to the United States because of its geographic position as the gateway to the Caribbean and its proximity to the Panama Canal. The United States felt it hardly could denounce Trujillo as a dictator when he was essential to the war effort. Political or ideological principle was of less consideration than the principle of survival in a time of grave national peril.

Nevertheless, attention came to be focused on the ideological orientation of Trujillo and the attitude of the United States toward the dictatorship, especially with the rise of the totalitarian threat around the world in the late 1930's and the expansion of hostilities in World War II. As expressed in a great deal of its wartime declarations and propaganda, the goal of the United States was to destroy dictatorial regimes in the name of democ-

Trujillo reviews Marines upon his arrival at Union Station, Wash D.C., July 6, 1939. *United Press International Photo*

Trujillo drinking toast with Senator Theodore Green, Chairman of Foreign Relations Committee, in the Senate Restaurant, July 7, 1939. *United Press International Photo*

racy. Anti-dictatorial elements expressed disillusionment with the apparently paradoxical posture of the Good Neighbor and continued to insist that pressure be applied against Trujillo and other dictators. When Trujillo arrived in Washington for a state visit on July 6, 1939, Carleton Beals, chairman of the Committee for Dominican Democracy, sent a telegram to President Roosevelt calling attention to the "inappropriateness of endorsing home grown dictators" such as Trujillo while condemning the European variety.[31]

Soon proposals were being made to subordinate the principle of nonintervention to the ideal of democracy. Among Latin Americans, one of the most vocal exponents of this idea was

Víctor Raúl Haya de la Torre, leader of the Peruvian *alianza popular revolucionaria americana* (APRA), who argued for intervention designed to overthrow dictatorial governments and support democracies. Haya asserted that "no action is the worst kind of intervention." He pressed for *buena intervención* ("good intervention") aimed at facilitating democracy. And he complained that while the United States condemned dictatorial governments in Europe, it never censured Latin American dictators and even maintained "the best possible relations with them." [32]

Trujillo's cooperation with the United States against Nazi Germany did appear to be an anomolous situation, as the dictator joined in expressing antipathy toward other dictators in the name of democracy. One cannot but note the irony of President Roosevelt's remark to Trujillo about "the democratic ideals and moral values which we hold dear" — or of Trujillo's statement that "we are at war alongside the United States in defense of democracy and civilization." [33] Trujillo played the anti-Nazi game, and from the standpoint of the United States the defeat of Nazi Germany became an all-important objective. Thus cooperation was sought and appreciated in all quarters, which included Latin American dictators.

Some official coolness toward the Trujillo regime appeared in 1944. That year Ellis O. Briggs was appointed United States Ambassador to Ciudad Trujillo, and he tried to maintain only the most circumspect formal contacts with the dictator. He particularly tried to avoid those public appearances which Trujillo manipulated in order to convey the impression that the United States cordially supported his government. A July 5, 1944, dispatch from Ambassador Briggs to the State Department contained the following:

> Trujillo is a dictator, indifferent to or even hostile to many of the fundamental principles for which our country stands. The fact that Trujillo has declared himself to be "on our side" in this war, and that he is collaborating with us in cer-

tain international matters should not blind us to the realities of his domestic administration nor to the implications within the important area of our general international relations, of our doing business with Trujillo on any except our own carefully considered terms.[34]

However, no outright opposition to Trujillo was forthcoming, certainly not to the extent recommended by the advocates of "good intervention." Briggs was succeeded as ambassador by George H. Butler in 1945. Ironically, Butler was the author of an article appearing in the July 15, 1945, edition of *The Department of State Bulletin,* which proposed multilateral intervention to enforce democracy in the western hemisphere.[35] The present writers have found no report of opposition to Trujillo during Ambassador Butler's tour.

Later in 1945 the most significant appeal made on behalf of collective intervention to promote democracy and protect human rights was the one made by the Uruguayan Minister of Foreign Affairs, Dr. Eduardo Rodríguez Larreta. Although his proposed policy of multilateral action was directed against the pro-Axis government of Argentina, it applied to all dictatorial regimes, and its author considered such action to be compatible with the principle of nonintervention.

On November 22, 1945, Dr. Larreta set forth his views in a note delivered to each of the American ambassadors in Montevideo. He stressed the "parallelism" between democracy and peace, and argued that nonintervention should not shield "the notorious and repeated violation by any republic of the elementary rights of man and of citizen." [36] Dr. Larreta contended that the nonintervention principle had been transcended by the American commitment to democracy and human rights. His advocacy of "multilateral collective intervention" was received enthusiastically by some American states but was rejected by the majority. The United States was first to respond and endorsed the proposal unreservedly,[37] happy to subscribe to a policy directed against Argentina and its pro-Axis policies.

There is little question that Trujillo's cooperation with the United States during World War II was based on expediency. He probably could not have pursued successfully any other policy, given the strategic importance of the Dominican Republic to the United States during the war. Moreover, cooperation was in his best interests, resulting in his receipt of economic and military aid and technical assistance from the United States. It does not follow, however, that the United States should have rejected Trujillo's cooperation because it was selfishly motivated. The threat of Nazi Germany was a transcending consideration, even though the fact of Trujillo's cooperating with the United States in the name of freedom and democracy was an anomolous one. The United States sought cooperation from all governments, including those of Latin American dictators.

4. THE DOMINICAN REPUBLIC AND POSTWAR CARIBBEAN CONFLICT

Exiles from Caribbean countries had always gathered in nearby republics to plan and execute revolutionary attempts against various regimes in the area, but this activity seemed to be extraordinary after World War II. According to one study, the Dominican Republic was directly involved in nine of twenty Caribbean "situations" that occurred between 1948 and 1959.[38] Trujillo accused other governments of designing plots to overthrow him, while those governments directed counter-charges at the generalissimo. Eventually some of these charges were brought before organs of the inter-American system. The problem for both the inter-American system and the United States was to reconcile two apparently conflicting principles: the doctrine of nonintervention with the doctrine of democratic development.[39]

Caribbean domestic and international strife were closely linked because of the leniency of a number of governments toward revolutionary activities carried on by political exiles in their countries. An organization known as the Caribbean Legion, which the liberal governments of the Caribbean region almost openly sponsored, was composed of political exiles and adventurers representing a broad spectrum of motivations, but which, in spite of differing motivations, was dedicated to overthrowing all dictatorships in the Caribbean. Top on the priority list of the Caribbean Legion were dictators Rafael Trujillo and Anastasio Somoza (of Nicaragua). The dictators in turn encouraged activities against their more "democratic" neighbors.

Two quotations from official sources sum up conditions in the Caribbean at this time. In 1950 an investigating team of the Council of the Organization of American States reported:

> The nationals of a given country not only try to fight against the government of their homeland, but also tend to congregate with those of other countries who have similar purposes. Many of those exiles are sincere and idealistic individuals who, being deprived of democratic guarantees in their native lands, inevitably strive to return to political life. Others are adventurers, professional revolutionaries, and mercenaries whose primary objective appears to be the promotion of illegal traffic in arms and expeditions against the countries with which they have no ties whatsoever.[40]

Agreeing with the COAS report, a Department of State official wrote the same year that whatever the motivations of the individual revolutionaries might be, their activities in the Caribbean Legion had involved territory whose use had violated their governments' international obligations and disrupted "friendly relations" among the countries of the Caribbean.[41]

As a result of these chronically bad relations, inter-American machinery designed for the peaceful settlement of disputes was set in motion. By supporting the use of multilateral procedures, as it had done some years before in the Haitian affair, the United States could continue to play the role of impartial good neighbor without being forced to favor one side or another openly, or having to ignore the serious situation of Caribbean instability.

The parties involved in the various disputes were the despotic regimes of the Dominican Republic and Nicaragua, the "reform" governments of Cuba, Guatemala and Costa Rica, and the not-easily-classifiable government of Haiti. In this study the issue of dictatorship versus democracy is of primary interest, but to identify the Caribbean conflict solely in terms of a confrontation between "democracies" and "dictatorships" would distort reality. In addition to conflicting ideologies, there were personal grudges and "adventurism" among the motivating factors of governments and individuals involved in the imbroglio.[42]

The first international conflict involving the Dominican Republic was with Cuba in the summer of 1947. The Caribbean Legion had organized a revolutionary expedition, using one of the keys off eastern Cuba (Cayo Confites) as a base of operations against the Trujillo regime. However, in response to international pressure resulting from widespread publicity, the Cuban government reversed its initial support of the expedition. It arrested the group of over 1,500 men preparing to leave for the Dominican Republic under the leadership of Dominican exiles General Juan Rodríguez García and the writer (later Dominican president) Juan Bosch.[43] The Dominican government denounced the attempted invasion as the work "of a Communist International Brigade."[44]

A year later the Dominican Republic and Cuba were again at odds over an alleged proposed invasion. On August 13, 1948, the Dominican government asked the Inter-American Peace Committee to resolve a dispute with Cuba, which was charged with organizing revolutionary forces against Trujillo. The Peace Committee, composed of representatives of Argentina, Brazil, Cuba, Mexico and the United States, undertook a painstaking investigation, heard the views of both parties and submitted a recommendation that direct negotiations be initiated between the disputants.[45] The report was accepted by both parties. The Cuban government, which had been strongly criticized by the Peace Committee's report, arrested the leaders of an expedition that was being organized against Trujillo, seizing the ships and aircraft that had been assembled.[46]

Meanwhile, the Trujillo regime had become involved in the "Roland Affair" with Haiti. On February 15, 1949, Haiti brought before the COAS a charge that the Dominican government was committing "moral acts of aggression." The Haitian Minister to Ecuador, Colonel Astrel Roland, in Ciudad Trujillo enroute to Haiti to answer charges of plotting revolution against his government, used the official Dominican radio to advocate a Haitian uprising against the government of Dumarsais Estimé. The COAS found no evidence to warrant its serving as the "Organ of Consultation" to consider the dispute under the Inter-American Treaty of Reciprocal Assistance (Rio Treaty of 1947). However, the Inter-American Peace Committee responded to the Haitian request to help resolve the dispute, and the committee pursued its investigations in that country and in the Dominican Republic. Finally, the two governments were persuaded to sign a joint declaration in which they promised not to tolerate activities directed against "other friendly nations." [47]

Despite a respite in the tension between Haiti and the Dominican Republic, trouble broke out in another Caribbean quarter. On the evening of June 19, 1949, an "airborne invasion" occurred at Luperón Bay, on the Dominican coast. This "invasion," involving two amphibious aircraft and about fifteen men (including three civilian pilots from the United States), was a fiasco from start to finish and was easily suppressed by Trujillo's forces. Trujillo accused Cuba and Guatemala of complicity in the "invasion" and of harboring and encouraging exiles to amass against him. He later broadened his attacks to include Mexico and Costa Rica.

All of the accused countries denied the charges, but the charges, counter-charges and debate continued through December, 1949. Trujillo claimed that he would bring the matter before the Inter-American Peace Committee, but he never formally filed a brief. Cuba, however, in denying Trujillo's charges, sent a letter to the Peace Committee on December 6, inviting it to visit Cuba and learn for itself the inaccuracy of Trujillo's claims. The invitation contained statements from several correspondents and journalists who had visited those places where Trujillo insisted exiles were being trained. The Peace Committee met on December 13 to discuss the Cuban invitation and replied to the Cuban government three days later. It thanked Cuba for its offer and cooperation, accepted the advanced evidence but said that it saw no reason to conduct an investigation and thus would take no action.[48]

Because of this tension in the Caribbean, the Inter-American Peace Committee had held an earlier meeting in August, 1949, at the request of the United States, to consider steps that could be taken to settle the various disputes. On September 14 the committee had presented a number of "conclusions" reflecting a series of recommendations for promoting peace in the Caribbean. In general, the Peace Committee's report summed up the "various principles and standards agreed on by the American Republics as necessary to maintain peace and security in the Western Hemisphere." The conclusions reiterated the basic Pan-American principle of nonintervention and recalled "the duty of each State to prevent its territory from being used for the preparation or initiation of aggression toward one or more States with which it is at peace." The report further expressed the desirability for American states to try avoiding hostile propaganda against one another and for maintaining "close and cordial diplomatic relations." Adherence to the principles and exercise of democracy was pointed to as "a common denominator of American political life." Finally, the report offered "once more the continuing willingness of the Inter-American Peace Committee to lend its services . . . for the pacific and friendly settlement" of conflicts, and pointed out that the inter-American system offered various methods of pacific settlement of disputes.[49]

Secretary of State Dean Acheson, in an address before the Pan American Society in New York on September 19, 1949, took a strong stand concerning the Caribbean turmoil. Plots, counterplots and "overt attempts at military adventure," he said, had created a situation in the Caribbean that was "repugnant to the entire fabric of the Inter-American System." The Secretary said that the United States would use its "strongest efforts" to oppose aggressive plots or acts wherever they occurred and "to defend the peace of the hemisphere." [50]

These admonitions produced no perceptible lessening of tension in Caribbean or Dominican affairs. In December, 1949, Trujillo renewed his charges of hostile activity on the part of Cuba and Guatemala. He called the Dominican Congress into special session and had himself empowered to "declare war" on any country permitting preparations for an invasion of his realm. This move brought a rebuke from Secretary Acheson: "This government deplores the action of the Government of the Dominican Republic in having brought up the possibility of the use of armed force for the purpose of 'war.'" [51]

Haiti reentered the scene on January 3, 1950; it went to the OAS delineating charges of a large-scale Dominican-supported plot to overthrow its government. Haiti invoked the Rio Treaty, asking that the "Organ of Consultation" (the Meeting of Ministers of Foreign Affairs) be summoned immediately. At a COAS meeting on January 6, the Haitian ambassador accused the Dominican government of violating the joint declaration of June 9, 1949, and insisted that the Dominicans had permitted Roland and other Haitian nationals to continue broadcasting and plotting.

The Trujillo government went beyond simply denying the Haitian charges: it called the council's attention to the "grave situation of the Caribbean zone" which had resulted in an attempted invasion of the Dominican Republic in June, 1949. It demanded a hearing on its long-standing contention that Cuba, Guatemala and other countries were fostering revolution against Trujillo's regime. The Dominican representative broadened the initial case of Haiti versus the Dominican Republic to include Cuba and Guatemala.

The OAS invoked the Rio Treaty and agreed to act provisionally as the "Organ of Consultation," calling for a Meeting of Foreign ministers (which was never held). The "Provisional Organ of Consultation" (the COAS) immediately appointed a committee to conduct an investigation in each of the four variously-accused countries. This committee comprised representatives of the governments of Bolivia, Colombia, Ecuador, the United States and Uruguay.[52]

The committee devoted ten weeks to its investigation, holding several hearings in Washington and making a series of visits to the four countries involved. An account of the investigation, completed on March 13, 1950, was contained in an extensive and plain-spoken report to the COAS (published on March 19), which substantiated the various charges that had been made.[53] It was equally severe in its criticisms of the Dominican Republic, Cuba and Guatemala, all of which were accused of plots and conspiracies that had kept the Caribbean in turmoil for the past three years. Haiti alone was found not to have engaged in any subversive activities or maneuvers. The committee recommended sanctions if the offending countries failed to keep the peace. In general, the report disclosed widespread unrest and governmental irresponsibility in the Caribbean.[54] Commenting on the report at a press conference on March 22, 1950, Secretary Acheson said that "the United States gives full support to the conclusions and recommendations presented by the Caribbean Investigating Committee.[55]

The COAS acknowledged that several claims had been substantiated and did not hesitate to place blame. Nevertheless, the COAS went beyond the immediate cases and presented resolutions of a larger scope. In weighing nonintervention against intervention in behalf of democracy, the COAS strongly favored the former. At its meeting of April 8, 1950, the COAS made a significant resolution regarding intervention and democracy. After noting "that both the principle of representative democracy and that of non-intervention are established in many inter-American pronouncements," and that there existed "some confusion of ideas as to the means of harmonizing the effective execution and application" of the two principles, the COAS declared that the principles of democracy "do not in any way and under any concept authorize any governments to violate inter-American commitments relative to the principle of nonintervention." [56]

Arthur P. Whitaker, referring to the COAS resolution, said that legally the council assumed a proper position, but in the case of the Dominican Republic the experience of many years indicated that if Trujillo could not be overthrown by forces coming from outside the country, he could not be overthrown at all; and now it seemed that the OAS was making such action impossible and was tending to be "a prop of established dictatorships in Latin America." But he conceded that there was "no significant support for the opposite thesis that the OAS should be used to support intervention against dictatorships." [57]

5. THE DOMINICAN DEBATE

During the last half of the 1950's, a furious debate raged over the proper posture the United States should have assumed toward Trujillo. Since 1930 both the regime of Rafael Trujillo and United States policy toward him had been severely attacked on the general grounds that dictatorship as such should be opposed. Criticism was especially pronounced during various phases of the Customs Receivership problem in the 1930's; the Haitian affair of 1937 and 1938; and the Caribbean turmoil that followed World War II. However, critical comment had never before posed as great a threat to the continued existence of the Dominican dictator, or as great a challenge to the assumptions of United States policy, as it did with the barrage of criticism and debate that commenced in 1956. A debate that continued until the dictator's death in 1961 was initiated with the Galíndez-Murphy case of 1956–1957.

Jesús M. Galíndez was a Spanish exile, ex-resident of the Dominican Republic and lecturer at Columbia University, who had written a bitterly anti-Trujillist book.[58] Galíndez mysteriously disappeared in New York on March 12, 1956. Gerald Murphy, a young aviator from Eugene, Oregon, who had been employed for several months as a co-pilot for the Dominican Airlines, disappeared in Ciudad Trujillo on December 3, 1956. Public attention was focused on these two events by freshman Congressman Charles O. Porter (D–Ore.), whose district included Murphy's hometown. Porter's theory was that Galíndez' book had motivated Trujillo to have the author kidnaped in New York, flown by Murphy from a Long Island airport to the Dominican Republic, delivered to Trujillo and finally murdered. Murphy, Porter said, did not know the nature of his mission at the time but later had become suspicious, had talked too much and had also been liquidated on Trujillo's orders.

More attention was drawn to the events by newspaper editorials and articles in popular magazines.[59] The State Department was in basic agreement with the press and Congressman Porter. The Dominican Secretary of State was informed that the United States took "a very serious view" of the case and could not accept the Dominican explanation of the disappearances on the basis of available evidence.[60]

The Dominican rebuttal was to dismiss Galíndez as a communist and to label all criticism as a "typical liberal smear job." [61] In reply to United States doubts of Dominican explanations, the Trujillo government protested that "to accept as conclusive in this matter an opinion to the contrary by the agencies of a foreign power would be equivalent to abdicating its sovereign rights as a state." [62] The most legitimate and enigmatic defender of Trujillo was the well-known champion of liberal causes, New York attorney Morris L. Ernst. The Dominican government retained Ernst to review the facts, and he concluded that no accusation connecting the Dominican Republic with the disappearance of Galíndez, or with Murphy's plane, was supported by "a scintilla of evidence." [63] Congressman Porter rhetorically asked how the report could be accepted, since Ernst had been paid by the accused.[64]

Whatever the merits of the case, general opinion, as it had been twenty years before at the time of the Haitian massacre, assumed Trujillo's guilt. The case set off a public controversy, carried out largely in the United States Congress, over the Dominican policy of the United States.

During the Galíndez-Murphy imbroglio, Congressman Porter had insisted that the United States should "revise present official policy of toleration, conciliation, and condonation of the Dominican tyranny." He raised his sights from the Galíndez-Murphy case to attack the general policy of the United States toward Trujillo. In the House of Representatives on February 28, 1957, Porter said that as he delved deeper into details surrounding the disappearance of Murphy, "it became apparent that we were dealing with the logical result of the present United States policy toward the Dominican Republic." Porter asked why, if the United States had taken a strong stand against communist tyranny, a "glove-hand approach" should be taken toward the tyranny of Trujillo.

As to what United States policy should be, Porter recommended first that the Ambassador to Ciudad Trujillo, William T. Pheiffer, be removed for showing undue cordiality to Trujillo. (Perhaps Porter had in mind Ambassador Pheiffer's public characterization of Trujillo as "an authentic genius who thinks and labors, primarily, in terms of the best interests of his people.)" [65] Porter also felt that the Galíndez-Murphy case should be submitted to the OAS. In addition, the United States should reduce the sugar quota for the Dominican Republic and terminate all Export-Import Bank loans, technical assistance and military aid. Finally, the United States should insist that Dominican Ambassador de Moya retract a speech delivered in San Francisco in which he insinuated that the Galíndez-Murphy cases were communist plots of which Porter was a dupe. If the Ambassador would not make the retraction, said Porter, he should be declared *persona non grata*.[66]

Trujillo was not without his apologists. Porter's attack invited a rebuttal from his congressional colleagues in both the Senate and House. Several legislators voiced opposition to Porter's stand for a variety of reasons, some more credible than others. One senator actually asserted that the widely held conviction that Trujillo was a dictator was loose talk. Senator George S. Long (D–La.) said he did not "speak in defense of dictators in general or of any dictatorship in particular," but he did not know that the Dominican government was a dictatorship because, after all, it held elections!

A little more convincingly the Senator said that even if Trujillo were a dictator, it was no business of the United States what type of government the people of the Dominican Republic had, "so long as that Government and its operations presents [sic] no danger to our own rights." Senator Long also felt that the many articles printed by Congressman Porter in the *Congressional Record* attacking Trujillo were simply "rehashes of ancient tales circulated throughout the Caribbean by dissident pamphleteers for many years, and which reeks [sic] with its communistic origin." Long said that it did not matter "what type of Government is maintained at Ciudad Trujillo, so long as it is not an atheistic Communist government which would endanger our own safety and security." The Senator further asserted that it was "the Communists who are behind the present smear campaign of the Dominican Republic," but he was making no accusation that Porter "knowingly" served the communist cause. Porter retorted that Long was implying that the Federal Bureau of Investigation and the State Department were also serving the communist cause, since their findings supported what Porter said.[67]

Senator Olin D. Johnston (D–S.C.) agreed with Senator Long. He felt that the Trujillo government was important to the United States for several reasons: It was a staunch friend, had provided a base in the guided missile program, was a foe of communism in the Caribbean and represented "stability and good government in an area of turmoil." Earlier, on July 25, 1956, Senator Johnston had extolled Trujillo in the United

States Senate after he had made a trip to the Dominican Republic. He said that "the sinister elements within the United States cannot escape responsibility for having participated in these unfounded attacks [on Trujillo] and thus willfully and knowingly advanced the cause of communism within our own hemisphere to the detriment of our allies and good neighbors." [68]

A year later, in an extreme but doubtlessly heartfelt statement, Senator Johnston again summed up his feelings and observations on the subjects of Trujillo and communism when he said that "the Dominican Republic has rendered a greater force [sic] in deterring the spread of communism in Latin America than any other country in the Caribbean area." [69]

Anti-Trujillists said that Senator Long and others failed to recognize that Trujillo tended to pin the communist label on all political opposition, and that "dictatorial regimes such as the Dominican Republic have perverted the anti-communist drive into a campaign to throttle all their opposition, most of it non-communist." [70]

Porter's main antagonist in the House was Representative B. Carroll Reece (D–Tenn.), who charged that Porter had overstepped proper bounds. Reece said that the United States could criticize Trujillo through such officials as the Secretary of State, but that official criticism was "a far cry from attempting to undermine or overturn an allied neighbor." Reece noted that the Dominican Republic was stable and that it enjoyed spiritual and material well-being, supported United States policies, had given the United States territory for military bases and had encouraged American investment. Reece said that "when a member of the Congress of the United States becomes a self-appointed international revolutionary, he necessarily imperils the entire delicate structure of international relations. . . . We are duty bound to observe the sovereign integrity of native government of every complexion no matter how repugnant they [sic] may seem to our concept of the body politic." Porter insisted that "yes, I do foment revolution against dictators, until I die," to which Reece rejoined that it was irresponsible to advocate revolution in the anti-communist Dominican Republic.[71]

The most effusive praise of Trujillo was the famous remark by Representative Gardner R. Withrow (R–Wis.) before the Dominican Congress in February, 1959. In his speech Withrow said that if Trujillo had been born in the United States, he would have become President.[72]

6. TRUJILLO'S TACTICS

Trujillo was always actively promoting his own cause. He had realized early in his career, undoubtedly as a result of realistic opportunism and his Marine Corps training, that his fortunes and those of the Dominican Republic (which he made synonymous) rested with the United States. Therefore he consistently cooperated with and supported the policies of the United States throughout the Cold War; he turned against the United States only in retaliation for its hostile attitude in the late 1950's and early 1960's (see Chapter IV).

Trujillo had continued his opportunistic and expediential cooperation with the United States after the conclusion of World War II. In the immediate postwar period, before the Cold War began, opportunist Trujillo sought to improve his relations with the Soviet Union, the great wartime ally of the United States – as well as create the appearance of democracy in the Dominican Republic. To these ends he established diplomatic relations with the Soviet Union and legalized the Dominican Communist party (Popular Socialist party). In addition, he encouraged the organization of other political parties, as well as the formation of labor unions. He used these "puppet" organizations for his own purposes, at one time making common cause with the communists.

In 1947, however, Trujillo suppressed all these groups and jailed many of their members, particularly those of the Popular

Socialist party. His suppression of Dominican communists was accompanied by much publicity because it demonstrated his apparent dedication to democracy and opposition to communism, for the confrontation between the United States and the Soviet Union had by then manifested itself. In addition, Trujillo realized that he ran the risk of losing control of these party and labor organizations if he tolerated them much longer.

Trujillo's supporters and his own official publications pointed to four facets of his regime for which they all said the United States should be thankful: effective anti-communism, economic and social progress, political stability and total cooperation with the United States. Trujillo also emphasized those areas of United States policy that favored his own position. One anti-Trujillo author accurately stated that the dictator "had his emissaries, his consuls and his Public Relations Department play up the Good Neighbor Policy to the hilt. Whenever the facts are written about the Dominican Republic under Trujillo, one of his representatives writes to say that they're false and, furthermore, it's bad for the Good Neighbor Policy and harms trade."[73] But Trujillo's anti-communism was advertised first and foremost. A Dominican author's laudatory pro-Trujillo work said that communism had clearly penetrated the western hemisphere and implied that Trujillo was the only real defender against international communism.[74]

In January, 1956, about the time the Dominican debate was becoming general and heated, the Dominican Embassy in Washington began publishing its monthly *A Look at the Dominican Republic*, which had an attractive format and was filled with good things about the Dominican Republic and the virtues of Trujillo. The start of publication coincided with the mounting anti-Trujillo campaign in the United States and perhaps was meant as a counteracting propaganda device. In general, the "Era of Trujillo" was extolled. Its unwavering stand against communism was stressed, along with the Dominican Republic as an investor's paradise. Articles claimed that industry had been expanded, disease eliminated and an efficient banking system initiated; in addition, no exchange controls were in effect, and there was an enviable credit rating to be enjoyed.

The publication described the Dominican Republic as a thriving tourist spot, a cultured land, a progressive country that had paid all its debts and one of the few nations in the world that was "not owing a nickel to Uncle Sam or anybody else." Also hailed was Trujillo's humanitarian "open door" policy toward the world's refugees; cited were the Jewish colony at Sosúa begun in 1941 and the settling of 2,000 Spanish farmers in 1955 on "choice land." Favorable speeches by United States congressmen made in the United States and in the Dominican Republic were reprinted, some referring to the Galíndez case, some hailing Trujillo's stand against communism, others simply complimentary in general.[75]

Apparently answering directly to his "anti-dictator" detractors, Trujillo was "interviewed" and quoted as saying that it was a mistake to apply all the criteria of United States democracy to other nations and expect them to work. With ironic understatement, Trujillo said that "it would not be truthful to say that the Dominican Republic functions the same way, democratically speaking, as the United States." He added that "we are daily perfecting a Dominican brand of democracy suitable to our own needs and idiosyncracies and in the future when illiteracy is more completely irradicated [sic] as a result of the vigorous drive we have undertaken, and when our advancements have been more completely stabilized, I feel certain the people will be ready for a more 'americanized' variety."

Trujillo purchased a great deal of advertising space in United States newspapers to promulgate his message and denounce his critics. In addition, the Dominican Republic became one of the major employers (along with several other governments) of lawyers, lobbyists and public relations experts hired to influence the Dominican sugar quota and attempt to establish a favorable image of the Trujillo regime. This was done both in accordance with and contrary to the Foreign Agents Registration Act, which had become law in 1938 and been broadened by amendments in 1939 and 1942. The law called for the registration of non-diplomatic representatives of foreign countries in the United States (including American citizens), periodic reports by them disclosing their activities, income and expenditures.

An article by Douglas Cater and Walter Pincus published in 1961, citing the Dominican Republic extensively as an example, detailed the many successful efforts to plant stories favorable to Trujillo in American news media. These stories were often written by public relations men and intended to be printed without any indication of their source. Such activity was in violation of the Foreign Agents Registration Act, which specified that any communications intended to influence "any section of the public with reference to the political or public interests, policies, or relations of a government of a foreign country" must be labeled clearly as such.[76]

In an exculpatory book published in 1963, a former Dominican Consul General in New York and later chief of Trujillo's secret police, Arturo Espaillat, declared that at least $5,000,000 was paid to some United States congressmen and State Department officials during the last five years of the Trujillo regime. He claimed that hundreds of Americans shared in money bribes and succumbed to sex lures in both the Dominican Republic and the United States. No recipients were named in the book, but Espaillat said that the complete list of names which had been kept in the Dominican Republic had been removed by the United States State Department after Trujillo's assassination.[77] The State Department, with good reason, questioned Espaillat's credibility as a witness and expressed no surprise at the "absurd" charges.

Thus it is apparent that from the end of World War II until the late 1950's, the United States generally remained aloof from the internal politics of the Dominican Republic and attempted to maintain cooperative relations irrespective of dictatorial practices. Nonintervention continued to be one of the major keys to policy for fifteen years after the war, much as it had been

for the preceding decade and a half. Originally, the policy thinking appears to have been that intervention had not achieved
its goals but had evoked serious hostility in Latin America. Official neutrality toward a dictator seemed to be better than intervention. Even though the United States did not consider Trujillo the most desirable ally, it was loath to oppose him.

However, the contradictory nature of Latin American criticism of United States policies created a dilemma for the United
States. Latin Americans voiced objection to the rigid adherence
to nonintervention, and some even charged that the United
States preferred dictators to more democratic governments.
Yet while they argued that the United States should "do something" about Trujillo, any hint of intervention also brought
vigorous dissent. In balancing this debate over the values of
intervention for democracy as against nonintervention, the
weight appears to be in favor of the latter viewpoint.

IV THE PROBLEM OF MUTUAL SECURITY

After the outbreak of World War II, a vexing problem of
United States relations with the Trujillo government was the
extending of foreign assistance, particularly military aid, to
the dictatorial regime for mutual security purposes. This chapter is devoted primarily to evaluating the validity of the charge
that United States military assistance, from the eve of World
War II until the last months of Trujillo's rule, either intentionally or inadvertently supported Trujillo and helped keep
him in power. A note on economic cooperation and technical
assistance is included at the end of the chapter.

1. WARTIME COOPERATION

The question of military cooperation between the United
States and the Dominican Republic to promote hemispheric
security did not arise until war in Europe appeared likely. Prior
to the fall of France in 1940, the objective of United States
strategy was to maintain American neutrality, at the same time
developing a defensive system aimed primarily at protecting
the Panama Canal. Other hemispheric defense concerns were
the Natal region of Brazil, which seemed vulnerable to any attempted German invasion, and submarine attacks in the ship-
ping lanes of the Caribbean Sea, Gulf of Mexico and Atlantic
Ocean.[1] After the United States entered the war in December,
1941, the building of a Caribbean defense system became even
more important.

The Dominican Republic was important to the security of

the United States and the hemisphere during World War II if only because of its strategic position on the eastern approaches to the Caribbean Sea and the Panama Canal, and as part of the island chain leading from Natal to Florida. The Dominican Republic was also a source of certain foodstuffs and materials imported by the United States during the war (e.g., rice and sugar, and bauxite).

By the time war broke out in Europe in September, 1939, the United States and the other American republics, including the Dominican Republic, had issued the expected neutrality proclamations. The Foreign Ministers of the American Republics, meeting at Panama in September and October, 1939, decided to establish and patrol a neutrality zone. However, since most parties to the declaration were unable to patrol their own coastal waters, the United States felt obliged to establish military bases and do this for them. The Dominican Republic put its facilities at the disposal of the United States in December, 1939, signing an agreement that opened its harbors, bays and territorial waters to United States patrol vessels.[2]

During a 1939 visit to Laurence Duggan, Chief of the State Department's Latin American Affairs Division, Trujillo made known his desire to obtain 4,000 Springfield rifles to replace the Spanish Mausers then in use by his army. He assumed that President Roosevelt could simply order them made available from surplus United States stock. Duggan replied that to grant the request would require an act of Congress, since existing legislation for arms shipments to Latin America did not include rifles. He told Trujillo that in the event of a surplus of Springfields, the Department of State would consider a formal request from the Dominican government.[3] This episode is a reminder that a program of military aid and standardization of equipment had not yet been initiated, and that the United States was unable to supply small arms to Trujillo legally.

With the necessities of war, however, a variety of military goods was made available to the Dominican Republic. In September, 1940, the Dominican Republic received an Export-

Import Bank loan of $5,000,000 both for arms purchases and for the development of bases and harbors for use jointly with the United States.[4] In March, 1941, the Lend-Lease act ended legal restrictions on supplying arms to Latin America by empowering the President of the United States to transfer defense articles to those Latin American governments whose defense was deemed vital to that of the United States. On May 6, 1941, the Dominican Republic became the first Latin American state eligible for Lend-Lease aid. In August, 1941, two agreements were signed in Washington, by whose terms the United States agreed to transfer "armaments and munitions of war to a total value of about $1,600,000" to the Dominican Republic. The Dominicans were to pay in advance for the goods they received.[5]

The amount of Lend-Lease aid to Latin America during World War II was nearly $459,422,000, of which Brazil, Mexico, Chile and Peru — in that order — accounted for most of the total. The Dominican Republic's total receipts up to September 2, 1945, were $1,590,108. Included in this amount was $521,000 for naval materiel and $391,000 for aircraft and spares.[6]

In 1941 the Dominican government gave the United States permission to build a naval base near the Bay of Samaná. On the day after Pearl Harbor it declared war on Japan, and four days later on Germany and Italy.[7] Shortly thereafter, the United States asked and was granted permission to utilize Dominican airports, to fly over the country and its territorial waters, and to station maintenance personnel in the Dominican Republic. In addition, a four-year naval-mission agreement requested by Trujillo was signed in January, 1943; that year the United States supplied three sub-chasers to help the Dominican coast guard and air force in patrol activities.[8] Later a Marine Corps air mission arrived and devoted itself to the training of Dominican pilots, and a number of Dominicans were sent to the United States for flight training.

Stirred by the growing totalitarian threat around the world in the late 1930's and during the war itself, serious charges were made by Dominican exiles and sensational North American writers that Trujillo was a Nazi, or at least pro-fascist, and was actively aiding the German cause.[9] The present writers have discovered no evidence to support these accusations. But whether or not Trujillo had Axis leanings, the geographic position of the Dominican Republic in the Caribbean meant that the United States could not risk any Axis infiltration. Trujillo decided to cooperate with the United States; he could do little else. His attitude was undoubtedly influenced by his early opportunistic realization that his fortunes and those of the Dominican Republic, which he made synonymous, rested with the United States.

Attention came to be focused on Trujillo's dictatorial practices and the attitude of the United States toward them. United States wartime propaganda expressed its goal as the destruction of dictatorial regimes in the name of democracy. Anti-dictatorial elements claimed disillusionment with the apparently paradoxical posture of the United States; these elements complained that though the dictatorial governments of Europe were condemned, friendly relations were being maintained with dictators like Trujillo.[10] Such critics failed to distinguish between wartime slogans and policy determinants, or to recognize that the war was essentially a struggle against powerful aggressive military forces. The primary objectives of the United States in Latin America during the war were to achieve political stability and cooperation in preventing Axis influence, and these it got from Trujillo. To secure and maintain these goals, the United States could hardly denounce Trujillo. Democratic principle was of less consideration than cooperation during a period of grave national peril.

However, another criticism concerning military relations — this time voiced by Ellis O. Briggs, the United States ambassador in Ciudad Trujillo — seems to have been a valid one (see Chapter III). In a September, 1944, dispatch to Washington, Briggs criticized United States military attachés and the War Department for not complying with his efforts and those of the State Department to refrain from praising Trujillo and to avoid maintaining close relations with the dictator's government. He recommended guidelines of conduct for United States military officials when visiting or assigned to the Dominican Republic and other Caribbean republics.[11]

After the end of World War II, in November, 1945, Trujillo requested an export license for a large quantity of munitions that he had bought in the United States. His request was rejected the next month, and Spruille Braden, then Assistant Secretary of State for American Republic Affairs, expressed his policy (and provided a good example of American naïveté) in an *aide-memoire:*

> The Government and people of the United States necessarily have a warmer feeling of friendship for and a greater desire to cooperate with those governments which rest upon periodically and freely expressed consent of the governed. This Government has over the past years observed the situation in the Dominican Republic and has been unable to perceive that democratic principles have been observed there in theory or in practice. The foregoing conclusion is based upon the lack of freedom of speech, freedom of the press, and freedom of assembly, as well as upon the suppression of all political opposition and the existence of a one-party system. To furnish large amounts of ammunition in the face of such a system might be held to constitute both intervention in the internal political affairs of the Dominican Republic and support for the practices just mentioned. In the opinion of the United States, the foregoing observations constitute sufficient reason to refuse to furnish the arms and ammunition requested.[12]

Not surprisingly, Trujillo considered himself rebuked and was irate. This rejection was an important factor in his subsequent decision to build his own arms and munitions factory.[13]

2. POSTWAR MILITARY RELATIONS TO 1961

The special Conference for the Maintenance of Continental Peace and Security, held at Rio de Janeiro in 1947, produced the Inter-American Treaty of Reciprocal Assistance (Rio Treaty). Those in attendance agreed that an attack against any member of the regional alliance would be considered an attack on all. The United States from then on maintained that the "corner-stone" of its military relations with Latin America was the Rio Treaty and that United States programs were to be carried out within its broad context.[14] With the outbreak of the Korean War, military cooperation was based upon the assumptions that the western hemisphere was threatened by "Communist aggression both from within and without," and that inter-American secur-ity was vital to all nations and was therefore a common respon-sibility.[15] Standardization of military organization, training, methods and equipment—all oriented toward the United States and devoted to mutual security—was considered desirable in order to discourage Latin American purchases elsewhere. The United States also wanted to insure the accessibility of strategic raw materials.

From the end of World War II until 1952, the United States had no well-organized program of military assistance to Latin America. Throughout the immediate postwar era the United States was preoccupied with Europe, and Latin America was peripheral to its foreign policy considerations. On two occa-sions—in 1946 and 1947—President Truman asked Congress for authority to put a program of inter-American military co-operation into effect.[16] Congress refused both requests, and some Latin American governments reacted by purchasing arms and military equipment from Europe. The Dominican Repub-lic bought a number of British aircraft. The United States con-tinued to supply some military equipment under the Lend-Lease Act, but only that which had been committed previously for delivery as of the end of the war.

From September, 1945, until April, 1949, the Dominican

Republic received a total of $27,258.76 in aircraft and aeronautical material, vessels and other watercraft, and miscellaneous military equipment from the United States.[17] In April, 1949, the Dominican government paid the $92,691 balance due on its account, discharging in full its Lend-Lease obligations assumed in August, 1941.

Another legal basis for the continued supply of military equipment during the immediate postwar period was the Surplus Property Act of 1944, which authorized direct sales of United States military surpluses at reduced prices. By May, 1949, Trujillo had purchased a number of small arms, vessels and pieces of artillery, paying $23,000 for material that was procured at a cost of $500,000.[18] In 1949 Congress passed the Mutual Defense Assistance Act, enabling Latin American countries to purchase arms in the United States, but no grant aid was available. The Dominican Republic received no supplies under this act.[19]

Between 1949 and 1957 the United States and the Dominican Republic negotiated several military-related conventions. In 1949 the United States established the Atlantic Missile Range for long-range missile testing from the Florida mainland to Ascension Island. In November, 1951, the Dominican Republic agreed to permit missiles to pass over its territory.[20]

The most important basis for United States-Dominican military relations after 1947 was the Mutual Security Act of 1951, passed in response to the stimulus of the Korean War. The Latin American portions of the agreement were conceived in part by a desire to end Latin American purchases in Europe and also thereby facilitate the standardization of arms in the hemisphere. This act made the provision of military assistance contingent upon the recipient's participation in "missions important to the defense of the Western Hemisphere." [21]

Under the provisions of the Mutual Security Act, the Dominican Republic was able to make cash purchases of weapons and equipment for uses considered important to hemispheric defense, such as anti-submarine patrol and coastal defense. Direct grants of military equipment in addition to purchases were also authorized for selected Latin American countries whose assistance was considered essential to hemispheric defense. Eventually twelve of the twenty Latin American republics signed bilateral Mutual Defense Assistance agreements with the United States. The Dominican Republic was among the first to sign (on March 6, 1953), thus agreeing to maintain a portion of its armed forces exclusively for the collective defense mission outlined in the Rio Treaty of 1947. The agreement, which was terminated the month after Trujillo's death in 1961, provided in part that "assistance shall be so provided as to promote the defense of the Hemisphere and shall be in accordance with regional defense plans." [22] From the beginning of the military assistance program in fiscal 1952 through fiscal 1961, the total value of United States military deliveries to the Dominican Republic was approximately $6,100,000 out of a Latin American total of approximately $336,000,000.[23]

The establishment of military missions was another feature of the mutual security program. In 1956 Air Force and Navy Service Training missions were sent to handle equipment furnished under the mutual defense agreement.[24] Part of the program involved training Dominican officers at United States military schools. This became the focus of a ludicrous controversy in 1958 as a result of the non-military interests of one officer. He was twenty-nine-year-old Rafael Leonidas (Ramfis) Trujillo, Jr., the dictator's playboy son, who had been commissioned a colonel at the age of four and promoted to brigadier general at nine. He was now head of the Dominican Air Force.

Sensational headlines announced that Ramfis had failed a United States Army Command and General Staff College course at Fort Leavenworth, Kansas, because he had not attended classes and, instead, had spent most of his time in Hollywood. While his wife and six children remained at home, Ramfis made lavish gifts to movie actresses and stirred the United States Congress to indignation. Congressmen were disturbed in particular over the relationship between Ramfis' indiscretion and the fact that he was in the United States ostensibly for a program being financed through foreign aid. The Dominican ambassador in Washington protested the attacks in a telegram to Congress explaining that Ramfis was not spending foreign aid money on his spree, that he received a monthly allowance of $50,000 from his father, and that, anyway, he was buying American.[25]

The Trujillos were defended in the House on June 18, 1958, by Representative Overton Brooks (D–La.), who referred to the Dominican Republic as the "bulwark which has protected our southeastern sea frontier from atheistic communism" and as "our loyal ally . . . so long friendly to us." The Dominican Republic had objected specifically, said Congressman Brooks, to

Ramfis Trujillo, Chief of the Dominican Air Force, greeting a U.S. general officer, date unknown. *Courtesy of the OAS*

attacks on Ramfis, "who is the highest military authority in his country and who, in the past few months has shown a propension to carry on a friendship with and associate himself with the highest circles of society existing on our West Coast." [26] That was probably the best euphemism of the day.

At the time of this "Ramfis imbroglio," another comic-opera incident occurred. A Dominican senator, in a speech to his colleagues, complained of the lack of United States appreciation of his country's "fullest cooperation" and "unquestionable friendship." Distressed that the United States Congress had been hostile toward the Dominican Republic with respect to the military aid program, the senator said: "In that hundred million dollar project our country is assigned the small amount of $600,000 to be invested in the United States itself for the purchase of equipment that is to be employed solely in the interest of the United States and of its program for collective security." [27]

He then presented a draft resolution, unanimously approved by Trujillo's rubber-stamp National Congress on June 18, 1958, which terminated the Mutual Defense Agreement, the Atlantic Missile Range Agreement and several other conventions between the two states. A short time later, Senators William O. Eastland (D–Miss.) and William E. Jenner (R–Ind.) spoke before a joint session of the Dominican Congress in which they praised Trujillo and the Dominican Republic highly. In direct response to this praise, the Dominican Congress adopted other resolutions that rescinded the one terminating its agreements with the United States. [28]

During the postwar years both the regime of Rafael Trujillo and United States policy toward him came under mounting attack, which culminated in a general public and governmental debate in the late 1950's. In the realm of military relations, Trujillo's detractors and his apologists engaged in a great deal of rhetoric.

It was in 1957 that Representative Porter of Oregon waged an energetic and articulate crusade against Trujillo and insisted, among other things, that no further military aid be extended to the Trujillo regime.[29] Representative B. Carroll Reece (D–Tenn.), who was Porter's main antagonist in the House, Senators Alexander Wiley (R–Wis.) and Olin D. Johnston (D–S.C.), noted approvingly Trujillo's professed anti-communism and political stability, his cooperation in World War II and his military agreements with the United States after the war.[30]

In 1958 other senators joined the fray. Wayne Morse (D–Ore.) "deplored a military program of the United States for the benefit of dictators in South America [sic] such as Trujillo." [31] William J. Proxmire (D–Wis.) offered an amendment to the Mutual Security Act that would have prohibited aid specifically to the Dominican Republic. Referring to the oft-stated opinion that "if we refuse to give military assistance to the Dominican Republic, we may compromise the long-range missile proving ground," Proxmire said, "I happen to think that would be well worthwhile." Joseph Clark characterized himself as a pragmatist who was unwilling to take the same chances with American security as was Senator Proxmire.[32] Theodore Francis Green (D–R.I.) felt that the Proxmire amendment was based on two misconceptions: first, that to furnish aid meant that the United States approved of the recipient country's government in power; and second, that if aid were cut off, such action would bring about desirable changes in the country so deprived. Senator Green noted that aid to the Dominican Republic had always been small and that stopping it would probably make little difference and simply precipitate a hostile reaction.[33]

Military policy toward Trujillo began to change during the latter part of the Eisenhower administration. The change was facilitated by Trujillo's increasing unpopularity in both the United States and Latin America and by the Latin American opinion that the United States was too kind to dictators. The adverse publicity associated with the disappearance of Jesús de Galíndez, and the subsequent disagreement between the United States and Dominican governments over the facts of the case, was a contributing factor. Relations between the two countries were also exacerbated by the international turmoil that existed among Caribbean nations and involved the Dominican Republic as well.

The United States began to limit the amount of aid made available to Trujillo and impose restrictions upon the kinds of armaments and munitions he could buy in the United States. In 1958, shortly after it imposed an arms embargo on the Batista government in Cuba, the United States stopped providing Trujillo with arms. Trujillo requested the recall of the United States Air Force Mission and began to make military equipment available to fellow dictator Batista to aid the Cuban leader's struggle against Fidel Castro. In 1960, although the Dominican Republic was scheduled to receive $445,000 in aid, the United States announced that it was cutting off military assistance.[34]

The cutoff coincided with Trujillo's unsuccessful attempt to kill the president of Venezuela and with subsequent diplomatic and economic sanctions applied by the United States and other members of the Organization of American States. The Kennedy administration continued to deny aid to Trujillo. The issue was closed when Trujillo was assassinated on May 30, 1961.

Criticism that United States military assistance kept Trujillo in power was prevalent from 1945 to 1961. During the Cold War the United States military establishment wielded great influence. Its main concern in the case of the Dominican Republic was to align the Trujillo regime on the side of the United States, and little attention was paid to the political or psychological aspects of the problem of assistance until after 1960. The test for aid and cooperation was simple: Was the Dominican Republic on the side of the United States? Trujillo's government easily passed the test. It mattered little that the United States in no way equated aid with approval of Trujillo, for such an interpretation was made of the United States position whether or not the dictator was coddled.

A lack of political sensitivity in the use of military aid does not mean that such aid kept Trujillo in power however. It is important to note that during the first ten years of the "Era of

Trujillo," when the dictator was consolidating his position, he received no military assistance from the United States. It was not until World War II that Trujillo began to receive aid. There is little difficulty in justifying military relations in the context of a world war and the threat to hemispheric security. While criticism of official praise for opportunist Trujillo's professed anti-communism and military cooperation is well founded, serious doubt exists that military assistance was responsible for Trujillo's survival after the war. In the first place the amount of aid was small. From 1945 until 1961 the United States made military shipments worth $8,200,000 under the Mutual Security Program.[35] Furthermore, Trujillo had little difficulty in getting military goods from sources other than the United States.

3. TRUJILLO'S MILITARY ESTABLISHMENT

Trujillo's interests and tactics must be considered a factor limiting United States actions. At the end of World War II, Trujillo developed his own source of supply for certain kinds of arms and munitions, because the United States would not respond fully to his requests for military equipment. As a result he constructed an arms factory at San Cristóbal. To get the military equipment he needed and could not produce at his armory or buy from the United States, he turned to willing European suppliers. With the exception of conventional aircraft and small naval vessels, Trujillo had far more success obtaining arms equipment and munitions in Europe (principally from England, France, Spain and Sweden) than in the United States (either from governmental stocks or from private suppliers with the necessary export licenses).

Trujillo persistently demanded that the United States sell him military equipment at discount rates, and he resorted to an extensive lobbying and public relations campaign in an effort to get congressional legislation passed or amended. He attempted to influence the United States armed forces, especially the Army, to support his requests against the negatively disposed State Department. Drawing on various international sources and developing his own internal source of arms and munitions, Trujillo developed one of the largest and most powerful military establishments in the Caribbean after World War II. And after 1950 both his air force and navy assumed proportions far greater than those of most other Caribbean nations.

Following World War II a German war veteran, Otto Winterer, who claimed to be an ex-*Luftwaffe* major, came to the Dominican Republic and convinced General Trujillo of the value of having an elite military organization patterned after Hitler's *Luftwaffe*. Trujillo created such a group in the form of an air force with its own autonomous army and armor. This force, designed to serve as Trujillo's personally loyal counterpoise to the other services, especially the army, included paratroops, infantry and the only tanks in the country. The pilots, most of whom had been trained during World War II by the United States, were a professionally competent and highly privileged group. The force soon became a major diversion for Trujillo's oldest son, Ramfis.

In 1947 the first in a series of incidents occurred to produce increasing turmoil in the Caribbean and exacerbate relations between the Trujillo regime and its neighbors. These incidents were caused by the activities of various Caribbean and Central American exiles, soon known collectively as the "Caribbean Legion," who plotted to invade the Dominican Republic and overthrow General Trujillo. The first planned expedition from Cuba — the Cayo Confites Affair — failed because the Cuban government finally reversed its policy and arrested the participants.[36] Trujillo's response, reenforced by a one-plane invasion (out of six aircraft sent) of Luperón in 1949, was to engage in an arms buildup. Because he was unable to purchase all of the arms he desired in either the United States or Europe, he accepted the plan of a Hungarian refugee, imported a number of European arms technicians (mainly Hungarian and Italian) and built his own *amería* (arsenal) in San Cristóbal.[37] The arsenal soon achieved high standards of quality workmanship and was capable of producing various types of munitions and weapons (for example, carbines, machine guns, mortars and anti-tank guns), as well as of rebuilding heavier weapons.[38] Trujillo not only achieved considerable self-reliance in the production of lighter weapons, but he developed a surplus that he sold to various Latin American governments.[39]

Trujillo took particular interest in building a Dominican navy, hoping to compete with his Caribbean neighbors, especially Cuba, Mexico and Venezuela. The navy was the one service for which he welcomed American advisors. Contrary to his usual policies of training his officers at home, he would permit certain selected naval officers to go to the United States in order to receive professional and technical instruction.[40]

After Fidel Castro assumed power on January 1, 1959, the activities of the revolutionary government of Cuba contributed to Caribbean turmoil. Trujillo, whose foreign image was already seriously impaired, responded not only by an arms build-up but also by an attempt to create his own Foreign Legion. Since the United States had stopped providing military equipment in 1958, he once again turned to European suppliers. In 1959 he created by means of a special tax a $50,000,000 National Defense Fund for the purchase of arms (only an amount somewhat in excess of $6,000,000 was actually spent for arms—the rest he appropriated to himself). It was the highest military budget in Dominican history.[41] Part of the $6,000,000 was spent on an arms-buying spree, whose acquisitions included a dozen French tanks and a number of British Vampire jets.

Trujillo had been shocked by Castro's success in the face of Batista's overwhelming military strength (to which Trujillo had contributed). Therefore he decided to organize a kind of Foreign Legion for dealing with guerrillas. He planned his elite group of fighting men after the French and Spanish foreign legionnaires. He was never able to create the large, efficient force he had originally envisioned, but his recruiters in Europe did attract a number of men, primarily from France, Greece,

Spain and Yugoslavia, by promising jobs and high salaries. In addition, some soldiers of fortune in the Caribbean were enticed to join. According to Howard Wiarda, three auxiliary forces were established in the late 1950's involving "a reported 5,000 men." [42]

The series of exile invasions that occurred in the Dominican Republic (as well as in Panama and Nicaragua) in 1959 provoked responses within and outside the Dominican Republic. In addition to Trujillo's concerted purchase of arms and his efforts to create a Foreign Legion, there were many acts of terror and repression. These resulted in disaffection or rejection on the part of many Dominicans, especially diplomats, government officials and some military officers. Furthermore, his increased military expenditures contributed greatly to a worsening economic crisis.[43]

A brief discussion of the nature of the military forces developed by Trujillo is necessary for examining the contention that the United States armed and supported Trujillo and thereby enabled him to stay in power. Figure 1 provides the major frame of reference.[44] Although this general military inventory was published in 1966, it is essentially the same as that which existed at the time of Trujillo's assassination in 1961. Particularly in the case of military equipment (airplanes, ships, tanks and artillery), few changes occurred during the five-year period after Trujillo. If there were fewer items of equipment in 1966, it was because some had become obsolete and were scrapped.

Trujillo had greatly increased the magnitude of military expenditures during his regime. The percentage of the national budget earmarked for military use rose from 11.5 per cent in 1931 to 25 per cent in 1957, reaching a high of almost 50 per cent in 1959.[45] His army was the largest service, receiving the largest share of defense appropriations, but it was the most inefficient and unprofessional as a result of his policies of nepotism and constant rotation, and his stress upon loyalty rather than competence. Trujillo insulated the army and the national police from United States influence; usually he would not permit more than minimal contact with United States military ad-

Defense Budget	$33,600,000
Population	3,451,700
Manpower in A.F.	18,500
Defense as % of GNP	3.2%

ARMY
  Manpower   12,000 men
  General   Small, but organized along U.S. lines
  Equipment   Light weapons
                    Armored cars

NAVY
  Manpower   3,500 men
  General   Operating with 33 vessels
  Equipment   *Vessels*
                    2 frigates
                    1 Presidential yacht
                    5 corvettes
                    5 patrol vessels
                    3 landing craft
                    4 Coast Guard vessels
                    3 motor launches
                    2 oilers
                    3 auxiliaries
                    5 tugs

AIR FORCE
  Manpower   3,500 men
  General   Small but efficient air force, numbering about 240
                    aircraft.
  Equipment   *Aircraft*
                    12 D.H. Vampire fighter-bombers
                    12 NAA F-51D fighter-bombers
                    11 Republic F-47D fighter-bombers
                     5 Boeing B-17G bombers
                     7 Douglas B-26 bombers
                       Stearman PT-17 trainers
                       NAA T-6 trainers
                       Beech T-11 trainers
                       C-46 transports
                       D.H. Beaver transports
                       Convair PBY-5A transports
                       Cessna 170 liaison
                     2 Sikorsky S-55 helicopters

Miscellaneous Data

Defense Agreements   Rio Pact
MAP Type Assistance
  received from   U.S.   Internal Security Forces   10,000 men

FIGURE 1

Source: Laurence L. Ewing and Robert C. Sellers (eds.), *The Reference Handbook of the Armed Forces of the World* (1966 ed.; Washington, D.C.: Robert C. Sellers & Associates, 1966). Reproduced by permission of the publishers.

visors (he preferred those from the Spanish army). He sent very few officers outside for training, and then preferably to Spain or to other Latin American countries. He intentionally kept his army at a low level, both in terms of training and equipment, and saw to it that only light weapons and limited amounts of ammunition were available. Although Trujillo generally distrusted his six-brigade army, he did organize the 4th Brigade as an autonomous unit, insured that it was the best equipped and trained, and made it personally loyal to him. This brigade was the only one that had armor and heavy artillery; there was a combat battalion with armored vehicles but no tanks, and another with heavy field artillery (152 mm Spanish artillery).[46]

Trujillo was interested in the operational efficiency of the Dominican navy. As a result, he permitted considerable contact between United States and Dominican naval personnel. He also sent numbers of his enlisted men and commissioned officers to the Canal Zone and to the United States for professional training. Consequently, the Dominican navy, which had a contingent of marines until 1959 but no air arm, became the most professional of his services. Most of the vessels were acquired from the United States, mostly during World War II and the immediate postwar period. In the 1950's Trujillo acquired a few non-combat vessels. The remainder of the vessels were acquired from Canada and England, and most were of World War II vintage.[47] In 1957 Trujillo's navy consisted of thirty-nine combat and auxiliary vessels, including two destroyers, eight frigates, six patrol boats and seven coast guard boats.[48]

The Dominican air force, which Trujillo especially favored during his last few years, got its start during World War II with the assistance of the United States, especially the Marine Corps pilot training mission sent in 1943. In 1940 Dominican personnel in the rudimentary air force consisted of ten officers and several non-commissioned officers.[49] By the end of 1952, the same year that the *Escuadrón de Caza "Ramfis"* under the command of Lieutenant General Ramfis Trujillo was created, there were 131 aircraft in the air force. Most of them were of United

States manufacture and of World War II vintage, but a few were from the 1930's. At least a dozen English Beaufighters and Mosquitos were included in the force.[50] Ernesto Vega states that by 1954 the air force consisted of 156 aircraft, although he does not give the total of each type.[51] Since the United States made no jet aircraft available to Trujillo, he bought them from England and Sweden.

Like the *Luftwaffe*, Trujillo's air force had its own combat troops, artillery and the only tanks in the country. These were light tanks, most of which came from France and Sweden; only a few were from the United States. The same pattern applied to the national origin of manufacture and/or purchase of artillery and mortars for both the army and the air force. About 10 per cent of the artillery and mortars was obtained from the United States. The bulk of the mortars (60 mm, 81 mm and 120 mm) came from Brazil, France and Spain. Cannons, howitzers and recoilless rifles came from England, Germany, Spain and Sweden. Trujillo obtained rifles from at least half a dozen European countries, machine guns from Italy and Spain, armored cars from Sweden.[52] Thus the United States government was in an unfavorable position to control the nature or number of armaments Trujillo employed to maintain his regime in power.

A caveat should be entered at this point. Although United States aid was far from decisive in Trujillo's maintenance of power, it was nevertheless a factor. Aid itself was inconsequential, but when combined with other factors, such as United States neutrality toward the Trujillo regime ("non-intervention"), it may have been more important than if it were the only consideration. The subtle interplay of the various elements of United States policy and its effect on Trujillo will be considered in the final chapter.

4. A NOTE ON ECONOMIC AND TECHNICAL ASSISTANCE

The Trujillo government received no direct public economic assistance from the United States during or after World War

II. Some Export-Import Bank credits were authorized for the Dominican Republic, but none were actually disbursed. The regular importation and purchase of Dominican sugar, which had commenced during the 1930's, as well as of foodstuffs and minerals during the war, are not usually categorized as "economic assistance," although the Dominican Republic did benefit economically.

A foodstuffs program in the Caribbean was inaugurated in 1942. That year President Roosevelt issued a directive to the Department of Agriculture to establish a revolving fund of $250,000 of Lend-Lease money to finance the accumulation and stockpiling of food supplies for the Caribbean area. Food was purchased and sold in the Caribbean area, and the proceeds were put back into the fund. The Dominican Republic was included in this program. In 1943 the United States purchased the entire Dominican export production of meat, corn, rice, peanut meal and sugar. In February, 1944, a United States-Dominican agreement was concluded whereby the entire exportable surplus of several Dominican food products would be sold to the United States through the Foreign Economics Administration in order to help meet shortages of food in the Caribbean and other areas.[53]

Trujillo had always been unhappy about Cuba's large sugar quota and its favored position in the United States market. He regularly lobbied to get the Dominican quota increased. The size of the quota for his major earner of foreign exchange increased over the years, mainly as a result of increased consumption in the United States, although his persistent lobbying played at least a minor role. By 1959 the Dominican quota was almost 81,500 short tons and in 1960 almost 131,000.[54] These figures, however, are only partial ones, for there was an additional "non-quota" category. In 1960 the "non-quota" quantity of Dominican sugar was almost 322,000 short tons.[55] Also, in 1960, when the Cuban quota was cut in July and redistributed, the Dominican Republic got almost 30,000 additional short tons. The effect of this bonus was reduced by the Department of Agriculture's requirement that the Trujillo government pay an additional tax of two cents per pound,[56] which was part of the United States' attempt to cooperate with the sanctions against Trujillo that had been voted by the OAS in August, 1960.

Technical assistance was made available to the Dominican Republic on only a small scale. In 1939 President Roosevelt established the Interdepartmental Committee on Scientific and Cultural Cooperation to administer operations of various governmental departments and agencies offering their services to other governments. The Dominican Republic was one of fifteen Latin American countries selected for the establishment of agricultural and experiment stations that operated during the war.[57] The wartime agency of the Coordinator of Inter-American Affairs (IIAA), set up in 1942 as an operating agency in various technical fields, carried on several projects in health and sanitation in the Dominican Republic.[58] As of September 30, 1946, the United States had contributed $400,000 and the Dominican Republic $175,000 to the cooperative health program. All these programs began theoretically as war measures and were designed "to combat Nazi totalitarian influences," [59] among other things. Some of these programs continued to function for a few years after the war; others were taken over by the Dominican Republic.

Technical assistance was revitalized with the worldwide Point Four program, later included in the Mutual Security Program. A "General Technical Assistance Agreement" was concluded between the United States and Trujillo governments early in 1951. A program in agriculture and natural resources was started in 1952, in industry and mining in 1953, and in transportation in 1955; the education program already in existence was continued, as was a rubber research program that had been carried on by the United States Department of Agriculture since 1942.[60] By 1957 technical assistance was again limited to an education program which included projects in vocational education, industrial arts and rural school teacher training.[61] The following table enables one to note the extent of technical assistance over the years since World War II:

UNITED STATES TECHNICAL ASSISTANCE OBLIGATIONS TO THE DOMINICAN
REPUBLIC, 1946–1960
(in thousands of dollars, by fiscal years)

1946 – 207	1954 – 229
1947 – 198	1955 – 362
1948 – 72	1956 – 537
1949 – 8	1957 – 210
1950 – 19	1958 – 163
1951 – 84	1959 – 219
1952 – 187	1960 – 253
1953 – 318	

FIGURE 2

Sources: U.S. Department of Commerce, *Foreign Aid by the United States Government, 1940–1951* (1952); Department of Commerce, *Foreign Grants and Credits* (1952 and 1953); Foreign Operations Administration, *Operations Report* (1954 and 1955); International Cooperation Administration, *Operations Report* (1955–1960).

V ACCOMMODATION TO CHANGE

The essential problem the United States faced in its relations with Trujillo between 1959 and 1961 was adapting to the changing Latin American political scene by opposing Trujillo without violating the nonintervention principle. The United States confronted the problem by acting unilaterally on its own and multilaterally through the Organization of American States. This attempt to accommodate to changes involving Latin American dictatorship, democracy and communism without violating nonintervention pledges was reflected in the proceedings of the Fifth and Sixth Meetings of Ministers of Foreign Affairs (in 1959 and 1960, respectively), and in subsequent developments between the Dominican Republic and the United States.

1. THE POLICY DILEMMA

In its Dominican relations during the last few years of the Trujillo era, the United States experienced something of the standard dilemma of the times regarding its policies toward Latin American dictatorial regimes: Despite restrictions imposed by the principle of nonintervention, the United States was accused of ignoring the democratic aspirations of others, thus defying a trend toward representative government in Latin America. Once Trujillo fell from power, the United States would again be identified with an unpopular figure and held responsible for problems accompanying the aftermath of dictatorship.

The United States was clearly sensitive to this problem. Despite Washington's rationale during the Dominican debate

beginning in 1956 (discussed in Chapter II) that opposition to
Trujillo would violate the principle of nonintervention, the
United States was not unresponsive to its critics. On occasion
the United States would admit that perhaps it had been overly
friendly to dictatorial regimes.[1]

During the last two years of the Eisenhower administration,
the orientation of the Latin American policy of the United States
began to change. The major catalyst for change was Vice-President Nixon's hostile reception during his 1958 Latin American
"good will" tour, especially in Peru and Venezuela. The saliva,
rocks and insults hurled at Nixon reflected Latin American dissatisfaction with United States policies toward dictators, among
other things. However, the policy change was further motivated
by the judgment that dictators bequeath a political vacuum to
their successors, which foments the communist alternative.
Therefore the best way to oppose communism is by opposing
oppressive regimes. Once dictators have been deposed, their
countries are vulnerable to political chaos and communist subversion.

The United States did not immediately act upon this judgment
concerning the link between dictatorship and communism.
Vice-President Nixon, after returning from his harrowing Latin
American tour, recommended that the United States extend a
"cool handshake" to dictators and an *abrazo* to democracies.
His views were echoed by Dr. Milton Eisenhower (see Chapter
I). Beyond these moderate proposals, however, the United
States was unwilling to oppose dictators as late as 1959. In the
case of Trujillo, this unwillingness was made clear during the
revival of Caribbean conflict in the late 1950's and at the Fifth
Meeting of Foreign Ministers in 1959.

2. CARIBBEAN TENSION AND THE FIFTH MEETING
   OF MINISTERS

In 1959 Caribbean instability again involved the Trujillo
regime. When Cuban dictator Fulgencio Batista abandoned the

field on January 1, after his defeat by Fidel Castro in the Cuban revolution, he fled to the Dominican Republic, thus joining deposed Argentine dictator Juan Perón, who had already sought and gained refuge there. Trujillo and Batista had had many differences, but after the United States ceased its military aid to Cuba, Trujillo had sold military equipment to Batista. Castro had hated Trujillo on ideological grounds as well as for supporting Batista. Now his hatred of Trujillo was intensified when asylum was granted the former Cuban dictator.

Castro announced his determination not only to carry out a thoroughgoing social revolution in Cuba itself, but also to work for the speedy elimination of all remaining military dictatorships in Latin America, beginning with the Caribbean area. Although Castro later became a dictator professing communism, the issue in 1959 appeared to be the same as it had been before the post-World War II international strife in the Caribbean: democracy versus dictatorship. Almost immediately after Castro came to power in Cuba, he initiated a "war of nerves" against the dictatorship of Rafael Trujillo. Cuba and the Dominican Republic became the principal rivals in Caribbean international politics.

In 1959 three "invasions"—of Panama, Nicaragua and the Dominican Republic—produced considerable tension in the Caribbean area. Although communism was not an issue, the revolutionary government of Cuba was a major contributor to Caribbean tension. In mid-June of 1959 the Dominican Republic was "invaded" twice by revolutionary groups of various nationalities at Constanza, Maimón and a point near Estero Hondo. The intruding forces numbered some 56 men brought in by aircraft and about 140 by yachts, all originating in Cuba. The Dominican government claimed to have "annihilated" the invaders.[2] On July 2, 1959, the Dominicans appealed to the Council of the Organization of American States for action under the Rio Treaty, accusing both Cuba and Venezuela of participating in the preparation of the recent "invasions."

The Dominican Republic also charged Cuba and Venezuela

with preparing new exile landings and appealed to the OAS to intervene. The Cuban and Venezuelan governments denied the charges, insisting they would not permit an OAS investigation of complaints on their territories. When Trujillo threatened attacks on their governments, they issued counter-threats that were equally precipitous. On July 10 the Dominican Republic unexpectedly withdrew its charges,[3] apparently recognizing that little support would be forthcoming from the other OAS members. By this time Trujillo had lost his support in the inter-American community, and the United States was becoming more and more impatient with him. Nevertheless the United States and several Latin American states felt that the time had come to convene a meeting of the American foreign ministers to discuss the Caribbean situation. The COAS decided at its July 13 meeting to convoke a Meeting of the Ministers of Foreign Affairs.

The Fifth Meeting of Foreign Ministers was held at Santiago de Chile in August, 1959. Its purpose was to reconcile the increasing demand for democratic progress and economic and social change in Latin America (particularly in the Caribbean) with traditional inter-American principles of peaceful relations and nonintervention in the internal affairs of others.[4] A few states favored a compromise of the nonintervention principle in order to oppose dictatorial regimes (*viz.*, those of the Dominican Republic and Haiti), promote democracy and protect human rights.

The United States Secretary of State, Christian A. Herter, took a strong stand for nonintervention, which received strong support from most of the other delegations present. Herter noted four principles expressed in the Charter of the OAS that were particularly applicable to the situation: nonintervention, collective security, the effective exercise of representative democracy and respect for human rights, and cooperation for economic and social progress. He emphasized the principle of nonintervention over the other three. Herter's strong stand, based on the idea that overthrowing oppressive regimes would produce disorder and tension and give political opportunity to the communists,[5] exemplified the Latin American policy of the Eisenhower administration.

What was wrong with the United States position was that under the circumstances it appeared to rebuke Cuba and Venezuela — both of which favored compromising the nonintervention principle for OAS action against Trujillo,[6] and were, in addition, the apparent centers of anti-dictatorial, pro-democratic movements.

Notwithstanding the arguments of Cuba and Venezuela, the overwhelming majority of delegates opposed any compromise of the nonintervention principle, which was manifested in several provisions of the Final Act. However, in the Declaration of Santiago, the meeting strongly condemned dictatorial governments without mentioning specific names. Thus the Fifth Meeting of Ministers reflected certain changes in the intensity of feeling about nonintervention. An awareness of greater regional responsibility for democracy was reflected in the discussions. The nonintervention principle was viewed in other than absolute terms; it was looked upon as it related to certain dictatorial regimes in the Caribbean. The ministers, although reaffirming the nonintervention principle, apparently no longer wanted to allow it to be a shield for dictatorial practices. A number of important topics relating to the relationship between nonintervention, representative democracy and human rights were referred to various agencies for study and for the preparation of reports and drafts for future consideration.[7]

3. PRELUDE TO THE SIXTH MEETING OF FOREIGN MINISTERS

A number of events occurring in 1959 and 1960 prompted another Meeting of Foreign Ministers in 1960. Its focus was primarily on the Dominican Republic rather than divided among most of the other states of the Caribbean region, as had been the case in the past. The Inter-American Peace Committee played a major role in reporting and publicizing the activities of the Dominican Republic. Also important was a special investigating committee of the Council of the Organization of American States. The United States was represented on both committees.

The Peace Committee prepared two major reports, in keeping with its mandate at the Fifth Meeting of Ministers in 1959 to ascertain the contribution to Caribbean tension of the violation of human rights and the non-exercise of democracy. The first [8] was published April 14, 1960, and the second [9] nearly four months later, on August 5. The first report, which reflected six months' work by two subcommittees of the Peace Committee, stressed that the promotion of democracy and the protection of human rights would be the best means for eliminating political tensions. But its most important statement concerned the principle of nonintervention, which the committee regarded as transcending any commitment to democracy and human rights. According to the report, the committee "took a firm position in favor of the peaceful achievement, without foreign intervention, of the political goals" of the American peoples. Accordingly, the committee could "under no circumstances suggest any formula that would violate the nonintervention principle or the solemn inter-American commitments which have as their aim the preservation of the right of each state to work out its own political destiny."

The second report discussed four incidents that had been investigated by the Peace Committee throughout 1959 and 1960. The two incidents involving the Dominican Republic will be examined here.

On November 19, 1959, an aircraft dropped pamphlets by mistake over the island of Curaçao, a Dutch possession. These pamphlets, destined originally for a Venezuelan city, called for the Venezuelan armed forces to revolt against the government of President Betancourt. In a note of November 25, 1959, the Venezuelan representative to the COAS asked the Inter-American Peace Committee to investigate the incident and at the same time charged the Dominican government with complicity. After completing an investigation the Peace Committee concluded that the flight to drop the pamphlets inciting revolution in Venezuela "could not have been carried out without the connivance of the Dominican authorities."

The second case discussed in the August report resulted from a Venezuelan note of February 17, 1960, requesting that the Peace Committee "investigate the flagrant violations of human rights by the Government of the Dominican Republic, which are aggravating tensions in the Caribbean." The Peace Committee attempted to visit the Dominican Republic and conduct an on-the-spot survey; however, the Dominican government refused to permit entry. As an alternative approach the committee requested information from member states, discussed the problem with both Dominican and Venezuelan representatives and received testimony in Washington, D.C.

The Peace Committee ultimately concluded "that international tensions in the Caribbean region have been aggravated by flagrant and widespread violations of human rights which have been committed and continue to be committed in the Dominican Republic." Among these violations were "the denial of free assembly and of free speech, arbitrary arrests, cruel and inhuman treatment of political prisoners, and the use of intimidation and terror as political weapons." The report concluded that the violations of human rights in the Dominican Republic "have increased the tensions existing in the Caribbean region," which would continue to increase as long as those violations persisted.

Despite this opinion by the Peace Committee, the Inter-American Juridical Committee stated in a subsequent report that there was no legal basis in the OAS Charter for collective action "in defense of democracy, for its maintenance or for its restoration." [10] The Dominican government reacted to the Peace Committee report by stating before the COAS on June 22, 1960, "that the pronouncement amounts to an intervention in the internal affairs of the Dominican Republic."

Two incidents occurring in April and June, 1960, respectively, led to a Meeting of Foreign Ministers to consider certain acts carried out by the Dominican Republic. These two incidents, following the earlier unsuccessful attempt to drop pamphlets inciting revolution against the government of Venezuela, reflected an accelerated drive by Trujillo against his Venezuelan antagonist and leading member of the Latin American "democratic left," President Rómulo Betancourt. This drive finally culminated in an attempt to assassinate the Venezuelan chief of state.

The first incident involved a military uprising in April, 1960, in San Cristóbal, Venezuela. The uprising was led by General Castro León, a former general in the Venezuelan army. An investigation disclosed that the Dominican government had issued passports to León and other instigators of the uprising.

At the time of the uprising and shortly thereafter, an important but unofficial conference was being held in Venezuela to focus on the problems of democracy and human rights, and the nonintervention principle. The conference passed a number of resolutions condemning four dictatorships in Latin America: the Dominican Republic, Haiti, Nicaragua and Paraguay. The conference — the Second Inter-American Conference for Democracy and Freedom — meeting in Maracay, Venezuela, from April 22 to 26, 1960, was attended by a number of leading liberals (including, in addition to President Betancourt of Venezuela, José Figueres, former president of Costa Rica; Gonzalo J. Facio, Costa Rica's ambassador to the United States; and Robert J. Alexander, professor at Rutgers University). Important opinions were expressed, but no governmental responsibilities resulted from the conference. President Betancourt, in his address to the opening session, advocated collective sanctions of nonrecognition and economic isolation against those states violating human rights, and the application of "a rigorous multilateral preventive cordon" around such regimes. The conference subscribed to the acceptance and application of the Rodríguez Larreta Doctrine, and welcomed the action of the Inter-American Peace Committee in the Dominican Republic.[11]

Far more serious than the Dominican-supported uprising in Venezuela was the attempt to assassinate President Betancourt by detonating a planted bomb near his passing automobile. This incident resulted in Venezuela's request for another meeting of the Foreign Ministers and for invocation of the Rio Treaty (under Article 6) "to consider the acts of intervention and aggression by the Government of the Dominican Republic against the Government of Venezuela, which culminated in the attempt upon the life of the Venezuelan Chief of State." The COAS met in Washington on July 6 and 8, 1960, to consider the Venezuelan request.

The United States representative, Ambassador John C. Dreier, stated that the evidence submitted had persuaded the United States to believe that the situation under consideration met the requirements of Article 6 of the Rio Treaty and that the Organ of Consultation called for was appropriate.[12] On July

Venezuelan President Betancourt's destroyed auto after Trujillo's unsuccessful assassination attempt, June 24, 1960. *Courtesy Oficina Central de Información (Caracas)*

8 by a vote of nineteen to zero, the COAS agreed to convoke the Sixth Meeting of Consultation of the American Foreign Ministers and to appoint a committee that would investigate the Venezuelan charges and report to the foreign ministers.

The five-member investigating committee, composed of representatives from Argentina, Mexico, Panama, Uruguay and the United States, examined the Venezuelan allegations and heard the Dominican denials and countercharges. In addition, the committee examined many documents, drew on the work and information of the Peace Committee, and visited both Caracas and Ciudad Trujillo. The committee's report, presented to the council on August 8, 1960, included detailed discussions of the three acts that comprised the Venezuelan protest against the Trujillo regime: [13] first, the attempt in November, 1959, to drop leaflets on a Venezuelan city inciting revolution against the government; second, the Venezuelan military uprising in April, 1960; and third, and most important, the assassination attempt against President Betancourt in June, 1960. Complicity of the Trujillo government was established in all three instances. With regard to the assassination effort, the report said that the persons implicated in the attempt "received moral support and material assistance from high officials of the Government of the Dominican Republic."

4. THE SIXTH MEETING OF FOREIGN MINISTERS

The Sixth Meeting of Foreign Ministers met in San José, Costa Rica, from August 16 to 21, 1960.[14] The major objective was to determine what action the OAS should take against the Dominican government in view of the investigating committee's report, which had first been presented to the council and was now before the Ministers of Foreign Affairs. The discussion among Latin American delegates during the early stages of the meeting did not embrace the usual preoccupation with nonintervention (this came later in response to the United States delegate's proposal). However, the Dominican Republic predictably denied the accusations and accused Venezuela, along with the Peace Committee, of intervention.

There were two reasons for the initial absence of debate on the principle of nonintervention. First, the Trujillo regime was almost universally disliked and opposed in Latin America. Second, the Dominican government itself, by its acts, had violated the nonintervention principle. However, there was no Latin American desire or will to intervene and honor other American commitments—the promotion of democracy and the protection of human rights. Instead, it was the aim of the United States to use Trujillo's violation of nonintervention vis-à-vis Venezuela as a pretext for converting the OAS into "an anti-dictatorial alliance." [15]

While the Latin American ministers favored sanctions as a means of punishing the Trujillo government, the United States representative, Secretary of State Herter, advocated an unprecedented role for the OAS. His proposal reflected a shift in policy attributable to the impact of Castro's rise to power. The shift was away from nonintervention as far as dictators were concerned—and toward a renewed interest in promoting democracy.[16] Thus a new means to the end of maintaining stability and preventing communist influence was embraced. The OAS was to be the instrument for bringing about democratic change in the Dominican government and for removing Trujillo from power. Such change would obviate the "political vacuum problem" and the resultant threat of communist inroads following in the wake of a dictator's overthrow, as had just happened in Cuba after Batista.

As later discussion revealed, Herter opposed the application of sanctions favored by most Latin American republics, preferring instead that the OAS agree to sponsor free elections in the Dominican Republic. He accepted the indictment against the Dominican government and stated his belief that its "grave acts against the sovereignty of Venezuela" deserved the condemnation of the meeting. But he said he doubted the efficacy of applying sanctions in order to move the Dominican Republic toward representative democracy.

His alternative was that the Dominican Republic agree to receive a special OAS committee to make certain that free elections were held under committee supervision. Herter's proposal, which provided for OAS involvement to force democratic reform in Dominican politics, "was clearly an attempt to use the sanctions provided for by the Rio Treaty as leverage to guide Dominican politics into non-Communist channels." [17] His recommended approach, especially its implications as recognized by the Latin American ministers, provoked a typical debate on the principle of nonintervention. Consequently, the United States abandoned the "free elections" proposal and joined the Latin American consensus.

On August 20, by a vote of nineteen to zero (under OAS rules neither the Dominican Republic nor Venezuela had the right to participate in the voting), the council passed a resolution which echoed the investigating committee's conclusion that persons implicated in the attempt on the life of President Betancourt had received "moral and material assistance from high officials of the Government of the Dominican Republic." The Dominican government was "condemned emphatically" and declared guilty of "intervention and aggression" which justified collective action under Article 6 of the Rio Treaty. The foreign ministers agreed to the "breaking of diplomatic relations of all member states with the Dominican Republic," and "partial interruption of economic relations . . . beginning with the immediate suspension of trade in arms and implements of war of every kind." The COAS was authorized to discontinue the measures by a two-thirds affirmative vote of the members "at such time as the Government of the Dominican Republic should cease to constitute a danger to the peace and security of the hemisphere." In the meantime, the council could also consider the "feasibility and desirability" of extending the suspension of trade to other articles.[18]

Seven Latin American states had already broken diplomatic relations with the Dominican Republic before the San José meeting. The United States joined the remaining American republics in severing diplomatic ties with the Trujillo regime. On August 26, 1960, a United States official delivered a note to the Dominican foreign office in Ciudad Trujillo advising that the United States was severing diplomatic relations and requesting that the Dominican diplomatic mission to Washington be recalled. Prior to the foreign ministers' decision, the United States had suspended "trade in arms and implements of war" with the Trujillo government. In January, 1961, the United States banned the export of trucks, parts, crude oil, gasoline and other petroleum products to the Dominican Republic.[19]

The COAS appointed a special committee to observe the effects of the various measures with a view to recommending lifting the sanctions when it became convinced that the Dominican government had demonstrated a willingness to abide by inter-American principles. The committee's first report—on December 21, 1960—concluded "that there has been no substantial change in the attitude of the Government of the Dominican Republic toward the basic principles of the Inter-American System." The committee recommended not only that sanctions be continued but also that they be extended to include petroleum and petroleum products, trucks and spare parts.[20] These recommendations were considered and accepted by the COAS on January 4, 1961, by a vote of fourteen to one. The United States voted affirmatively, six nations abstained and Brazil was the lone dissenter.

Brazil felt that an increase in sanctions was both hasty and "inappropriate," that it would "jeopardize the long-range unity and solidarity of the Americas, and above all it would immediately bring about the aggravation of a situation which might take an unforeseeable turn." In a philosophical vein Brazil observed that "the real solution in such cases does not lie in the progressive application of coercive measures, but at the higher, more constructive, long-range level of moral sanctions and persuasion, which will not endanger inter-American solidarity but preserve the unity of the system and encourage the gradual evolution of the country into a living democracy." Concerning OAS sanctions against the Dominican Republic, Brazil stated that they "had as their purpose not the condemnation of the domestic government of a country—which would violate the principle of non-intervention, the cornerstone of the inter-American System—but the condemnation of acts of aggression and intervention which were perfectly determined and duly verified." [21]

5. THE MEANING OF MULTILATERAL CONDEMNATION

In the United States and in Latin America, opponents of dictators, and anti-Trujillists in particular, applauded the OAS action and the concurrence of the United States. Others protested, however. Senator Olin Johnston (D–S.C.) told the Senate on August 29, 1960, that the action was "a stab in the back by our government to a friend"; that Trujillo, who had been called the "Caesar of the Caribbean" now had a "Brutus of his own"; and that "stupidity and misplaced idealism has led us to turn our backs on anti-communists and support forces intent on ousting a formerly friendly government." [22]

In a more sophisticated manner, William Manger, former Assistant Secretary General of the OAS, said that the Meeting of Foreign Ministers had sacrificed principles to expediency. He said that in response to popular demand the Rio Treaty had been used to punish rather than restrain, which was an abuse of one of the basic instruments of the inter-American system. Manger felt that the OAS had undertaken a responsibility it could never fulfill; that is, once the Trujillo dictatorship came to an end, the OAS could not ascertain that democracy would automatically follow in the Dominican Republic. Moreover, he asked, what advantage "would there be for the Dominican people or for the inter-American community to get rid of Trujillo only to have him replaced by a Castro?" [23]

Actually, condemnation of the Dominican Republic and the

application of sanctions against it was significant for two reasons: (1) This was the first time the OAS had taken such strong action against one of its members, and (2) to Latin Americans this action in no way compromised the principle of nonintervention. However, the Latin American community was not yet willing to modify the nonintervention principle in order to promote democracy and protect human rights. In the context of the San José meeting, nonintervention transcended any commitments to democracy and human rights.

Thus the American community did not take action against the Dominican Republic because that regime had failed to observe democratic principles or had violated human rights, although both these charges could be documented adequately. Nor did Latin America fear, as did the United States, that communism would find fertile ground in the Dominican Republic as a result of Trujillo's oppressive policies. Instead, the OAS action was prompted mainly by the Dominican attempt to assassinate President Betancourt, which the OAS regarded as both a violation of the nonintervention principle and an act of aggression. Because it had committed this act, the Dominican government could no longer utilize the nonintervention principle to rationalize its desired insulation from community action.

6. UNILATERAL REPUDIATION

The United States attempted to align its own unilateral policies with the spirit of the multilateral OAS condemnation of the Dominican Republic. The role of the Dominican Republic in the government-controlled international sugar market in the United States was an important issue in the unilateral repudiation of the Trujillo dictatorship.

The Sugar Act of 1948, which was to expire on December 31, 1960, became a subject of great controversy with the passage of the Sugar Act Extension of 1961. Under the 1948 act the United States had limited the amount of foreign sugar that might be placed on its domestic market. This restriction took the form of quotas on imports and on domestic production as well. The effect was to prevent low-cost foreign sugar from flooding the market and injuring the domestic industry, and to maintain a relatively high United States price compared to the world price. The difference of two cents per pound made it highly profitable for foreign nations to sell in the United States, if they could obtain quotas.[24]

When the 86th Congress turned its attention to new sugar legislation in 1960, it faced a number of circumstances that made simply an extension of the act beyond the scheduled date of expiration all but impossible. Initially, the most important factor was the deterioration of United States-Cuban relations after January, 1959, and establishment of the revolutionary Castro government in Cuba. President Eisenhower asked Congress to empower him to cut the Cuban quota. After considerable debate Congress extended the Sugar Act to March 31, 1961. The President was authorized to assign Cuba any reduced allocation he determined was in the national interest; he was also empowered to reallocate the quotas by means of a specified formula and to specific countries named by Congress to make up the Cuban deficit.

Noting the action taken by the Foreign Ministers Meeting at San José, President Eisenhower, in a message to Congress in August, 1960, requested discretion in the purchase of Dominican sugar and for authority to take away the reallocated quota for the Dominican Republic. The President pointed out that considering the reduced amount of sugar being purchased from Cuba under the new Sugar Act, the Dominican Republic's new allocation represented a sizable increase in its quota. Such imports would give the Dominican Republic "a large sugar bonus embarrassing to the United States in the conduct of our foreign relations throughout the hemisphere," the President said. Thus he asked for legislation that would allow the Dominican share to be purchased instead from any foreign country without regard to allocation.[25]

Hearings were held, and in support of the President's request for legislation Acting Secretary of State C. Douglas Dillon stated before the House Committee on Agriculture that "it is apparent that the U.S. Government would be in an extremely equivocal position if our Government were now to grant to the Dominican Republic an economic benefit by authorizing the additional purchase of nearly four times as much sugar as the United States imported from that country last year." [26] The House and Senate passed different versions of a resolution (HR 13062) to grant the President's request, but these proposals never went to conference and died when Congress adjourned. President Eisenhower's attempt to take away the sugar import from the Dominican Republic was blocked by two Trujillo supporters, Senators James Eastland (D–Miss.) and Allen Ellender

Vice-President Richard M. Nixon and Trujillo exchange *abrazos* in the Dominican Republic, November 1960. *United Press International Photo*

(D–La.). Lacking authority to reduce the Dominican quota, the President imposed a fee of two cents per pound on sugar purchased from the Dominican Republic, an action the Sugar Act authorized him to take at his own discretion. This action canceled the amount per pound over the world price that the United States paid for quota sugar.[27]

In late September, 1960, the governments of Venezuela and the United States exchanged *aides mémoires* concerning the Dominican sugar quota. The Venezuelan government was concerned over the recent authorizations for United States purchases of sugar in the Dominican Republic. The United States in turn gave assurances of its continued opposition to the Trujillo regime and tried to explain the equivocal position as a regrettable product of its constitutional process.[28]

In the meantime a Presidential election took place in the United States. During the campaign the subsequent winner, Senator John F. Kennedy, said that the United States' decision to oppose Trujillo had been wise, for an anti-dictator wave had swept Latin America during the preceding ten years. In this connection he rejected the view that the only alternative to dictatorship was a communist dictator.[29] Once in office and confronted by the question of sugar legislation, President Kennedy supported the prior appeal of the Eisenhower administration for authority to decrease the Dominican quota.

In February, 1961, after a new Congress had convened, Representative Harold Cooley (D–N.C.), chairman of the House Agriculture Committee, introduced a bill to extend the Sugar Act to December 31, 1962, without changing the allocation system, a proposal that would assure the Dominican Republic its share of the import quota. President Kennedy asked Congress to extend the act to the date proposed by Cooley; however, in a letter to Speaker of the House Sam Rayburn, Secretary of State Dean Rusk asked that the Dominican Republic be denied any special benefits under the new law. A compromise bill was finally passed by both houses and signed by the President on March 31, 1961. Sugar legislation was thereby extended to June

30, 1962, and the Dominican Republic was specifically denied a share of the Cuban cut.[30]

Under the COAS resolution the United States was not required to desist from buying Dominican sugar, but supporters of such a policy felt that the United States would be placed in an equivocal position by continuing to buy. It was argued that since the United States was trying to achieve OAS unity against Castro as well, this was an acutely embarrassing position. Nevertheless, the proposal to remove the Dominican bonus was subjected to sharp criticism. The main fear seemed to be that the Trujillo regime might be replaced by something worse.

Concern developed in certain quarters over the possibility that Cuban communism might attempt to gain control in the Dominican Republic. The concern was especially great after Premier Fidel Castro's May 1, 1961, statement in which he described Cuba as a "Socialist Republic." For example, Representative W. R. Poage (D–Tex.) deplored the fact that the Sugar Act was "designed to be used as an instrumentality of power in foreign relations" involving discriminatory treatment of the Dominican Republic. He feared that if the Trujillo government were overthrown it would be succeeded either by "the direct agents of Mr. Castro or a Castro-type communist government." If not overthrown, he argued, Trujillo could not be expected to accept the abuse and continue to maintain his strong anti-communist position.[31] And Representative Cooley was quoted as saying that he "hated like hell to see a country trying to be friendly get kicked in the teeth," especially since Trujillo was not the only dictator sharing in the sugar quota.[32]

The New York Times reported that in a letter to Trujillo dated April 21, 1960, Senator Johnston of South Carolina suggested that Trujillo enlist the American Legion's support to achieve a better public image for the Dominican Republic in the United States. An improved image, he believed, would help the Dominicans win a larger sugar quota in the United States market. Almost four years later in December, 1963, *The New York Times* reported that Senator Johnston "emphasized his belief that his advice to the Dominican government in 1960 was completely justified." He was quoted as saying: "Let me tell you one thing. That Government down there was anti-Communist to the core, more so than I've ever seen." [33]

The Kennedy administration confirmed in July, 1962, that some six weeks before Trujillo was assassinated, on April 16 and 17, 1961, Robert D. Murphy, former Under-Secretary of State, had gone on a confidential mission to the Dominican Republic for President Kennedy. Murphy had been "informally assisted" by Igor Cassini, a New York society columnist who wrote under the name of "Cholly Knickerbocker." Cassini was a friend of prominent figures in the Trujillo regime, including playboy-diplomat Porfirio Rubirosa, who gave Cassini information suggesting a threat of revolution in the Dominican Republic. Cassini informed the President's father, Joseph P. Kennedy, in February, 1961, who passed the information on to the President.

Murphy's mission resulted in a "reporting" memorandum that subsequently reached President Kennedy, but no action was recommended and none was taken. Cassini said in a later interview that the talks "dealt with the possibility of leading the Trujillo Government to a liberalization of its policies." At this same time reports from the Dominican Consul General in New York indicated that Trujillo was hopeful of arranging a meeting with the President or his father "in an effort to win a reversal of United States diplomatic and economic sanctions from the conference of 1960." [34]

Igor Cassini and his dress-designer brother Oleg were at this time directors of Martial, Inc., a New York public relations concern that handled foreign accounts and was registered with the Justice Department under the Foreign Agents Registration Act of 1938. The Dominican Republic was not registered as a Martial account, however. Igor Cassini and R. Paul Englander, who had been associated with Martial, Inc., were indicted in February, 1963, for failing to register as publicity agents for Trujillo; Cassini was accused of sharing fees of almost $200,000 for spreading "political propaganda" to improve the tarnished image of the Trujillo government during the period June, 1959, to November, 1961, in violation of the Foreign Agents Registration Act. (On November 8, 1963, Cassini and Englander pleaded *nolo contendere;* they were subsequently fined $10,000 each and placed on six months' probation.) [35]

7. "DEMOCRATIZATION" OF THE DOMINICAN REPUBLIC

Because of the August, 1960, OAS decision and subsequent independent United States action, Trujillo faced the biggest threat of his thirty years as absolute ruler of the Dominican Republic. A news magazine at the time noted the additional external threats posed by Cuba and by Dominican exiles, and pointed out the internal economic distress caused by three years of drought, low market prices for Dominican exports, decreased tourist trade, large arms-spending in Europe and friction with the Roman Catholic Church.[36]

Trujillo announced that he and his entire family were retiring from public life. Brother Héctor Bienvenido Trujillo resigned as president, allegedly because of ill-health. Rafael Leonidas "Ramfis" Trujillo, Jr., resigned the chairmanship of the combined Chiefs of Staff and left for Geneva. Vice-President Joaquín Balaguer was ostensibly brought in as president to "democratize" the country, but in reality he ruled only as a figurehead for Trujillo. The opposition was "encouraged" to participate in elections announced for the coming year, and general amnesty for political prisoners was promised. However, Trujillo had resorted to democratic masquerades before. Secretary of State Herter understated the generally skeptical view of most observers when he remarked at a press conference that it was not clear whether the new changes were ones of real substance or were simply a reshuffling of the same old regime.[37]

The Dominican government under General Trujillo had committed itself to holding national congressional and presidential elections in return for removal of OAS sanctions. Senator George

A. Smathers (D–Fla.) took the initiative with General Trujillo that resulted in a visit by three North American political scientists to the Dominican Republic in June, 1960, to study the electoral climate. Smathers headed a Senate unit on Latin American trade, which had conducted a ten-nation tour in early 1960. It was during the unit's visit to the Dominican Republic in February that Smathers had met with Trujillo and had encouraged the general to start moving in the direction of democratic government. The Senator warned that if Trujillo did not democratize his government, communism might be the only alternative. Trujillo promised to hold local elections in fifteen months and national elections within two years, and to permit the presence of foreign observers at the time of the elections. Trujillo also consented to Senator Smathers' proposal that a private group of scholars visit the Dominican Republic to ascertain the capabilities and facilities available for holding national elections.[38]

Smathers then contacted the American Political Science Association, which secured the agreement of three political scientists to visit the Dominican Republic. They were Dr. Franklin L. Burdette of the University of Maryland, Richard M. Scammon of the Governmental Affairs Institute and Dr. Henry Wells of the University of Pennsylvania. The trio examined electoral conditions in the Dominican Republic and prepared a report containing their observations and conclusions.[39]

This generally optimistic report found that, in terms of electoral mechanics, the Dominican Republic was in a fairly good position to hold free elections. It observed that literacy was higher there than that in some other Latin American countries whose citizens had voted successfully, that communications and transportation facilities were adequate, and that the electoral laws were "administratively sound." The report stressed the need for a truly secret ballot, for freedom to form political parties, and for freedom from reprisals after the elections. In their conclusion the political scientists defined the central problem affecting the possibility of free Dominican elections: "Whether such free elections are held depends in the final analysis on the will and response of Generalissimo Trujillo."

In 1960 Trujillo's opportunism and expediency led him to approach communism in response to United States and Latin American opposition to his oppressive regime. His movement away from alignment with the United States and the OAS occurred in the months before the OAS voted sanctions against his government. Early that year Trujillo took the initiative and worked out a détente with Fidel Castro, previously a Dominican Republic *bête noire*. The new alignment was reflected in the broadcasts of *La Voz Dominicana* and *Radio Caribe,* which stopped castigating Castro and began attacking the United States in Marxian terms. In June, the same month Trujillo attempted to kill his leading democratic critic, the president of Venezuela, the Dominican Communist party was legalized. The *New York Herald Tribune* reported on May 10, 1961, that Castro and Trujillo, in the face of rising Latin American and United States pressure, had signed a "Hitler-Stalin" non-aggression pact. (The Dominican Republic denied the existence of such a pact.)

Trujillo also attempted to establish contacts and relations with the Soviet Union and with Eastern European countries. Sympathetic gestures were made toward Premier Nikita Khrushchev, and Dominican emissaries were sent to Moscow. However, in early September, 1961, the Soviet Union initiated a move in the United Nations Security Council to endorse OAS sanctions under Article 53 of the UN Charter. The Soviet resolution was defeated and the Security Council voted instead to "take note" of the OAS measures.

The Soviet objective in requesting Security Council approval of the OAS action against the Dominican Republic was to establish the Security Council's competence in regional enforcement actions. Legal and political implications related to the unsuccessful Soviet move were that the Soviet Union would have been able to cast its veto in preventing regional enforcement actions, thus establishing a precedent for Soviet opposition in the eventuality of OAS sanctions against Cuba.[40] In the words of Robert D. Crassweller, "the Russian flirtation had failed, but it had existed from the first only as a cynical leverage against the United States, a tactic of intimidation, and the failure of the Russians to cooperate was no reason to abandon the anti-United States posture." [41]

Four months later, on May 30, 1961, the thirty-one-year regime of General-President Trujillo came to an end with his assassination. Although it appeared that the major impediment to change and reform in the Dominican Republic had been removed, OAS sanctions were not removed until January, 1962 — seventeen months after they had first been applied and seven months after the dictator's death. During this latter period the United States worked through the OAS in an attempt to reorient certain basic institutions in the Dominican Republic, primarily the military forces, in keeping with the policy goals of the Kennedy administration. [42]

8. CONCLUSION

During the last years of the Eisenhower administration and the early months of the Kennedy Presidency, the United States abandoned its policy of non-opposition to Trujillo. This change of policy indicated in part a judgment that Trujillo's end was probably not far away at the time and a desire not to be identified with Trujillo and his legacy when he departed, as the United States had been with dictators in Colombia, Cuba and Venezuela. Open repudiation of Trujillo, however reluctantly tendered and modified by the fear of creating new problems, reflected a new flexibility in United States policy means. A few years previously the United States would not have seriously considered violating the principle of nonintervention. Now, however, it was felt that the time had come to adjust to what appeared to be a new political order in Latin America and not to defy an apparent trend toward popular government.

Despite the fact that the United States had joined in recognizing "effective democracy" and nonintervention as basic principles of the inter-American system, the limitations of effective

Dominican democracy were too obvious to make democracy a criterion for friendly relations. These relations were governed by considerations more practical than the observance of democratic processes. Nevertheless, doctrinaire pro-democratic pressure, such as that from Congressman Porter, had its effect on influencing the decision to oppose Trujillo.

The Latin American mood at the Foreign Ministers Meeting also helped condition the change in United States policy. The charge against Trujillo was as much that he was a dictator as that he was disturbing the peace of the hemisphere. The formal indictment against Trujillo specified aggression and intervention. However, the tyrannical character of the Trujillo regime was certainly on the minds of many, and his great unpopularity as a dictator made it easy to vote sanctions for the crime of violating the sacred principle of nonintervention.

However, it would be a mistake to regard the reversal of United States or OAS policy as having been motivated solely by the fact that Trujillo was a tyrant, or by an expectation of the early triumph of Dominican democracy. It is true that the United States made a whole-hearted effort to establish democracy in the Dominican Republic after Trujillo's death, but it is evident that Washington was also prepared to act on the basis of the uncertain advent of democracy.[43] The United States seemed to be saying to Dominicans, "Don't go Communist" as much as it was urging them, "Go democratic."

We may conclude that ideological pressure had its influence on the change of policy, but that decisions by and large were not based on abstract considerations but rather on the peculiar circumstances of the case and the nature of the objectives being sought. The single overriding objective was to create stability in the Dominican Republic, and the new policy indicated an evaluation that it was doubtful whether stability through Trujillo's dictatorial methods could long endure.

VI THE AFTERMATH OF DICTATORSHIP

Important to an evaluation of United States policy toward Trujillo, and significant for actions toward dictators in general, are problems resulting from the aftermath of his dictatorship. While the present writers are well aware that *trujillismo* survives today in the Dominican Republic in certain military and civilian circles, it is beyond the scope of this study to go deeply into United States-Dominican relations since the death of Trujillo. The dramatic and complex events of the intervention of 1965 and the period since then involve many issues beyond the problem of dictatorship and democracy. Nevertheless, a brief review of the years since Trujillo's death is necessary before any conclusions about relations with dictators can be drawn. The fact of Trujillo's many years of autocratic rule presented policy dilemmas for the United States after he had left the scene and the Dominican Republic began to move from dictatorship to something else. (The attempt to deal with continuing Trujilloism was a major factor contributing to the civil war and intervention of 1965.) The purpose of this chapter is to analyze attempts by the United States and the Organization of American States to influence events in the Dominican Republic after 1960, based on the idea that Trujilloism did not end with the demise of Trujillo.

1. THE POST-TRUJILLO SITUATION

After Trujillo's death on the night of May 30, 1961, the most urgent political questions in the Dominican Republic involved the problem of succession. Both before and after the assassination, observers predicted that the Dominican Republic would follow one of three roads into its political future: It would either revert to dictatorship, degenerate into anarchy or communism, or embrace democracy.[1] A power struggle among several political groups began immediately after Trujillo's death, and each of these alternatives seemed possible at one time or another. But at this writing the unfinished struggle has produced none of them on a continuing basis.

An immediate question after Trujillo's death was whether or not the sanctions imposed by the OAS against the Trujillo regime in 1960 should be continued. Trujillo's heirs said they would try to bring about the gradual development of democracy and to respect the civil rights of Dominican citizens. Since they were being pressured by the continuing OAS sanctions and a great deal of international attention as well, they did relax certain aspects of governmental control and forced into exile a few of the worst Trujillo associates. The dictator's two "general" brothers, Arismendi and Héctor, left the country. The government promised amnesty for all political prisoners, a safe return for exiles and free elections in 1962. However, the efficient police-state apparatus was not dismantled. And though Ramfis disavowed political ambitions for himself, he did not give up control of the armed forces, which were an inherent part of Dominican political life.

After a six-week period of surprising calm following Trujillo's death, the first violent opposition to the government began. It was triggered primarily by returning exiles and students. Balaguer and Ramfis encountered increasing opposition and demands that the president resign and all members of the Trujillo family leave the Dominican Republic. The new regime found that dismounting the dictatorial tiger was difficult to accomplish gracefully.

In September, 1960, the Council of the OAS had appointed a special committee to observe the effects of the sanctions imposed upon the Trujillo government and to make recommendations concerning their continuation (see Chapter V). The committee met on June 2, 1961, three days after Trujillo's death, and decided to send a fact-finding subcommittee to the Dominican Republic to determine the need for continuing the OAS measures against the Dominican government. The subcommittee was composed of representatives from Colombia, Panama, the United States and Uruguay.

The team visited the Dominican Republic from June 7 until June 15. In its subsequent report to the special committee on July 2, 1961, these observations were made:

(a) that there has been no substantial change in the character and policies of the Dominican government;

(b) that officials implicated in the attempt on the life of the president of the Republic of Venezuela on June 24, 1960, continue to hold positions in the government;

(c) that the Dominican officials who issued the diplomatic passports used by Venezuelans participating in the April, 1960, military uprising in San Cristóbal, Venezuela, also remain in the government;

(d) that the General Amnesty Law is not being applied, or at least not effectively so;

(e) that there have been repressive acts against Dominican citizens; and

(f) that it is not known what has become of various Dominican citizens.[2]

The report noted the Dominican government's declaration of intentions regarding democratic progress, but said that it was too early "to determine the degree of change that may have occurred in the character and policies of the Dominican Government." The subcommittee recommended continued observation of Dominican activities. Thus no concrete conclusions were reached, and the sanctions remained in effect.

On July 13 President Balaguer sent a letter to the COAS indicating his government's willingness to cooperate "to bring about the discontinuation" of OAS sanctions, and welcomed another subcommittee visit. The subcommittee again visited the Dominican Republic from September 12 until October 1. Its second report, presented to the special committee on November 10, again noted the gap between the government's claims of progress and its opponents' charges of continued violations. The report was influenced more by critics of the Dominican government than by its defenders. After acknowledging a limited amount of progress in the "program of democratization" and a degree of change since its last report, the subcommittee concluded "that greater progress than that which has been attained so far should be evidenced before the conclusion can be reached that the Dominican Government has ceased to be a danger to the peace and security of the Continent." Continued observation was recommended.[3]

Meanwhile, on August 29, 1961, the Dominican ambassador to the OAS made a report to the special OAS committee restating his government's intention to bring about a democratic transformation, and expressing the wish that the OAS subcommittee return promptly to observe the progress of Dominican democratization.[4] On September 12, 1961, an OAS inspection team arrived in the Dominican Republic to study the possibility of easing sanctions, check the progress of democracy since Trujillo's assassination, and find out if free elections were possible in 1962. Riots greeted the subcommittee, for the now-active political opposition groups were just as anxious to have the sanctions continued as the ruling regime was to end them. Despite a rapidly deteriorating economic situation, the opposition did not want the sanctions lifted until concessions had been won from the government, for it was feared that their removal might strengthen the government to the point where the opposition might once again be throttled.

President Balaguer, on the other hand, strongly urged the OAS to end the sanctions, claiming they had hurt his nation severely, and warned that his government might be replaced by a communist dictatorship if they were continued. No doubt the lifting of sanctions was considered vital, too, because the Dominican Republic remained ineligible for United States financial aid or expansion of its sugar quota while they remained in force.

President Balaguer stated his case on October 2, 1961, during a brief visit to the United Nations, where in a remarkable speech he enumerated Trujillo's many crimes, including the assassination attempt against Betancourt in June, 1960. "But," Balaguer said, "it is not fair that the punishment should continue after the death of the culprit."

In addition to the work of the special committee, the Inter-American Commission on Human Rights was also active at the time. From its establishment in October, 1960, through early 1961, it had received an increasing number of complaints from Dominicans concerning the violation of human rights by the Trujillo government. In April, 1961, the month prior to Trujillo's assassination, the commission had begun preparing a document on the various aspects of human rights in the Dominican Republic. The document was completed in September, 1961, almost four months after Trujillo's death.[5]

Because of continuing complaints of human rights violations by the new Dominican government, the commission visited the Dominican Republic from October 22 to 28, 1961. The Dominican government had agreed to the visit but asked that the study be limited to events occurring after the Trujillo assassination. Based on this fact-finding tour, the commission sent a note to the Balaguer government on November 8, 1961, stating that the principal violators of human rights were groups of *paleros* ("stick men") whom Balaguer himself had denounced over the radio in October. The police and army, the note said, had failed to take action against the *paleros,* and both were criticized for their own excesses during the political disorders and student riots. Finally, the note cited the lack of freedom of speech and expression, the denial of freedom for the labor movement, and the mass political deportations.[6]

Recommendations were presented to the OAS. The commission noted that the most flagrant violations of human rights had occurred during the Trujillo regime, and that the situation had improved under Balaguer. The note pointed out that since the start of 1962 the commission had received no complaints concerning human rights violations from the Dominican Republic.

During this post-Trujillo period the United States became cautiously but increasingly sympathetic toward the new regime. After an initial period of reserve during which the Kennedy administration warned the OAS against haste in lifting the sanctions, a more conciliatory approach was adopted. At a news conference on August 22, 1961, Secretary of State Rusk said that the United States regarded "many of the moves toward democratization" in the Dominican Republic as "highly constructive." [7] On September 5 the State Department raised its consulate in Ciudad Trujillo to the status of a consulate general.[8] Then, on November 14, the State Department recommended to the OAS that some of the sanctions be lifted as a "gesture of encouragement" to the Dominican Republic in view of its recent steps toward democracy.[9] But the following day the proposal was withdrawn when word reached Washington that the two Trujillo brothers had returned to the Dominican Republic.

The episode of the "wicked uncles" in November, 1961, was a brief but dramatic power struggle in which some members of the Trujillo family attempted to regain control of the Dominican Republic. Generals Héctor and José Trujillo returned to the Dominican Republic from "vacations" abroad in an attempt to reimpose the dictatorship. Young Ramfis resigned his military position and fled. These events prompted Secretary Rusk to state publicly that the United States would not permit the Trujillo family to regain power.[10] At a press conference on November 18, Rusk said that the Trujillo brothers might be planning to overthrow Balaguer, and that the United States was considering "further measures" to safeguard recent Dominican progress toward democracy.[11]

The next day a United States naval task force of eight vessels with eighteen hundred marines aboard approached within three miles of the Dominican coast, in view of the capital.[12] In addition, the anti-Trujillo opposition mobilized. Certain military elements opposed to a Trujillo takeover rallied behind Balaguer. Most important was the air force, led by Major General Pedro Rafael Rodríguez Echavarría. As a result of this combined external and internal pressure, the uncles were prevented from carrying out their coup. The Trujillo brothers, along with another twenty-seven members of the Trujillo family and a number of associates, fled the country. Thus the United States was instrumental in affecting a facet of Dominican politics by use of the old method of threatening armed intervention.

Balaguer now found himself in a shaky position, although he announced that he had achieved full control of the country with the support of the "entire Dominican military establishment." General Rodríguez was named Secretary of State for the Armed Forces. The major opposition groups had supported Balaguer against the Trujillos, but they did not intend for him to remain in office. He carried the stigma of an ex-Trujillo-picked president. Now that the last of the dynasty had left, Balaguer was politically unacceptable. In demanding elimination of the last vestiges of Trujilloism, the opposition parties also opposed the continued presence of General Rodríguez, who had supported Balaguer during the attempted coup. Disorders and violence mounted, with the aim of dislodging Balaguer, and a state of emergency was declared.[13]

Finally, on December 17, 1961, in response to the demands of opposition groups and to continued political strife (and with United States and OAS assistance), a provisional government was established in the form of a seven-man Council of State, headed by Balaguer. He agreed that when the OAS terminated its sanctions, he would resign from the council and another member, Dr. Rafael F. Bonnelly, would become president. General elections were promised by late 1962. President Kennedy commended the "impressive demonstration of statesmanship and responsibility by all concerned," and promised to support the prompt lifting of sanctions.

On November 20, 1961, the day after the last of the Trujillos had departed, the OAS special committee had decided that a third subcommittee trip was necessary. It visited the Dominican Republic from November 20 to 26, and its subsequent report, published on December 20, recommended that the sanctions be lifted.[14] The report was formally submitted to the COAS on January 4, 1962. That day, seventeen months after they had been imposed, all sanctions against the Dominican Republic were terminated.

In January, 1962, shortly after the sanctions were lifted, a *golpe de estado* was attempted. On the night of January 17, General Rodríguez Echavarría staged a bloodless coup and led a short-lived military-civilian combination junta that replaced the Council of State. The United States voiced official dismay but did not send the fleet to Dominican waters, nor was any OAS action proposed. However, the junta did not survive because the rest of the armed forces rallied in support of the council.[15] Only forty-eight hours after the coup, the junta fell to the council it had just overthrown. Rodríguez Echavarría and four of his fellow junta members were arrested by air force officers in the counter-coup, and Rafael Bonnelly was again proclaimed president and head of the seven-man Council of State. On March 9 both Rodríguez Echavarría and Balaguer were flown to Puerto Rico in exile.

The Council of State served as the provisional government until February, 1963. This was a period of intermittent political, economic and military crises characterized by factional maneuvering, outbreaks of civil strife and frustrating United States-Dominican relations. (John Bartlow Martin, who had undertaken a special Dominican study mission for President Kennedy in September, 1961, was accredited as ambassador in March, 1962.) Nevertheless, the Council of State was able to begin preparations for the forthcoming elections scheduled in December, 1962. An extensive campaign was begun to instruct Dominican citizens in their voting rights.

Eight political parties, both old and new, representing the political spectrum from left to right, began campaigning for the presidency and for seats in the national assembly. The main contenders were the *Partido Revolucionario Dominicana* (Dominican Revolutionary Party — PRD), a party to the left of center; and the *Unión Cívica Nacional* (National Civic Union — UCN), a party to the right of center.

The PRD's chief, as well as its presidential candidate, was Juan Bosch, one of the country's leading literary figures and long-time foe of the late Trujillo.[16] Bosch had been in exile for twenty-five years in several Latin American states until his return to the Dominican Republic in October, 1961. While still in exile he had helped form the PRD in 1939. He based his campaign on reform and stood for what he referred to as "democratic leftism." His campaign focused on the peasants, promising them land reform, and he pledged the future nationalization of foreign property and business.

Viriato Alberto Fiallo, a country physician, was the UCN's presidential nominee. He had remained in the Dominican Republic during the Trujillo era and had led a clandestine movement against the generalissimo. He had also participated in formation of the UCN. Fiallo and the UCN drew their major support from landowners, shopkeepers and professional people.[17] Both candidates were friendly to the United States, although the Kennedy administration seemed to favor the PRD because its views were more in keeping with the reformist goals of the Alliance for Progress. Nevertheless, the United States pledged to support the winner of the election, whomever he might be.

In late November, the month before the national elections, the Dominican representative to the OAS Council requested that the Secretary General select a group of distinguished American educators, jurists and publicists to come to the Dominican Republic for the dual purpose of participating in a symposium on democracy and observing the national elections. The Secretary General selected forty-six persons to be participants and observers, representing all the American Republics except Cuba, Haiti and Mexico, plus the OAS, the Technical Assistance Mission and the Inter-American Development Bank. The United States was represented by thirteen individuals.[18]

Finally, on December 2, 1962, some nineteen months after Trujillo's assassination, the OAS-supervised national elections were held. Over one million Dominicans went to the polls, representing almost 70 per cent of the electorate. This first free and honest election since 1924 resulted in the election of Juan Bosch as president by a two-to-one margin over Viriato A. Fiallo, and in a solid majority for the PRD in the national assembly.[19] The inauguration of Bosch as president on February 27, 1963, and the formation of a fourteen-member cabinet early the next month, marked the end of the era of Trujillo and the beginning of a unique period in Dominican history.[20]

Shortly after Bosch's inauguration another chapter was written in the long record of animosity between the Dominican Republic and its cohabitant on the island of Hispaniola, Haiti, which was ruled with an iron hand by François "Papa Doc" Duvalier. In late April, 1963, Duvalier's police broke into the Dominican Embassy in Port-au-Prince to search for anti-government Haitians who had been granted asylum.[21] Although Haiti had refused to grant safe-conduct passes to these political refugees, this was the first time its police had violated the extraterritoriality of a diplomatic mission in order to capture political refugees. The situation was further complicated by the presence in Haiti of certain members of the Trujillo family and by rumors that they were plotting with Duvalier to assassinate Bosch.[22]

The Dominican navy put to sea, and tanks and troops moved to the border. Bosch publicly called Duvalier a mad tyrant and issued an ultimatum on April 28 threatening to use force against Haiti if the situation were not "rectified" within twenty-four hours.[23] On the same day the Dominican Republic went to the OAS and charged Haiti with threatening the peace of the hemisphere, presenting ten specific charges against the Haitian government.[24] The OAS persuaded the Bosch administration to extend its ultimatum for twelve hours until it could investigate, and sent a fact-finding mission at once.[25]

In the face of the Dominican massing of troops along the Haitian border, as well as a Venezuelan pledge of military support for the Dominican Republic and the stationing of United States naval units offshore ("to evacuate nationals"), the Haitian government announced its compliance with Dominican demands. A few more threats were required, however, before Duvalier implemented his promises and allowed the Haitian political prisoners to leave his domain, thus ending the three-week imbroglio.

Some commentators believed that Bosch had reacted the way he did in order to divert Dominican attention from domestic problems. Bosch had encountered internal as well as international problems almost from the day he took office—and the former were largely attributable to the legacy of Trujillo. Although a dedicated and honest man, Bosch was a poor organizer and an uncompromising idealist. He alienated one group after another. He lost his supporters' backing because he was unable to fulfill his reform commitments to them; he alienated his conservative critics because he made only limited efforts to compromise with them. In fact, those who opposed him were intransigent and refused to cooperate with him from the very beginning. Bosch's final undoing, which was used as a pretext by his opponents, was alienating the armed forces by permitting extreme leftists to return from exile and failing to take a strong anti-communist stand.[26] Unfounded rumors that Bosch was creating his own rival military force increased the military's fear and suspicion.

Finally, at dawn on September 25, 1963, a widely predicted coup overthrew Bosch and dissolved the National Assembly after only seven months in office. The prime mover was General Elías Wessin y Wessin, commander of the San Isidro air base garrison, who had helped exile the members of the Trujillo family in late 1961. The rationale for the coup was Bosch's "softness on communism" and his responsibility for "plunging the country into chaos." Two days after the coup a three-man civilian provisional government was named, although the armed forces had real power. Bosch left the Dominican Republic for exile in Puerto Rico on September 29, 1963. Thus ended in disappointment the United States- and OAS-backed Dominican democratic experiment.

2. UNITED STATES ASSISTANCE POLICIES

After Trujillo's assassination the general policy of the United States was to assist democratic elements in the Dominican Republic and to oppose strongly any attempts to reestablish autocracy or to begin a Castro-inspired revolution. Trujillo's death on May 30, 1961, occurred about midway between President Kennedy's formal proposal of the Alliance for Progress (March 15) and its acceptance as a hemispheric commitment at Punta del Este, Uruguay (the following August). Consistent with the stated ends and means of the Alliance, the United States opposed solutions to Dominican problems advocated by the extreme right or left, and sought to promote a moderate program of social reform. The United States felt it had a vested interest in the success of Dominican progress toward democracy by steering between the positions of both the extreme left (Cuba) and the right (Trujillo era). If successful, such progress was to confirm the United States' wisdom in adopting a new approach to Latin American problems—and would underscore the potentialities of the Alliance for Progress in combating communist subversion as a substitute for unilateral intervention and cooperation with dictators.

Complete United States support of Dominican efforts to move toward democracy was evidenced in early 1962. On January 6, two days after sanctions were lifted, diplomatic relations were resumed. The Latin American director of AID, Teodoro Moscoso, led an economic mission to the Dominican Republic. An agreement was signed by the two governments on January 11, providing for economic aid and a Peace Corps mission.[27] Immediately after the Rodríguez coup on January 17, the United States halted its steps toward renewal of aid and trade. But when the Council of State was restored two days later, the pledge of aid was promptly renewed and official gratification was voiced that "constitutional government had been reaffirmed." In late January an Alliance for Progress official and a mission from the Inter-American Development Bank were sent to the Dominican Republic. On February 17 the United States and the Dominican Republic signed an agreement giving the latter a twenty-year credit of $25,000,000 at the low interest rate of three-fourths of 1 per cent. The following year, in early January, 1963, President-elect Bosch was welcomed to Washington to discuss his country's problems and its role in the Alliance for Progress. During his four-day visit he had discussions with President Kennedy and Moscoso.

The problem of the Dominican sugar quota was also resolved. In January, 1962, the United States Congress had temporarily assigned an additional amount to the basic quota as assistance to the newly established Council of State for its "transition to democracy." But under the new Sugar Act of June 30, 1962, the Dominican quota was reduced and no additional "Cuban windfall" was granted. The Dominicans protested that any decrease of the quota would interrupt their democratic progress. On July 5 Congress approved an amendment to give an extra allotment to several Latin American countries, which included an award of considerable tonnage for the Dominican Republic.

During this post-Trujillo period of turmoil, the Kennedy administration was redirecting the major thrust of its military assistance programs in Latin America from hemispheric defense to internal security. The Foreign Assistance Act of 1961, replacing the Mutual Security Act of 1954, retained anti-submarine warfare as the only vestige of hemispheric defense.[28] The new emphasis on internal security was reflected in the stress placed upon engaging the Latin American armed forces in civic action, training them in counter-insurgency, and improving their technical and professional competence.[29]

In the Dominican Republic, the United States attempted to develop the Dominican National Police as an effective non-

political law and order force while at the same time trying to
de-Trujilloize the armed forces, particularly the army, and
convert them from their traditional role as a political-military
force.[30] The United States believed that it could have a great
impact upon the former — and could perhaps remake it — but
realized that its influence upon the latter was limited. As part
of this plan the national police were granted autonomy, sep-
arated from the Ministry of Defense, where they had been under
Trujillo, and placed in the Ministry of the Interior. Their size
was increased so they could better control the streets and more
effectively stabilize any emergency situation. United States
military aid programs concentrated on training them in riot
prevention and control. These steps were accompanied by
attempts to neutralize the political role of the armed forces by
reducing their size (particularly that of the army), improving
their professional competence and training them in civic action
and counter-insurgency.

After the rioting in late 1961 and early 1962, during which
the national police had lost control of the streets in downtown
Santo Domingo, two Spanish-speaking detectives from the Los
Angeles Police Department were sent to the Dominican Republic to train the Dominican police in riot control and investiga-
tive and communications procedures. These training efforts
helped the police bring order to the streets.[31]

The United States found it could do little with the armed
services, either through de-Trujilloization or reduction in size.
No meaningful distinction could be drawn between the *Trujilloistas* and the non-*Trujilloistas,* for almost everyone had been
compromised by the dictator. Reducing the size of this preserve
and cutting the military budget increased the risks of a coup.
The Council of State already had enough problems to deal with
and was unwilling to take this risk. As a result, the United States
attempted to transform the nature of Dominican military services
by stressing training and improving professional competence.
Its efforts along these lines were not extensive during 1962 and
did not assume meaningful proportions until 1963 and 1964. In

March, 1962, for example, the Military Assistance Advisory Group (MAAG), which had been closed in February, 1960, was reopened, but it had only five members. An agreement was signed that same month, providing for military assistance "either for the purpose of internal security requirements or for the purpose of defense missions which are important to the maintenance of peace and security in the Western Hemisphere." However, it did not become effective until June, 1964.[32]

President Bosch's inauguration in February, 1963, stimulated an acceleration of United States military, economic and technical assistance. The Kennedy administration decided to use the Dominican Republic to prove the methodology of the Alliance for Progress, for the Bosch administration represented a constitutional and legitimate government, dedicated to change and reform, which had come to power less than two years after the end of an all-pervasive dictatorship.

In the military area the MAAG increased its strength from five members to forty-five. Provision for equipment, parts and supplies was increased. More civic action projects were undertaken. Greater numbers of Dominican military personnel were sent to the Canal Zone and to the United States for professional and technical training. The United States increased its efforts to improve the professionalism of the national police through military assistance — an AID-sponsored public safety team worked with the police, for example.

President Bosch had his own ideas, however. He distrusted the national police and feared their growing power and effectiveness. He also shared the general populace's view of them as Trujillo's gestapo. As a result he cut off their funds, shortly after assuming office, and thus undermined the United States training program.[33] Nor was Bosch willing to reduce the budget and size of the armed forces, and retire some of the old-line Trujillo holdovers as the United States wished, although he was able to reduce some graft and corruption at the upper echelons. President Bosch supported civic action programs, but he saw little need for counter-insurgency programs.

When President Bosch was overthrown by a coup in September, 1963, the United States responded by severing diplomatic relations, withholding recognition of the new government, suspending all assistance and recalling almost all personnel. This response ended a number of economic development projects which the United States undertook again when relations were reestablished.[34] The Dominican military chiefs set up a conservative three-man junta and expressed interest in reestablishing relations with the United States and the resumption of economic assistance. The junta broadened its political base and scheduled elections for 1965. In mid-December, 1963, the new Johnson administration recognized the junta, and three months later a new ambassador, William Tapley Bennett, arrived. In late January, 1964, economic and military programs were resumed.

3. UNITED STATES–DOMINICAN RELATIONS SINCE 1964

Despite the coup, which was led by the army and backed by rightist groups, the new government was dominated by the same elite families that had survived with relative prosperity under Trujillo and had turned over power to Bosch seven months earlier. Eventually, Donald Reid Cabral, an automobile dealer who had served in the Council of State before the Bosch presidency, emerged as president of the junta and as the dominant figure in government. He pursued an austerity program and attempted to stabilize the regime.

The United States resumed relations with the Dominican Republic and supported the Reid government. North American officials were pleased with the Dominican leader's apparent willingness to institute certain reforms in the armed forces. His efforts involved limiting their exorbitant fringe benefits and the smuggling monopoly, forcing out certain old-line officers, and cutting their budget. The military assistance agreement that had been signed in 1962 became effective in June, 1964, and the MAAG was reopened. The civic action program, initiated by the United States in October, 1964, and operated on an *ad hoc* basis, was resumed. President Reid cooperated with the United States by stressing counterinsurgency training. An increasing number of Dominicans were sent to receive such training in the United States, and Mobile Training Teams from Fort Bragg supervised similar programs in the Dominican Republic.[35]

The military reforms caused increasing dissension in the armed forces. Senior old-guard army officers (the "San Cristóbal group") who bore the brunt of the reforms, favored ousting Reid and recalling former president Balaguer from exile. On the other hand a group of young officers interested in some reform as well as their own advancement, complained that the retirement of old-line Trujilloist officers was not proceeding rapidly enough. This group also favored removing the Reid government but desired the return of former president Bosch and the PRD.[36]

On April 24, 1965, the pro-Bosch army faction, known as the "constitutional" or "rebel" group, staged a coup that turned into a civil war. Supported by a few defecting military units and thousands of civilians in Santo Domingo, they removed Reid from office. The rebels were first headed by José Rafael Molina of the PRD, but he was replaced a few days later by Colonel Francisco Caamaño. The opposing faction was referred to as "military" or "loyalist." It enjoyed the support of most of the military units and the national police. General Antonio Imbert, who had participated in the assassination of Trujillo, emerged as head of the "loyalists." This faction did not support the Reid government but advocated Balaguer's return; they seemed most interested in preventing the return of Bosch.[37]

The four-day period from April 24 to 28 was one of turmoil and uncertainty. The United States helped to set up a three-man military junta as the "legal" body representing the "military" faction. Civilians supporting the "constitutionalists" acquired arms when they managed to capture the national police arsenal. (This was the first time since the military occupation of 1916-1924 that a sizable group of ordinary citizens was in possession of arms, an unthinkable situation during the Trujillo era.) The populace turned on the national police, scapegoat of the Trujillo legacy, and vented their hatred by beating and killing many of them. Aircraft from San Isidro strafed the National Palace during negotiations between the opposing factions, which galvanized the "constitutionalists" to action and resulted in a rapid polarization of the opponents. Military advantage fluctuated between the two sides, as first one faction and then the other seemed to gain the upper hand in the streets.[38]

Thereafter, for more than four months, the city of Santo Domingo was the locale of a civil war and for the landing of American troops. United States intervention began on the eve-

Trujillo's palace, next door to the U.S. Embassy, serving as the headquarters, Commander of U.S. Forces, during the 1965 intervention, May 14, 1965. *U.S. Army Photo*

ning of April 28, 1965, with the landing of 405 marines. Beginning two days later the complement of troops was increased, reaching a high of approximately 23,000 ashore in the vicinity of Santo Domingo.

Initial justification for the intervention was to protect the lives of foreign nationals in the Dominican Republic. President Johnson's press release the night of April 28 stated that Dominican authorities could no longer guarantee the safety of American lives and had requested military assistance for that purpose.[39] Two days later Johnson noted a changing situation. In a broadcast to the American public, he referred to "signs that people trained outside the Dominican Republic are seeking to gain control."[40] Then, on May 2, in a major address to the nation, he

U.S. Marines locating a sniper target in Santo Domingo, May 8, 1965.
Dept. of Defense Photo (Marine Corps)

declared that communist leaders, many of them trained in Cuba, had joined the revolution, taking more and more control. He lamented that "what began as a popular democratic revolution" had been "seized and placed into the hands of a band of Communist conspirators." Now the American goal, in addition to protecting the lives of its nationals, was "to help prevent another Communist state in this hemisphere." [41]

The United States had attempted to obtain OAS endorsement of its action from the initial troop landing. It had concentrated upon the creation of an Inter-American Peace Force to serve as the instrument for settling hostilities and forming an interim government. After considerable debate the OAS passed a resolution in May creating the Peace Force, and later that month the United States military command was transformed into an OAS force. With the arrival of contingents from Latin America, the United States began withdrawing some of its troops. However, the Latin American presence in the peace force during the summer of 1965 was essentially a token one, as the percentage of Latin American troops was small. [42]

Meanwhile, negotiations for a settlement remained stalemated. In an attempt to break the impasse, President Johnson sent a high-level four-man mission (composed of McGeorge Bundy, Jack Hood Vaughn, Thomas C. Mann and Cyrus R. Vance). They suggested a coalition government under the interim presidency of Bosch's former minister of agriculture, Antonio Guzmán. The proposal suited Colonel Caamaño, but General Imbert opposed it, believing that victory was imminent and there was no need to compromise. The United States then applied economic pressures to Imbert. It had been paying the salaries of Dominican civil servants and military personnel, and it now threatened to suspend the payments. This pressure was ineffective, however, as General Imbert remained intractable throughout the negotiations.

In early June the OAS sent a three-member Ad Hoc Committee to the Dominican Republic, composed of representatives from Brazil, El Salvador and the United States (Ellsworth

Bunker). The committee presented a Declaration to the Dominican People, which provided for termination of the armed struggle, surrender to the OAS of all arms held by civilians, formation of a provisional government and the holding of general elections.[43] Although neither faction accepted this declaration, it served as a basis for discussions that led to later agreement.

Negotiations for a settlement continued throughout July and August; they revolved around the composition of the provisional government, particularly the nomination of a provisional president. It became clear that the only person acceptable to both sides would have to be a respected "moderate." This led finally to the acceptance of Dr. Héctor García-Godoy, a businessman and former diplomat. Then ensued the far more difficult negotiations over terms of the final acts.

In early August the Ad Hoc Committee presented a new proposal for a settlement, called the Act of Dominican Reconciliation, which this time provided the basis for a final accord. Several provisions of this act posed problems of persisting difficulty for both the provisional president and the Peace Force. These provisions called for the immediate "demilitarization and disarmament" of civilians in the constitutionalist zone, ordered the armed forces to return to their barracks, specified the reincorporation of constitutionalist units "in the armed forces without discrimination or reprisal," and insisted that "no officer or enlisted man of the armed forces will be submitted to court martial or subject to punishment of any kind for acts, except common crimes, committed since April 23, 1965." [44]

The Act of Dominican Reconciliation was signed in late August. In early September, more than four months after the Dominican crisis had begun and the United States had landed troops, the provisional government and President García-Godoy assumed control in preparation for holding elections in the spring of 1966.[45]

During this difficult period García-Godoy's government achieved reasonable stability and survived only because of the

Peace Force, which also served as a buffer between the left and the right. However, one major objective of the Act of Dominican Reconciliation was not realized—the disarming of civilians and the collection of arms. Despite the assistance of the Peace Force, this problem was passed on to the future government. Under the circumstances the general maintenance of conditions permitting political campaigns was in itself an important achievement and a credit to the provisional government.

The two major presidential candidates in the 1966 campaign were Dr. Joaquín Balaguer, the Reformist party nominee, and Juan Bosch of the PRD. On June 1 the Dominican electorate went to the polls in what were fair and free elections observed by the OAS. Dr. Balaguer defeated Bosch by receiving over 56 per cent of the votes cast. Bosch won only 39 per cent of the total; Dr. Rafael Bonnelly, the candidate of the National Integration Movement, won about 3 per cent; and the pro-Castro 14th of June Movement garnered less than 1 per cent. Dr. Balaguer was inaugurated on July 1, 1966.

In his inaugural address, after announcing an austerity program and the need for continued United States economic assistance, President Balaguer stressed the need to eliminate corruption and graft in the bureaucracy and military services. In the weeks that followed, he formed his cabinet and then reached an agreement with Bosch and the opposition PRD, second largest political party, about a policy of military reforms and PRD cooperation.

President Balaguer honored this agreement by replacing the head of the national police and sending a number of officers from various branches of the armed forces abroad to serve as military attachés or to pursue their professional education. A number of these changes, particularly the transfer of military personnel, were carried out during the continued presence of the Peace Force, which was recognized as a backstop to the Dominican president. Finally, in late September, 1966, the Peace Force, by then reduced to a strength of less than 5,000, was withdrawn from the Dominican Republic. Thus ended the sixteen-month role of the Peace Force, which had assured the mandate of the provisional government and the initial policies of President Balaguer.

4. CONCLUSIONS ON THE POST-TRUJILLO PERIOD

The limited success of United States policies since the death of Trujillo in 1961 stems from the nature of Dominican society. Although that society's various facets — economic, military, political and social — are interrelated, the United States focused on the military and economic factors at the expense of the political. The need to change the Dominican milieu as a prerequisite for the possible development of a civilian-controlled military force has been rejected in the belief that a Dominican military force would be the catalyst for transforming Dominican society and thereby solving its chronic problems. This was to be done through professional and technical training, since the United States was in no position to take on the army and purge it.

Another factor limiting United States capabilities is the lack of experience of American civilian and military officials responsible for carrying out policy. Military attachés played an important role in the Dominican Republic from 1962 on, but most of them lacked sufficient experience or training to prepare them for such positions. There is no sub-specialty in the military services to prepare officers for attaché duty. Frequently, the pressures of time do not permit the attaché to complete the intensified preparatory program, and he may be assigned to a country without knowing its language. Tours of duty tend to end at about the time an officer really becomes effective, having learned the language, established rapport with his domestic military counterparts and set up a network of contacts.

Furthermore, some observers have noted the rivalry between embassy personnel and representatives of the armed services in the Dominican Republic. A lack of coordination and an undermining of State Department policies by the Department of Defense imposes another limit on American policy implementation. In addition, rivalries between the military services in the United States may be transplanted to foreign countries.[46]

The United States has confused the relationship between economics and politics in approaching a solution to Dominican turmoil since the demise of Trujillo. Not only has an attempt been made to use economic and technical assistance to fill the vacuum of political underdevelopment attributable to Trujillo, but economic development has been assumed to be the key to democratic political change. The attempt to fill the political vacuum with economic aid probably arises from impatience for tangible results and from the glaring economic needs and deficiencies of the Dominican economy, also in part attributable to Trujillo. The United States has also taken refuge in the economic facet because it is "safer" than the political. The magnitude and nature of United States assistance to the Dominican Republic indicates an overwhelming economic bias.

By comparison, although it was content with the order and stability of the Dominican Republic during the Trujillo regime and considered the country "safe" in the Cold War, the United States did make some aid available. The magnitude of assistance increased once the Kennedy administration decided to use the Dominican Republic to prove the methodology of the Alliance for Progress after Trujillo had left the scene. The total amount of post-Trujillo economic aid, as of June 30, 1969, was approximately $175,000,000. These programs have made a contribution to economic development and probably should be continued, but they cannot compensate for political underdevelopment.

The fallacy that economic development produces democratic political change is strongly conditioned by the United States' unique economic-political history, which is inapplicable to the Dominican experience. Here is one more example of the frequently noted error of judging another national set of needs according to one's own standards. The basic reality of the Dominican situation and the key to its future political development is the lack of experienced, moderate and responsible political leaders. This is the legacy of authoritarian governments over a long period of time.

The real problem of the Dominican Republic, which the coalition government and the elections of 1966 and 1970 have not solved, is not to keep all political parties and factions satisfied; it is to persuade them to settle their disagreements by peaceful, responsible means and to refrain from branding any group that disagrees with them as being communistic. The necessary bridge that must be built between the non-extreme left and right is the province of political development and Dominican leadership; it cannot be constructed through efforts of the United States, no matter how great the magnitude and variety of economic assistance.

VII   THE QUEST FOR STABILITY
AND DEMOCRACY

A dilemma the United States faced during the Trujillo era was the commitment to representative democracy in Latin America on the one hand and the maintenance of political stability, especially in the Caribbean area, on the other. This dilemma came to the fore after the United States accepted the principle of nonintervention as the cornerstone of the inter-American system and as an important part of its own policies in the 1930's. This chapter will address the questions raised by postulating—and attempting to reconcile—both stability and democracy as policy goals. It will also provide a conclusion to the entire study, for it is concerned with the very heart of the problem of United States policy toward non-democratic governments in Latin America as exemplified by the Trujillo case: In the quest for stability and democracy, what attitude toward dictators should be assumed?

1. DOMINICAN STABILITY AS A GOAL OF POLICY

The political history of most Caribbean states, including the Dominican Republic, has been marked by political instability. Abrupt changes in chief executives by irregular and violent means has been a common phenomenon. Historically, instability and its accompanying violence and economic backwardness led to European intervention or, from the North American point of view, necessitated United States intervention to preempt extrahemispheric interference. In recent times, instability has offered opportunity to extremist groups the United States has considered inimical to its interests.

The interests of the United States as a major status-quo nation are best served in a secure, stable, peaceful world. Thus a politically stable Caribbean area has been a traditional goal of United States policy. Since at least the turn of the century — three decades before Trujillo came to power — the Caribbean region has been the object of considerable United States attention and concern. Over the years the policy issue has not been whether stability was desirable, but rather the best means of achieving it.

Stability in the Dominican Republic and avoidance of European control were the primary objectives of the later-discredited United States fiscal and military intervention that preceded the Trujillo era. After the techniques of direct intervention were abandoned, the goal of stability remained the same, although sought through persuasion and cooperation rather than coercion and paternalism.

Military assistance and small technical assistance programs were designed with the goal of stability in mind. Technical assistance was aimed at helping achieve a degree of economic progress that would support political stability. Military assistance was more extensively utilized as an instrument of policy aimed at helping to establish conditions of internal order that were considered essential to the security and welfare of the United States. Likewise, after the war, military aid was extended for the avowed purpose of strengthening the Dominican capability to contribute to hemispheric defense against the Soviet Union. But the fact that military equipment was given parsimoniously and was obsolete in quality indicated no major concern with defense against external aggression. The United States would have been required to assume the preponderant military burden in the event of an attack on the western hemisphere.

On occasion, American officials would candidly state that military aid was primarily aimed at achieving internal stability.

For example, in 1958 the Secretary of Defense testified before the Senate Foreign Relations Committee that the military program in Latin America was "primarily for the purpose of the maintenance of internal security and also a very modest preparation for defense against any incursion from offshore."[1] In the late 1950's and early 1960's the greatest threat to stability was considered to be "internal communist subversion," especially after the success of Fidel Castro in Cuba.

During more than three decades in power, Generalissimo Trujillo achieved a period of political stability unparalleled in Dominican history, but he did so by oppressive and totalitarian means. For the most part the United States accommodated the military dictatorship, regarding Trujillo as conducive at least to temporary stability. Even though stability under Trujillo's rule meant a dictatorial status quo, the United States hesitated to oppose the dictator, at least until the late 1950's.

However, increasing Caribbean instability in international politics involving the Dominican Republic after World War II became more and more of a problem for the United States and the Organization of American States. United States opposition to Trujillo after 1960 and the post-Trujillo effort to establish constitutional democracy in the Dominican Republic through the OAS were largely directed toward the goal of stability. This shift in policy reflected a judgment on the part of the United States that representative democracy was the best means by which to achieve the general Dominican welfare that was essential to peaceful political processes.

One might question the policy of promoting political stability by supporting Trujillo's overthrow and then endorsing free elections. Perhaps the very opposite should have been done; that is, the military dictatorship which, in fact, had ruled the Dominican Republic for over thirty years should have been strengthened. One reason this was not done stems directly from the problem of succession in a dictatorship. It was evident in 1960 that Trujillo would soon leave the scene and that the process of moving from dictatorship to an alternative system was likely to be disorderly at best. The United States hoped to avoid as much disorder as possible by holding free and honest elections in which all political parties would have equal opportunity.[2] This change of policy indicated a United States evaluation that stability through Trujillo's methods could no longer endure.

Upon committing itself to open repudiation of Trujillo and pressing for his removal, the United States generated a new policy problem: What could be done to insure that future Dominican governments would be more desirable than Trujillo's, and to what extent could United States actions be successful in determining the future of the Dominican political system? This problem became an urgent one as the Trujillo era drew to a close with the dictator's assassination in 1961.

The United States, along with the OAS, was active in guiding the political direction of the Dominican Republic in the post-Trujillo period. In the decade (at this writing) since the dictator's death, Dominicans have been governed by an interim president who was forced to resign; a Council of State; an elected president who was overthrown by a military coup after seven months in office; another Council of State that evolved into the Reid government which was overthrown, precipitating a civil war; a provisional government and president; and another elected president who was inaugurated in 1966 and reelected to office in 1970.

During these years in which there were only two elected presidents, the Dominican Republic has experienced demonstrations and strikes, anarchy and violence, riots and civil war, attempts at control by both the far right and far left, and the landing of United States troops and a United States-dominated Inter-American Peace Force in the 1965 civil war. Today inequities still exist in Dominican society, and the Balaguer government remains threatened by continuing economic problems and political polarization and factionalism. Although these are disquieting signs, it appears that the Dominican Republic is achieving a degree of stability in the post-Trujillo period following a hectic transition, but at an increasing political cost.

In view of the efforts made since Trujillo's death, should the United States, in its quest for political stability in the Dominican Republic, have opposed Trujillo and tried to promote Dominican democracy and solicit Latin American support long before 1961?

2. THE IDEAL OF DEMOCRACY AND THE REALITY OF TRUJILLO

Representative democracy has long been expounded as a historic pillar of Pan-Americanism, and its promotion has been declared an integral part of the inter-American system. From the early International Conferences of American States, especially after World War I, before the United States had accepted the nonintervention principle, members of the regional system had regularly committed themselves to representative democracy and the protection of human rights. It would appear that this commitment at least implied an obligation to oppose nondemocratic governments, particularly despotic and oppressive ones. It was partly on this ground that United States relations with the Trujillo government were criticized; viz., that its commitment to representative democracy and human rights had been sacrificed in order to support Trujillo because his regime had assured economic and political stability.

Although the United States had attempted to organize and use the OAS as an "anti-communist alliance" on several occasions (and it had served in that capacity to varying degrees, in the Korean War and Guatemala in the early 1950's, for example, and against Cuba in 1962), the OAS first operated as an "anti-dictatorial alliance" against the Dominican Republic in 1960. Imposing OAS sanctions against the Trujillo government by the Sixth Meeting of Ministers in 1960 was the result of a special set of circumstances that had not prevailed before. These circumstances permitted collective action against a dictator for the first time – primarily because, by attempting to kill Betancourt,

Trujillo had violated the nonintervention principle, not because he was a dictator and had violated human rights. It is doubtful that action would have been taken had he not committed an act of intervention.

The relationship between commitments to representative democracy, nonintervention and the protection of human rights, and how to reconcile them, has posed a policy dilemma for the United States. The Latin American states and the United States view the relationship and the dilemma in different ways, which is primarily attributable to the considerable power disparities that exist between Latin and North America. Commitments to representative democracy and human rights in both Latin America and the United States are viewed as ideals imposing a moral obligation. Although these commitments are contained in a series of American agreements, declarations and resolutions, the consensus in the inter-American community is that they do not impose any legal obligation. Democracy has never been defined, nor have means been specified for making representative democracy operational. Such a task, if desired, is made difficult by the differing views about its theory and practice that exist in Latin America and the United States.

On the other hand nonintervention is considered an obligation as binding as a treaty commitment and is enshrined in the OAS Charter. The Latin American republics view nonintervention in an absolute and legal way, to which the commitment to democracy and human rights is subservient; they have a seemingly inexhaustible list of acts that constitute intervention. The United States, however, views nonintervention flexibly and as a legal commitment to be ignored under certain circumstances in the name of national security. In addition, within the context of the Cold War, most Latin American states have continued to regard nonintervention as their major bulwark against the power of the United States. They have been far more fearful of North American actions than of acts of infiltration or subversion by the Soviet Union – concerns with which the United States has been perennially preoccupied.

There has also been concern in Latin America that collective action by the OAS against dictatorial regimes, because of alleged United States omnipotence, would be applied against those Latin American governments whose conduct and nature did not conform to the North American view of democracy. In the words of Gordon Connell-Smith, who prefers to refer to inter-American relations as those between the "One" (the United States) and the "Twenty," the Latin view of the OAS is the following:

> . . . they look to it to impose a measure of restraint upon their powerful neighbour: to maintain the principle of non-intervention. Many do not accept the United States position on the Cold War and reject the idea of the OAS as an anti-communist alliance. They believe . . . that the United States is inclined to view any movement for substantial reform as communist-inspired, and they are extremely reluctant to give OAS support to what would in practice be action by the United States. They tend to be more afraid of United States policy to meet the Soviet challenge than of any threat from communism itself.[3]

The above indicates the policy dilemma posed for the United States by the nonintervention principle. As a result the OAS Charter is not an infallible guide to policy (perhaps this is why the charter is frequently violated by the United States when it feels its security is being threatened) because it treats both representative democracy and nonintervention as absolutes. However, the latter does transcend the former in operational terms, while policy is concerned with shifting priorities and relative values. Although the regional system provides for collective intervention, the inter-American consensus maintains that such action in behalf of representative democracy and human rights would violate nonintervention. This is true despite the argument that the elimination of dictatorial regimes and progress toward democracy would promote stability in the long run and thereby reduce the incidence of intervention. One writer has observed that "as long as the maintenance of 'sovereignty' [of which non-intervention is a corollary] is considered by the Latin Americans to be the primary function of the inter-American system, . . . [no] organ of the OAS can play a truly significant part in the advancement of democracy and human rights in the hemisphere." [4] This poses an impediment to the Latin American policy of the United States.

It should be recalled that immediately after World War II the United States favored collective intervention against dictatorial regimes. In 1946, in accordance with the Braden policy of outright opposition to dictators in the name of promoting democracy, the United States endorsed the Rodríguez Larreta Doctrine, which advocated inter-American intervention against dictators, also in the name of democracy. Most Latin American countries rejected this doctrine and adhered to the primacy of the nonintervention principle. Following the short-lived influence of Braden in United States policy-making, it was not until 1960 that the inter-American system — and the United States — took action against a dictator.

The collective economic and diplomatic sanctions that were voted against the Trujillo regime in August, 1960, as noted above, were not based on the oppressive and anti-democratic nature of Trujillo's government, although they were used as a lever to force Dominican reforms toward the direction of democracy and human rights. The sanctions were imposed because that government had violated the nonintervention principle when it attempted to kill President Betancourt. This was Trujillo's undoing; otherwise the nonintervention concept most likely would have continued to insulate him from accountability to the regional system, no matter how retrograde and cruel his rule. In response to Trujillo's intervention in Venezuela, the Inter-American Treaty of Reciprocal Assistance (Rio Treaty) was invoked, and sanctions were applied thereunder. This collective action had to meet the legal requirement of support by two-thirds of the OAS members, which was forthcoming. Thus to act legally fourteen affirmative votes were required; these — and more — were readily available for action against Trujillo but have not been available to promote representative democracy. If the United States acts unilaterally, it is guilty of intervention, which it is willing to commit only in opposing what it views as communist infractions of its national security.

It appears that the only alternative to the Trujillo regime, or to one like it, would have been another United States military intervention followed by years of military occupation, for Trujillo could not have been persuaded to give up his control. Such direct and forceful action was out of the question, however, nor was it a feasible policy alternative.

This study has suggested that the American policy-maker had few alternatives to his actions toward the Trujillo regime. United States policy reflected the realities of dealing with dictatorial governments, and exemplified the acceptance of certain unfortunate exigencies which the United States was in a poor position to alter or modify. Two basic factors must be considered here: the legacy of United States intervention in Latin America and the consequent Latin American demand for and United States acceptance of the principle of nonintervention as the prerequisite for inter-American cooperation; and the related policy goals of maintaining stability and preventing foreign control (first by European creditors, then by Nazi Germany, and finally by Soviet communism).

However, a number of criticisms of the United States' attitude toward Trujillo are in order. One can be justly critical of ostentatious demonstrations of friendship and camaraderie with dictators. This is particularly true of the praise given Trujillo's dedication to democracy, freedom and human rights, which allowed the dictator to use official American statements as apparent endorsements of his regime. One can also criticize and question the wisdom of the postwar preoccupation with anticommunism, especially after the death of Stalin, which seemed to transcend all other policy considerations. The anti-communist syndrome resulted in welcoming all comers to the struggle, no matter how oppressive or antithetical to the American value system they might be, conveying the impression that the United States not only supported totalitarian regimes but actually preferred them. It is most unfortunate that Castro's impetus was needed to bring about a tactical change in the Latin American policy of the United States vis-à-vis dictators and stability; that is, the realization that stability maintained by a dictator becomes instability once he passes from the scene.

3. POLITICAL DEVELOPMENT AND THE LIMITS OF U.S. POLICY

The United States must deal with reality, no matter how unfortunate it may be, and accept a number of limitations upon its capability to influence Latin American political development. By now the limitations of American power have become apparent on a worldwide scale. Just as military intervention in Vietnam has failed to achieve stated security goals, so have coercive measures in Latin America. At the same time even cooperative techniques aimed at progressive objectives in the other Americas have often been unsuccessful. The United States has been unable to promote hemispheric democracy largely for reasons beyond its control. It is difficult to prevent dictatorial or military regimes or even to bring about social and political change. By recognizing that there is no way out of this dilemma and that no solution exists in this regard, the Latin American policy of the United States would be more realistic and thereby improved.

While North American proximity and power are ever-present factors in hemisphere affairs, the United States is not truly omnipotent. The Trujillo experience, including its legacy, demonstrates that democracy cannot be imposed by an external force. The United States was unable to achieve its goal of creating a professional non-political Dominican national police force (during the 1916-1924 military occupation) that would protect future constitutional governments after United States-supervised elections were held. Once in office Trujillo used the national police as a vehicle to confirm his dictatorship, but after the dictator had been removed, it appeared that the principal obstacle to change and reform had been overcome.

The problem then was to reorient the existing armed forces to a position that had been desired forty years earlier. This was to be accomplished after Trujillo, through professional and technical training, since neither the United States nor the Dominican government were in a position to purge the army. Despite post-Trujillo efforts by the United States to transform the Dominican armed forces and promote social reform and political development (in part through large dollops of economic aid), the Dominican government today is basically conservative and elite-dominated. The armed forces remain the locus of political power.

The process of economic and political development, as illustrated by the Dominican Republic, poses limits to United States power. Although a certain amount of economic and political development (the "prerequisites" of democracy) is necessary for a democratic and representative government to flourish, the United States could not contribute to this process until the Trujillo regime. Until Trujillo's demise, it was not really possible for the OAS — especially with the United States working through it — and other outside instrumentalities to play a role. Some economic development occurred during the Trujillo era, but the political and human costs were too exorbitant to justify the progress. There was no political development under Trujillo in terms of people acquiring experience with the institutions and practices of participation essential to representative government.

The absence of dictatorship in itself does not insure democratic progress. If democracy is to develop, it must do so from within, and it requires slow cultivation. It is not for export, and depends primarily upon internal (Dominican) leadership rather than external (United States) direction. The role of the United States, by the very nature of political development, is a limited one. In this context United States policy may be criticized. There has been a constant tendency in the "pro-democratic" policies of the United States to focus on the procedures (especially the holding of elections) rather than the substance of democratic processes. Moreover, democratic policy seems to have been pursued in ethnocentric ideological terms, despite the vast social differences between the Dominican Republic and the United States.

The terms "democracy" and "constitutionalism" are not relevant to the Dominican national experience. Even when the government in power welcomes or permits outside assistance it is not possible to export a particular political-economic system. Whereas modern technology and technicians can be exported, this is not the case for the institutions and traditions of representative government. The latter must have an indigenous life, developing and evolving according to the economic, political and social configuration of the country in question.

All this suggests that, to a considerable degree, political forms are a matter for each state to work out on its own, and that the United States must stand ready to deal with dictators, militarists and other non-democratic regimes simply because they are there. If dictators are the end result of conditions rather than the cause of them, and if other socio-political causes better explain military intervention in political processes than does simple praetorian conspiracy, then opposition per sé would seem to be of little value.

A persistent and disturbing contention is that communists will gain control of social revolution as in Cuba unless the United States offers a democratic counter-ideology. The Alliance for Progress as originally formulated accepted this thesis and presented the issue as communism versus democracy. It was argued that a strong democratic left provides the best protection against the spread of communism because it tries to bring about social reform which undercuts the appeal of communist solutions. This would suggest that the dictatorship of Rafael Trujillo, where all political opposition was stifled, was preparing the way for communist success after the dictator's disappearance.

Despite a number of staggering problems in the Dominican Republic today, and the 1965 intervention notwithstanding, Cuba is not viewed as a "showcase for communism" exuding a universal appeal to reformers. The notion need not be accepted that a Cuban-type revolution would be embraced by Latin Americans as the only remaining solution to their problems. Coming to terms with a revolutionary Latin America is not so much a problem of promoting political ideology as it is of encouraging reform, and the two are not necessarily synonymous. This is not to downgrade the communist threat but to question whether communism would even spread throughout a largely non-democratic hemisphere. Dogmatizing democracy as the only alternative to communism is an unviable policy for the United States and a disservice to Latin Americans.

In recognizing the limits of United States power, one runs the danger of incorrectly concluding that the United States is without force or effectiveness, and perhaps even making a case that dictators should be supported. While non-democratic regimes may mean at least temporary stability, it would be erroneous to attempt to shore them up against revolutionary pressures. It does not follow that the United States should see to it that dictators are overthrown, for this in itself will not solve the problem of reform. However, while the United States will have to deal with non-democratic governments, there is no reason to justify such relationships on the theory that they are more stable than others. On the other hand the United States must, in general, accept military governments and be satisfied simply with trying to modify them. If they are overthrown, the United States may help as much as possible to divert revolutionary demands into constructive channels.

The authors do not propose that as a policy matter the United States should ignore the development of representative democracy in Latin America, nor that it should abandon its stand in favor of political democracy and the corollaries of social and economic justice and individual rights. It may be argued that ultimate stability depends on some form of open society and on a measure of broadly distributed economic prosperity and social justice. If this is true, then an unstable transition period between authoritarianism and something else is necessary before the ultimate ideal policy goal of stability can be realized.

The promotion of democracy in Latin America is a legitimate objective of United States policy in order to achieve ultimate stability, and measures should be employed to this end. But in pursuing policies aimed at assisting democratic development, we Americans must keep in mind the limits of our policy and contain our hopes within a manageable scope, avoiding false expectations. We must keep in mind that political development is a complicated process involving the interaction of political, social, psychological and economic factors—and that an ideological approach reduces policy to utopian dimensions and obscures alternatives to development. We must avoid demanding the desirable so as not to defeat the attainable. We must even be prepared for failure.

REFERENCES

CHAPTER I

1. For full examinations of ends-means analysis and the ideas of objectives, policy instruments, and capability, see James N. Rosenau (ed.), *International Politics and Foreign Policy: A Reader in Research and Theory* (New York: The Free Press of Glencoe, Inc., 1961), pp. 141–85, 254–67; and the revised edition (1969), pp. 167–98, 255–60; and K. J. Holsti, *International Politics: A Framework for Analysis* (Englewood Cliffs, N.J.: Prentice-Hall, Inc., 1967), chaps. V–XII.

2. See the discussion of national interest by Charles O. Lerche, *Foreign Policy of the American People* (3d ed.; Englewood Cliffs, N.J.: Prentice-Hall, Inc., 1967), pp. 9–14.

3. See discussions by Gordon Connell-Smith, *The Inter-American System* (London: Oxford University Press, 1966), Introduction, chaps. 1, 3, 5, 7 and 9, and postscript; Jerome Slater, *The OAS and United States Foreign Policy* (Columbus: Ohio State University Press, 1967), Introduction, chaps. I, III–V and VII; and Howard J. Wiarda, "The Context of United States Policy Toward the Dominican Republic: Background to the Revolution of 1965" (Paper presented to the Seminar on the Dominican Republic, Center for International Affairs, Harvard University, December 8, 1966).

4. J. Lloyd Mecham says: "The Caribbean area has been regarded by the United States as a regional unit to which it applied a distinctive set of policies. . . . American diplomacy has been so much concerned with the countries of the area that it is hardly an exaggeration to say that most of its major policy decisions and actions relating to Latin America originated in this region." *A Survey of United States–Latin American Relations* (Boston: Houghton Mifflin Co., 1965), p. 239.

5. The definitive work is Arthur P. Whitaker, *The Western Hemisphere Idea: Its Rise and Decline* (Ithaca, N.Y.: Cornell University Press, 1954).

6. C. O. Lerche, Jr., "Concepts of International Relations," Lecture Before the U.S. Army War College, Carlisle Barracks, Pa., October 3, 1961 (mimeograph), p. 7.

7. John C. Dreier, *The Organization of American States and the Hemisphere Crisis* (New York: Harper & Row, 1962), pp. 132–33. Italics in the original.

8. Quoted by William L. Neumann, Jr., *Recognition of Governments in the Americas* (Washington, D.C.: Foundation for Public Affairs, 1947), p. 3.

9. Charles G. Fenwick, "Intervention: Individual and Collective," *American Journal of International Law*, XXXIX (October, 1945), p. 653.

10. Arthur P. Whitaker sees the answer to the Wilsonian puzzle in what he calls the "civilizing mission": "In Wilson's own mind there was no inconsistency between his principles and practice, for with him the overriding principle was the principle of power—with its preponderance of power in the Western Hemisphere the United States had both the right and the duty to intervene in Latin America to perform its civilizing mission." *The Western Hemisphere Idea*, p. 121. Samuel Flagg Bemis says that Wilson's policy had an "ideological and missionary background originally deriving from Protestant Christianity and resting on the 'Gospel of Progress,'" the political reflection of which was "popular sovereignty and republican government as opposed to monarchy and totalitarianism." *The Latin American Policy of the United States* (New York: Harcourt Brace & Co., 1943), pp. 160–61.

11. Marvin Goldwert, *The Constabulary in the Dominican Republic and Nicaragua: Progeny and Legacy of United States Intervention* (Gainesville: University of Florida Press, 1962); Dana G. Munro, *Intervention and Dollar Diplomacy in the Caribbean, 1900–1921* (Princeton, N.J.: Princeton University Press, 1964); and Mecham, *A Survey of United States-Latin American Relations*, chaps. 10–12.

12. Bryce Wood, *The Making of the Good Neighbor Policy* (New York: Columbia University Press, 1961), p. 152.

13. *The Department of State Bulletin*, XIV (February 24, 1946), p. 296.

14. *Ibid.* (January 27, 1946), p. 103.

15. The official title of the State Department's publication was *Consultation Among the American Republics with Respect to the Argentine Situation* (Pub. No. 2473, February 24, 1946).

16. *The Department of State Bulletin,* XX (January 2, 1949), p. 30.

17. *Ibid.,* XXI (September 26, 1949), pp. 463–64.

18. *Ibid.,* XXII (May 22, 1950), pp. 797–99.

19. Pan American Union, *Alliance for Progress: Official Documents Emanating from the Special Meeting of the Inter-American Economic and Social Council at the Ministerial Level, Held in Punta del Este, Uruguay, from August 5 to 17, 1961* (Washington, D.C.: Pan American Union, 1961).

20. Reprinted from *The Department of State Bulletin,* L (June 29, 1964), pp. 995–1000.

21. For complete text see "Inter-American Solidarity: Safeguarding the Democratic Ideal," *Ibid.,* XIII (November 25, 1945), pp. 864–66.

22. Edgar S. Furniss, Jr., "The Inter-American System and Recent Caribbean Disputes," *International Organization,* IV (November, 1950), p. 586.

23. Department of State, *Peace in the Americas: A Résumé of Measures Undertaken Through the OAS to Preserve Peace* (Pub. 3964, International Organization and Conference Series II, American Republics 6, 1950), pp. 8–18.

24. Slater, *The OAS and United States Foreign Policy,* chap. VI, also points out a second instance where the OAS acted as an "anti-dictatorial alliance" with respect to the "Haitian-Dominican conflict of 1963." This time, however, the OAS stressed the maintenance of peace between the two disputants, resisting efforts by the Dominican Republic and the United States to have the OAS act to overthrow the Duvalier government.

25. Pan American Union, Council, Committee of Investigation, *Report Submitted by the Committee of the Council, Acting Provisionally as Organ of Consultation in the Case Presented by Venezuela, to comply with the Provisions of the Third Paragraph of the Resolution of July 8, 1960* (Washington, D.C.: Pan American Union, 1960).

26. Arthur P. Whitaker, *The United States and Argentina* (Cambridge: Harvard University Press, 1954), pp. 220–21.

27. *The Department of State Bulletin,* XL (January 19, 1959), p. 103.

28. *Arms and Politics in Latin America* (rev. ed.; New York: Frederick A. Praeger, 1961) and *Generals Vs. Presidents: Neo-Militarism in Latin America* (New York: Frederick A. Praeger, 1964).

29. "Military Assistance and Militarism in Latin America," *The Western Political Quarterly,* XVIII (June, 1965), pp. 382–92.

30. "Reflexiones sobre las dictaduras," *Cuadernos Americanos,* XI (julio-agosto 1952), pp. 57–63.

31. *United States Policy and the Third World* (Boston: Little, Brown & Co., 1967).

32. "The Nonmilitary Use of the Latin American Military: A More Realistic Approach to Arms Control and Economic Development," *Background*, VIII (November, 1964), pp. 161–73.

33. "Politics, Social Structure and Military Intervention in Latin America," *European Journal of Sociology*, II (1961), pp. 62–81.

34. *The Military and Society in Latin America* (Palo Alto, Cal.: Stanford University Press, 1964).

35. "The Role of the Military in Contemporary Latin American Politics," *The Western Political Quarterly*, XIII (September, 1960), pp. 747–62.

36. See David H. Bayley, "The Effects of Corruption in a Developing Nation," *The Western Political Quarterly*, XIX (December, 1966), pp. 719–32.

37. House Foreign Affairs Committee, *News Release*, April 6, 1966 (mimeographed), pp. 3–4.

38. Nelson A. Rockefeller, *Quality of Life in the Americas: Report of a U. S. Presidential Mission for the Western Hemisphere* (reprinted by Agency for International Development), p. 18.

39. See Robert T. Holt and John E. Turner, *The Political Basis of Economic Development: An Exploration in Comparative Political Analysis* (Princeton, N.J.: Van Nostrand Co., 1966). See also, Fred R. von der Mehden, *Politics in the Developing Nations* (Englewood Cliffs, N.J.: Prentice-Hall, 1964); Martin C. Needler, *Political Development in Latin America: Instability, Violence, and Evolutionary Change* (New York: Random House, 1968); and Lucian W. Pye, *Aspects of Political Development* (Boston: Little, Brown & Co., 1966).

CHAPTER II

1. Howard J. Wiarda, "The Context of United States Policy Toward the Dominican Republic: Background to the Revolution of 1965." Paper presented to the Seminar on the Dominican Republic, Center for International Affairs, Harvard University, December 8, 1966.

2. For text of the protocol see Department of State, *Papers Relating to the Foreign Relations of the United States*, 1905, pp. 311–12; beginning with correspondence of 1932, the volumes were published under the title *Foreign Relations of the United States: Diplomatic Papers*, hereafter cited as *Foreign Relations*, with year.

3. For text of the convention and proclamation by the President of the United States, see *ibid.*, 1907, pp. 307–10.

4. Dana G. Munro, *Intervention and Dollar Diplomacy in the Caribbean, 1900–1921* (Princeton, N.J.: Princeton University Press, 1964), p. 124.

5. Sumner Welles, *Naboth's Vineyard: The Dominican Republic, 1844–1924* (New York: Payson and Clarke, Ltd., 1928), II, p. 792.

6. David Charles MacMichael, *The United States and the Dominican Republic, 1871–1940: A Cycle in Caribbean Diplomacy* (unpublished doctoral dissertation, University of Oregon, 1964), p. 503. See also Munro, *Intervention and Dollar Diplomacy in the Caribbean*, pp. 531, 533–35; and Samuel Flagg Bemis, *The Latin American Policy of the United States: An Historical Interpretation* (New York: Harcourt, Brace & Co., 1943), p. 157.

7. For text of the proclamation see U.S. Senate Select Committee on Haiti and Santo Domingo, *Inquiry Into Occupation and Administration of Haiti and Santo Domingo*, 67th Cong., 1st Sess., 1922, pp. 90–94.

8. Welles, *Naboth's Vineyard*, pp. 802–18.

9. *Ibid.*, pp. 819–20.

10. Robert D. Heinl, Jr., *Soldiers of the Sea: The United States Marine Corps, 1775–1962* (Annapolis, Md.: United States Naval Institute, 1962), p. 251.

11. Harry A. Ellsworth, *One Hundred and Eighty Landings of United States Marines, 1800–1934* (Washington, D.C.: U.S. Navy, Historical Section, 1934), p. 71.

12. Clyde H. Metcalf, *History of the United States Marine Corps* (New York: G. P. Putnam & Sons, 1939), p. 355.

13. MacMichael, *The United States and the Dominican Republic*, p. 457.

14. Marvin Goldwert, *The Constabulary in the Dominican Republic and Nicaragua: Progeny and Legacy of United States Intervention* (Gainesville: University of Florida Press, 1962), pp. 2–3.

15. Munro, *Intervention and Dollar Diplomacy in the Caribbean*, p. 317.

16. Goldwert, *The Constabulary in the Dominican Republic and Nicaragua*, p. 12.

17. *Ibid.*, pp. 12–13.

18. A well-known legal scholar in the United States, Philip Mason Brown, justified the occupation in terms of international law in his "Armed Occupation of Santo Domingo," *American Journal of International Law*, XI (April, 1917), pp. 394–99. More typical views, however, were the condemnation by such students of Latin America as Otto

Schoenrich and Samuel Guy Inman, in George H. Blakeslee (ed.), *Mexico and the Caribbean: Clark University Addresses* (New York: G. E. Stechert, 1920).

19. Select Committee on Haiti and Santo Domingo, *Inquiry Into Occupation and Administration of Haiti and Santo Domingo.* See also Carl Kelsey, "The American Intervention in Haiti and the Dominican Republic," *Annals of the American Academy of Political and Social Science,* C (March, 1922), pp. 110–22; Professor Kelsey, of the University of Pennsylvania, visited the two countries under the aegis of the Academy.

20. For text of the 1924 treaty see *U.S. Treaty Series,* no. 726.

21. Goldwert, *The Constabulary in the Dominican Republic and Nicaragua,* p. vi.

22. A few of the more fulsome, eulogistic, often officially inspired accounts include: Joaquín Balaguer, *Dominican Reality: Biographic Sketch of a Country and a Regime* (Mexico, 1949); Laurence de Besault, *President Trujillo: His Work and the Dominican Republic* (Santiago, R.D.: Editorial del Diario, 1941); Pedro Gonzáles Blanco, *La era de Trujillo* (Ciudad Trujillo: Editora del Caribe, 1955); Ramón Marrero Aristy, *Trujillo: síntesis de su vida y su obra* (Ciudad Trujillo: Impresa Dominicana, 1953); Abelardo R. Nanita, *Trujillo* (Ciudad Trujillo: Editora del Caribe, 1954); José Antonio Osorio Lizarazo, *La isla iluminada* (Ciudad Trujillo: Editora del Caribe, 1953); Stanley Walker, *Biografía del generalissimo Rafael L. Trujillo* (New York: Caribbean Library, 1957). A sampling of the many scathing denunciations are: Jesús M. Galíndez, *La era de Trujillo: un estudio casuístico de dictadura hispano-americana* (Santiago de Chile: Editorial del Pacífico, 1956); William Khrem, *Democracia y tiranías en el caribe* (Mexico, D.F.: Unión Democrática Centro-americana, 1946); Francisco Girona, *The Misdeeds of the Bandit Trujillo* (n.p., 1937); and Germán E. Ornés, *Trujillo: Little Caesar of the Caribbean* (New York: Thomas Nelson & Sons, 1958). The only balanced, detailed account is Robert D. Crassweller's excellent biography, *Trujillo: The Life and Times of a Caribbean Dictator* (New York: Macmillan, 1966).

23. Goldwert, *The Constabulary in the Dominican Republic and Nicaragua,* p. 20.

24. *Foreign Relations,* 1930, II, pp. 699–717.

25. *Ibid.,* p. 708.

26. *Ibid.,* p. 711.

27. *Ibid.,* pp. 704–05, 714–15.

28. *Ibid.,* pp. 718–19.

29. *The New York Times,* May 17, 1930. An excellent treatment of the nature and extent of Trujillo's control is Howard J. Wiarda, *Dictatorship and Development: The Methods of Control in Trujillo's Dominican Republic* (Gainesville: University of Florida Press, 1969).

30. Hubert Herring, "Scandal of the Caribbean: The Dominican Republic," *Current History* (March, 1960), pp. 141–42.

31. Rafael Leonidas Trujillo Molina, *Message Addressed to His Countrymen on the Tenth Anniversary of Assuming the Political Direction of the Dominican People* (Ciudad Trujillo: Imp. Listín Diario, 1949), p. 4.

32. For example, Goldwert, *The Constabulary in the Dominican Republic and Nicaragua;* and Noel Henríquez, *La verdad sobre Trujillo: capítulos que se le olvidaron a Galíndez* (Habana: Luz Hilo, 1959).

33. Albert C. Hicks, *Blood in the Streets: The Life and Rule of Trujillo* (New York: Creative Age Press, 1946), pp. 88–89.

CHAPTFR III

1. Bryce Wood, *The Making of the Good Neighbor Policy* (New York: Columbia University Press, 1961), p. 152.

2. For the text of the 1907 convention, see *Foreign Relations* (1907), pt. 1, p. 307; the text of the treaty of 1924 is in Department of State, *U.S. Treaty Series,* no. 726.

3. Charles A. Thomson, "Dictatorship in the Dominican Republic," *Foreign Policy Reports* (April 15, 1936), p. 40.

4. Department of War, Bureau of Insular Affairs, General Receiver of Dominican Customs, *Report of the Dominican Customs Receivership Under the American-Dominican Convention of 1924, Together with a Summary of Commerce,* calendar year 1930, pp. 9–11 [hereafter cited as *Report of Customs Receivership,* with year]; and W. E. Dunn, Special Emergency Agent, Dominican Republic, *Report of the Special Emergency Agent for the Period October 23, 1931 to December 31, 1932* (n.p., n.d.), pp. 10–11 [contains a translation of the Emergency Law and several related executive decrees]. The status of the Dominican bonded indebtedness as of December 31, 1930, was as follows: (1) bond issue of April 5, 1922, for $6,700,000, combined with issue of April 1, 1926, for $3,300,000, totaling $10,000,000, maturing March 1, 1942 — $9,144,500 outstanding plus interest; (2) bond issue of January 10, 1927, for $5,000,000, and issue of January 27, 1928, for $5,000,000, totaling $10,000,000, maturing October 1, 1940 — $9,137,000 outstanding plus interest.

5. Department of State, *Press Releases,* November 14, 1931, p. 454; *Report of the Customs Receivership,* 1934, p. 6.

6. The Foreign Bondholders Council, Inc. had been established under the auspices of the United States government to provide an agency whereby bondholders could present their petitions for amelioration of the terms of the original obligations. *Report of the Customs Receivership,* 1934, p. 7.

7. *Ibid.,* pp. 7–9.

8. *Foreign Relations,* 1936, V, p. 444.

9. For the texts of some proposals submitted by both governments, see *Foreign Relations,* 1937, V, pp. 444–49, 453–61, 464–65; 1940, V, pp. 792–97.

10. Rafael Leonidas Trujillo y Molina, *The Evolution of Democracy in Santo Domingo,* 2d, ed. (Ciudad Trujillo: Editors del Caribe, 1955), p. 55; *Foreign Relations,* 1936, V, pp. 435–58; 1937, V, pp. 440–67; 1938, V, pp. 491–508; 1939, V, pp. 579–95; 1940, V, 792–830.

11. *Foreign Relations,* 1937, V, p. 452; 1939, V, p. 588.

12. *The New York Times,* September 23, 1939. An example of Trujillo's influence on Dominican policy, even when he was not the formal head of government, occurred at this time. With great candor President Peynado and Foreign Secretary Despradel informed Minister Norweb that negotiations on the treaty had been suspended until Trujillo's return from Washington, and that renewed conversations would depend entirely on his views. It was clear to Norweb that "no one in the Dominican Republic will touch the Convention question pending the return of General Trujillo." *Foreign Relations,* 1939, V, p. 587.

13. Text of convention in Department of State, *Treaty Series,* no. 965 (1941).

14. *Congressional Record,* vol. 87, p. 1027; *The Department of State Bulletin,* IV (March 22, 1941), p. 345; Manuel A. Peña Battle, *Contribución a una campaña. Cuatro discursos políticos* (Santiago, R.D.: Ed. el Diario, 1941).

15. *The Department of State Bulletin,* XVII (August 17, 1947), p. 341, and XXV (August 20, 1951), p. 299.

16. *The New York Times,* November 21, 1937.

17. *Ibid.,* November 7 and 9, 1937; Crassweller, *Trujillo,* pp. 153–56; Wood, *The Making of the Good Neighbor Policy,* p. 155.

18. *The New York Times,* December 22, 1937.

19. *The New York Times,* December 18, 1937.

20. J. Lloyd Mecham, *The United States and Inter-American Security, 1889–1960* (Austin: University of Texas Press, 1961), pp. 175–76.

21. (1) Treaty to Avoid or Prevent Conflicts Between the American States (Gondra Treaty, 1923); (2) General Convention of Inter-American Conciliation (1929); (3) General Treaty of Inter-American Arbitration (1929); (4) Additional Protocol to the General Convention of Inter-American Conciliation (1933); (5) Anti-War Treaty of Non-Aggression and Conciliation (Saavedra Lamas Treaty, 1933); (6) Convention to Coordinate, Extend and Assure the Fulfillment of the Existing Treaties between the American States (1936); (7) Inter-American Treaty on Good Offices and Mediation (1936); and (8) Treaty on the Prevention of Controversies (1936).

22. *Foreign Relations,* 1938, V, p. 196.

23. *Ibid.,* 1937, V, pp. 135–40.

24. Text of the Gondra Treaty in *ibid.,* 1923, I, p. 308, and of the General Convention of Inter-American Conciliation in *ibid.,* 1929, I, p. 653.

25. This position was defended in a full page advertisement in *The New York Times,* December 17, 1937. Even after the matter was settled, the Dominican Republic continued to protest.

26. *Congressional Record,* LXXXVII, pp. 2040 and 2043. Unfortunately for the cause of later anti-Trujillists, Fish changed his mind and publicly praised Trujillo; in 1942 he was implicated in a $25,000 "payoff" by the dictator, according to *Time* (August 17, 1942), pp. 18–19.

27. Pan American Union, *Bulletin,* LXXII (March, 1938), pp. 288–304; Department of State, *Press Releases,* March 19, 1938; *The Dominican Republic,* Vol. 5 (March, 1938), p. 1.

28. *Foreign Relations,* 1938, V, pp. 197–98.

29. *The New York Times,* May 21, 1939.

30. William Alex, "Are We Really Good Neighbors?" *The Pan American* (March, 1945), p. 32.

31. Text of Telegram in *The New York Times,* July 7, 1939.

32. Lewis Hanke, "Friendship Now With Latin America," *The Virginia Quarterly Review* (Autumn, 1946), p. 509; and Víctor Raúl Haya de la Torre, "Toward a Real Inter-Americanism," *Mexican Life,* XVIII (October, 1942), and his "Inter-American Democratic Front," *Free World,* IV (November, 1942).

33. For a few of the many examples, see *The Department of State Bul-*

letin, V (December 20, 1941), p. 547; VII (November 14, 1942), p. 912; X (June 10, 1944), p. 531. *The New York Times,* September 23, 1942.

34. *Foreign Relations,* 1944, VII, p. 1019. See also his memoirs, *Farewell to Foggy Bottom: The Recollections of a Career Diplomat* (New York: David McKay Co., 1964), pp. 221–25. Ambassador Briggs confirmed to the present writers in a letter dated April 29, 1968, that he had not been declared *persona non grata* in 1945 as some Dominican writers suggested.

35. See also *The Department of State Bulletin,* XV (July 21, 1946), p. 134.

36. Uruguay, Ministerio de Relaciones Exteriores, *Paralelismo entre la democracia y la paz. Protección internacional de los derechos del hombre. Acción colectiva en defensa de esos principios* (Montevideo: Sección Prensa, informaciones y publicaciones, 1946), pp. 7–12; and "Inter-American Solidarity: Safeguarding the Democratic Ideal," *U.S. Department of State Bulletin,* XIII (November 25, 1945), pp. 864–66.

37. "U.S. Adherence to Principle Opposing Oppressive Regimes Among American Republics," *The Department of State Bulletin,* XIII (December 2, 1945), p. 892. Ellis O. Briggs, Director of the Office of American Republic Affairs, stated in a November 20 speech at the University of Pennsylvania, two days before the release of Dr. Larreta's note, that the United States did not intend to intervene to impose democracy. "Pan America, a Post-War Estimate," *The Department of State Bulletin,* XIII (November 25, 1945), p. 869.

38. Northwestern University, "The Organization of American States," in U.S. Senate Committee on Foreign Relations, *United States–Latin American Relations,* 86th Cong., 2d Sess., Doc. No. 125, August 31, 1960, p. 216.

39. Edgar S. Furniss, Jr., "The Inter-American System and Recent Caribbean Disputes," *International Organization,* IV (November, 1950), pp. 593–94.

40. Pan American Union, *Inter-American Treaty of Reciprocal Assistance, Applications* (1964), I, p. 127. See also the excellent treatment by J. Lloyd Mecham, "Caribbean Turbulence (1949–1960)," chap. XIII of his *United States and Inter-American Security, 1889–1960* (Austin: University of Texas Press, 1961).

41. Leonard H. Pomeroy, "The International Trade and Traffic in Arms: Its Supervision and Control–II," *The Department of State Bulletin,* XXII (March 6, 1950), pp. 357–58.

42. Harry B. Murkland, "The Complicated Caribbean," *Current History* (January, 1950), p. 10; and Olive Holmes, "Dominican Dispute Tests Inter-American Systems," *Foreign Policy Bulletin,* XXXIX (February 17, 1950), N.P.

43. Miguel Jorrin, *Governments of Latin America* (New York: D. Van Nostrand Company, Inc., 1953), pp. 285–86.

44. *A Bulletin of the Dominican Embassy,* no. 43 (October 15, 1947).

45. Pan American Union, *Annals of the Organization of American States,* II (1950), pp. 24–25; Pan American Union, *Second Report of the Inter-American Peace Committee Submitted to the Tenth Inter-American Conference* (1954), pp. 5–6.

46. Pan American Union, *Bulletin,* LXXXII (October, 1948), p. 591.

47. *Inter-American Treaty of Reciprocal Assistance, Applications,* pp. 69–76; *Second Report of the Inter-American Peace Committee,* pp. 6–7; *Annals of the Organization of American States,* I (1949), pp. 217–19, 325–26; text of the joint declaration is in *The Department of State Bulletin,* XX (June 26, 1949), p. 833.

48. Pomeroy, "The International Trade and Traffic in Arms," p. 357. See also "The Caribbean Situation: U.S. Memorandum to the Inter-American Peace Committee," *The Department of State Bulletin,* XXI (September 26, 1949), pp. 450–54. [This is a document solicited by the committee, dated August 18, 1949, detailing activities of United States citizens in running aircraft and arms or working as aviators for exile groups]; and Inter-American Peace Committee, *Report to the Tenth Inter-American Conference* (1954).

49. *Peace in the Americas,* pp. 2–3, 5–7; and *The Department of State Bulletin,* XXI (October 31, 1949), pp. 665–67.

50. *The Department of State Bulletin,* XXI (September 26, 1949), p. 463.

51. *Ibid.* (December 26, 1949), p. 990.

52. Department of State, *Peace in the Americas: A Resume of Measures Undertaken Through the OAS to Preserve Peace* (Pub. No. 3964, International Organization and Conference Series II, American Republics 6, 1950), pp. 3–4. See also *The Department of State Bulletin,* XXII (February 20, 1950), pp. 279–82.

53. *Peace in the Americas,* p. 4.

54. Organization of American States, Investigating Committee of the Organ of Consultation, *Documents Submitted at the Meeting of March 13, 1950* (Pan American Union Document C-I-67-E); "Report of Spe-

cial Committee for the Caribbean," *Annals of the Organization of American States*, II (1950), pp. 23–24; and *Inter-American Treaty of Reciprocal Assistance, Applications*, pp. 79–155.

55. *Peace in the Americas*, p. 4.

56. *Ibid.*, pp. 8–18. See also *Inter-American Treaty of Reciprocal Assistance, Applications*, pp. 79–155; and Edward Jamison, "Keeping Peace in the Caribbean Area," *The Department of State Bulletin*, XXIII (July 3, 1950), pp. 18–25.

57. Arthur P. Whitaker, "The Organization of American States," *International Conciliation* (March, 1951), pp. 153–57.

58. Based on Galíndez' doctoral dissertation for Columbia University, *La Era de Trujillo*, published in Santiago de Chile by Editorial del Pacífico, S.A., in 1956.

59. Porter's speeches before the House of Representatives are published in the *Congressional Record*, CIII, pp. 2815–18. See also his articles in *Coronet* (June, 1957) and *The New Leader* (July 7–14, 1958). *Life* (February 25, 1957), pp. 24–31, carried a widely read article detailing "an amazing tale of intrigue, violence, and perhaps murder involving the Dominican Republic, which is run by the ruthless dictator Rafael Leonidas Trujillo." See editorials in *The New York Times*, June 24, 29, 1958 and July 8, 21, 1959. Also of interest are Noel Henríquez, *La verdad sobre Trujillo: capítulos que se le olvidaron a Galíndez* (Habana: Luz Hilo, 1959); Germán E. Ornes and John McCarter, "Trujillo: Little Caesar on Our Front Porch," *Harper's* (December, 1956), pp. 67–72.

60. *The Department of State Bulletin*, XXXVI (February 11, 1957), p. 221; (March 4, 1957), p. 349; (April 15, 1957), p. 610; and (June 24, 1957), pp. 1025–28.

61. Germán E. Ornes, *The Other Side of the Coin* (Washington: Embassy of the Dominican Republic, 1955); *A Look at the Dominican Republic*, I (June, 1956), p. 7; II (July, 1957), pp. 7–10; Juan Arce Medina, *An Open Letter to the Editors of Life re: the Galindez Murphy Case* (New York: Dominican Republic Cultural Society, n.d.).

62. *The Department of State Bulletin*, XXXVI (June 24, 1957), p. 1027.

63. Morris L. Ernst, *Report and Opinion in the Matter of Galindez* (New York: Sidney S. Baron and Co., Inc., 1958).

64. *Congressional Record*, CLIV, pp. 12860–67.

65. *Address of Hon. William T. Pheiffer, Ambassador of the United States of America to the Dominican Republic, at the Luncheon Meeting of the Miami Beach Rotary Club on March 6, 1956* (Ciudad Trujillo: Impresora Domi-

nicana, 1956). A few years earlier Ambassador Pheiffer's predecessor, Ralph H. Ackerman, had also publicly praised Trujillo in an address at the University of Santo Domingo on June 9, 1952. After receiving an honorary Doctorate of Philosophy, Ambassador Ackerman had said that United States relations with the Dominican Republic reflected a trend toward general international cooperation, that governments were showing greater interest in the welfare of their nation, and that "your own illustrious President, Rafael Leonidas Trujillo, gave illustration of this trend when . . . he reiterated an aspiration he has often voiced before, to raise the standard of living in the Dominican Republic so that his people may benefit from a fuller life. No one can gainsay the great benefits he has already succeeded in bringing about in the form of better educational facilities, hospitalization, water supplies, port facilities, roads, and every branch of economic activity." *The Department of State Bulletin,* XXVII (July 14, 1952), p. 52.

66. *Congressional Record,* CIII, pp. 2817–18, 11756–57.

67. *Ibid.,* pp. 4944–46, 5935, 5938, 6462, 7793–95.

68. *Ibid.,* pp. 9983–84, 10299–10300, 14349–50.

69. U.S. Senate Committee on the Judiciary, *Communist Problems in Latin America,* 85th Cong., 1st Sess., 1957, pp. 3–4.

70. Edwin Lieuwen, *Arms and Politics in Latin America* (New York: Frederick A. Praeger, 1960), p. 7.

71. *Congressional Record,* pp. 8868–69, 9052–53, 9219–20, 11538–39.

72. *Ibid.,* pp. 10266–67, 10270, 10273; CV, pp. 3164–65.

73. Albert C. Hicks, *Blood in the Streets: The Life and Rule of Trujillo* (New York: Creative Age Press, Inc., 1946), p. 91.

74. José Antonio Lizarazo, *El bacilo de Marx* (Ciudad Trujillo: Editorial La Nación, 1959); and his *Germen y proceso del anti-trujillismo en América* (Santiago, D.R.: Imp. Colombia, 1956).

75. Vol. 1, no. 2 (February, 1956), pp. 10–11; no. 6 (June, 1956), p. 5; Vol. 2, no. 4 (April, 1957), p. 3.

76. Douglas Cater and Walter Pincus, "The Foreign Legion of U.S. Public Relations," *Reporter* (December 22, 1960), pp. 15–22.

77. *Trujillo: The Last Caesar* (Chicago: Henry Regnery, 1963).

CHAPTER IV

1. J. Lloyd Mecham, *The United States and Inter-American Security, 1889–1960* (Austin: University of Texas Press, 1961), chaps. VII and

VIII; Laurence Duggan, *The Americas: The Search for Hemispheric Security* (New York: Henry Holt, 1949).

2. World Peace Foundation, *Documents on American Foreign Relations,* II (1939), pp. 208–16, and III (1940), p. 134.

3. *Foreign Relations,* 1939, V, pp. 579–80.

4. Mecham, *The United States and Inter-American Security,* pp. 195–96.

5. Texts of both agreements are in *Foreign Relations,* 1941, VII, pp. 253–55. The purpose of Lend-Lease in Latin America during World War II was ostensibly to help the American republics carry out hemisphere defense plans, but an official memorandum in 1940 listed but one reason for supplying arms to the Dominican Republic: "to insure internal stability." Stetson Conn and Byron Fairchild, *The Western Hemisphere: The Framework of Hemispheric Defense,* Vol. 12, pt. 1, of Department of the Army, *United States Army in World War II* (Washington, D.C.: Government Printing Office, 1960), p. 213.

6. U.S. House, Committee on Foreign Affairs, *Twenty-Ninth Report to Congress on Lend-Lease Operations,* 81st Cong., 2d. Sess., 1950, pp. 16–18.

7. *Foreign Relations,* 1941, VI, p. 87. At the time of Pearl Harbor, although the United States had military missions in thirteen Latin American countries, the Dominican Republic was not included — there was not even a naval attaché in the country. Mecham, *op. cit.,* p. 201; and Edwin Lieuwen, *Arms and Politics in Latin America* (rev. ed.; New York: Frederick A. Praeger, 1961), pp. 153, 190–91.

8. Ernesto Vega y Pagán, *Historia de las Fuerzas Armadas* (Ciudad Trujillo: Imp. Dominicana, 1955), II, p. 439.

9. Dominican Revolutionary Party, *Trujillo, A Nazi* (Mayagüez, P.R.: 1944): Juan Isidro Jimenez Grullón, *Una gestapo en América. Vida, tortura, agonía y muerto de presos políticos bajo la tiranía de Trujillo* (Habana: Ed. Lex., 1946), and by the same author, *La propaganda de Trujillo al desnudo* (Habana: Unión democrática antinazista dominicana, 1943); Selden Rodman, *Quisqueya: A History of the Dominican Republic* (Seattle: University of Washington Press, 1964), p. 143; Carleton Beals, "Caesar of the Caribbean," *Current History,* XLVIII (January, 1938), p. 34, and by the same author, *The Coming Struggle for Latin America* (Philadelphia: J. B. Lippincott, 1938), pp. 49–50, 82; and Albert C. Hicks, *Blood in the Streets* (New York: Creative Age Press, 1946), p. 89.

10. For example, Víctor Raúl Haya de la Torre, "Toward a Real Inter-Americanism," *Mexican Life,* XVIII (October, 1942), and his "Inter-American Democratic Front," *Free World,* IV (November, 1942);

and Carleton Beals, telegram to President Roosevelt, text in *The New York Times,* July 7, 1939.

11. *Foreign Relations,* 1944, VII, pp. 1015–24; see also Ellis O. Briggs, *Farewell to Foggy Bottom: The Recollection of a Career Diplomat* (New York: David McKay, 1964), pp. 221–25.

12. Quoted in Robert D. Crassweller, *Trujillo: The Life and Times of a Caribbean Dictator* (New York: Macmillan, 1966), p. 216.

13. Germán E. Ornes, *Trujillo, Little Caesar of the Caribbean* (New York: Thomas Nelson & Sons, 1958), p. 136.

14. U.S. House Committee on Foreign Affairs, *Mutual Security Act of 1951,* 86th Cong., 2d Sess., 1959, p. 729.

15. "Military Assistance to Latin America," *The Department of State Bulletin,* XXVIII (March 30, 1953), pp. 463–67.

16. U.S. House Committee on Foreign Affairs, *Inter-American Military Cooperation Act,* 79th Cong., 2d Sess., 1946.

17. U.S. Congress, *Twenty-Ninth Report to Congress on Lend-Lease Operations,* pp. 1, 16–18, 22–23. The total amount for all Lend-Lease (including World War II) paid by the Dominican Republic was $679,-247.71.

18. *The Department of State Bulletin,* XXI (September 26, 1949), pp. 479–81.

19. Agency for International Development, *U.S. Overseas Loans and Grants and Assistance from International Organizations, Obligations and Loan Authorizations, July 1, 1945–June 30, 1965* (1966).

20. Text of treaty in Department of State, *Treaties and Other International Agreements Series,* No. 2425 (1953). Other treaties included an "Air Transport Services Agreement" (July 19, 1949), an "Aviation Agreement" (August 11, 1950), an agreement for a "Cooperative Weather Stations Program" (July 25, and August 11, 1956), an agreement concerning "Atomic Energy Cooperation for Civil Uses" (June 15, 1956), and a "Navigation Agreement Establishing a LORAN Station at Cape Francis Viejo" (March 19, 1957). Texts, in the order listed above, can be found in *ibid.,* no. 1955 (1950), no. 2143 (1951), no. 3699 (1957), no. 3711 (1957), and no. 3780 (1957).

21. P.L. 165, 82d Cong., 1st Sess., approved October 10, 1951.

22. See text in *Treaties and Other International Agreements Series,* no. 2777 (1954).

23. Agency for International Development, *U.S. Overseas Loans and Grants . . .* (1966), p. 26.

24. Department of State, *United States Treaties, VII,* p. 3238; U.S.

Senate, Committee on Agriculture and Forestry, *A Review of United States Government Operations in Latin America,* 86th Cong., 1st Sess., 1959, p. 486.

25. *The Congressional Record,* CIV, pp. 8620 and 8719; and p. 8734.

26. *Ibid.,* pp. 11648–50.

27. Embassy of the Dominican Republic in Washington, *A Look at the Dominican Republic,* Vol. 3 (July, 1958), pp. 4–5.

28. *Ibid.* (September, 1958), pp. 3–6; and pp. 7–9.

29. Porter's speeches before the House of Representatives are published in *The Congressional Record,* CIII, pp. 2815–20. Also see his articles in *Coronet* (June, 1957) and *The New Leader* (July 7–14, 1958).

30. *The Congressional Record,* CIII, pp. 9983–84, 10299–300, 14348–50.

31. *Ibid.,* CIV, pp. 9472–73.

32. *Ibid.,* p. 10267.

33. *Ibid.,* pp. 10270 and 10273.

34. Crassweller, *Trujillo,* pp. 344, 423. Agency for International Development, *U.S. Overseas Loans and Grants* . . . (1966) reports "less than $50,000" for fiscal year, 1961.

35. Mutual security appropriations from 1945 to 1961 were higher to all Latin American countries than to the Dominican Republic except for El Salvador, the only one receiving less than the Dominican Republic. The Dominican amount of $8,200,000 may be compared to the following amounts received by other Caribbean states: Costa Rica, $10,000,000; Cuba, $13,300,000; El Salvador, $7,600,000; Guatemala, $74,000,000; Haiti, $43,600,000; Honduras, $18,400,000; Nicaragua, $10,000,000; Panama, $18,400,000; and Venezuela, $32,500,000. The Latin American total for this period was $889,900,000. Source: Agency for International Development, *U.S. Overseas Loans and Grants* . . . (1966).

36. John Frank Rye, *Tension and Conflicts in Cuba, Haita, and the Dominican Republic Between 1945 and 1959* (unpublished doctoral dissertation, American University, 1966), p. 89.

37. Ornes, *Trujillo,* pp. 136–37.

38. Interviews with Colonel Simmons and the Dominican Air Force and Army military attachés, Washington, D.C., on September 19, 1967; and Howard J. Wiarda, "The Politics of Civil-Military Relations in the Dominican Republic," *Journal of Inter-American Studies,* VII (October, 1965), p. 470; U.S. Senate Committee on Foreign Relations,

Study Mission in the Caribbean Area, 85th Cong., 2d Sess., 1958, pp. 11–12. Although varying reports exist of the actual weapons and munitions produced, there is general agreement that Trujillo's armory mass-produced revolvers (.38 cal.), automatic rifles (.30 cal.), sub-machine guns (.30 cal.), carbines, light machine guns (.30 cal. and 7.6 mm), and hand grenades. In addition, some mortars were produced as well as aerial bombs and various calibers of light artillery were rebuilt. Gun powder and dynamite were manufactured as well as the following munitions: .30 and .50 cal.; 7.6, 20, and 40 mm.

39. Conversation with Willard F. Barber, Professor of Government and Politics at the University of Maryland, on October 11, 1968.

40. Interview with Colonel Simmons.

41. Crassweller, *Trujillo,* pp. 346–47.

42. Howard Wiarda, *Dictatorship and Development: The Methods of Control in Trujillo's Dominican Republic* (Gainesville: University of Florida Press, 1968), p. 45. See also Crassweller, *Trujillo,* p. 347. This information also substantiated in interview with Colonel Simmons.

43. Rys, *Tension and Conflicts in Cuba, Haiti, and the Dominican Republic,* p. 201.

44. Although the military profile presented in Fig. I is generally accurate, it does not indicate that the air force had its own ground troops with artillery and the only tanks in the country. Also, the number of aircraft appears to be much too high; a figure of 100 is probably more realistic.

45. Crassweller, *Trujillo,* p. 346; and Wiarda, "The Politics of Civil-Military Relations in the Dominican Republic," p. 470. See also Dominican Republic, Secretariado Tecnico, Oficina de Planificación, *Bases Para el Desarrollo Nacional, Análisis de los problemas y perspectivas de la economía dominicana, Diciembre 1965,* table 29.

46. Interviews with Colonel Simmons and the Dominican Air Force and Army attachés.

47. For a description of each vessel, including its place and date of construction and manner of acquisition, see Raymond V. B. Blackman (ed.), *Jane's Fighting Ships, 1965–1966* (London: Sampson, Marston & Co., 1965).

48. Wiarda, "The Politics of Civil-Military Relations in the Dominican Republic," p. 470.

49. Vega, *Historia de las Fuerzas Armadas,* II, pp. 405–06.

50. *Ibid.,* pp. 497–98.

51. *Ibid.,* p. 504. Inadequate maintenance and a shortage of spare parts should be considered when judging the meaning of this figure.

52. Interviews with Brigadier General Simmons and with Norman E. Warner, Department of State, on February 23, 1967.

53. Department of State, *Executive Agreement Series,* No. 350 (1944) and no. 404 (1944).

54. U.S. Department of Agriculture, Agricultural Stabilization and Conservation Service, Sugar Division, *Sugar Statistics and Related Data,* Statistical Bull. No. 293, Vol. I, 1961, pp. 152–53, 157.

55. *Ibid.,* p. 153.

56. Crassweller, *Trujillo,* p. 429.

57. Philip M. Glick, *The Administration of Technical Assistance: Growth in the Americas* (Chicago: University of Chicago Press, 1957), p. 10.

58. *Executive Agreement Series,* no. 346 (1943).

59. U.S. Congress, House, Committee on Foreign Affairs, *Institute of Inter-American Affairs,* Hearings, 80th Cong., 1st Sess., 1947, pp. 11 and 49; and *The Department of State Bulletin,* XVI (May 18, 1947), p. 958.

60. *The Department of State Bulletin,* XXIV (March 12, 1951), p. 414; and National Planning Association, *Technical Cooperation in Latin America: Recommendations for the Future* (Washington: National Planning Association, 1956), pp. 177, 179, 180, 182.

61. James Minotto, "Central America and the Caribbean Area," survey no. 9 of U.S. Senate, Special Committee to Study the Foreign Aid Program, *Foreign Aid Program,* 85th Cong., 1st Sess., 1957, p. 1553. Detailed descriptions of most programs are presented in U.S. Congress, Committee on Agriculture and Forestry, *A Review of United States Government Operations in Latin America,* 86th Cong., 1st Sess., 1959, pp. 483–98. For the texts of the many technical assistance agreements, see the present bibliography.

CHAPTER V

1. See, for example, House Committee on Foreign Affairs, *Report on United States Relations with Latin America,* 86th Cong., 1st Sess., 1959, p. 3.

2. U.S. Department of State, *Inter-American Efforts to Relieve International Tensions in the Western Hemisphere, 1959–1960* (1962), pp. 5–18.

3. *The Department of State Bulletin,* XLI (July 27, 1959), pp. 136–37.

4. *Ibid.* (August 31, 1959), pp. 299–305.

5. *Ibid.,* p. 299.

6. Unión Panamericana, *Quinta Reunión de Consulta de Ministros de Relaciones Exteriores, Santiago, Chile, 1959* (1959), pp. 2–3.

7. See, for example, Inter-American Peace Committee, *Report of the Inter-American Peace Committee to the Fifth Meeting of Consultation of Ministers of Foreign Affairs* (1959). For discussion of the meeting, see George C. Compton, "Consultation at San Jose," *Américas*, XII (October, 1960), pp. 3–9, and "What About Intervention?" *Américas*, XI (November, 1959), pp. 3–6; and Charles G. Fenwick, "Intervention and the Inter-American Rule of Law," *American Journal of International Law*, LIII (October, 1959), pp. 873–76.

8. Pan American Union, Inter-American Peace Committee, *Special Report on the Relationship between Violations of Human Rights or the Non-exercise of Representative Democracy and the Political Tensions that Affect the Peace of the Hemisphere* (Washington, D.C.: Pan American Union, 1960).

9. Pan American Union, Inter-American Peace Committee, *Report of the Inter-American Peace Committee on the Seventh Meeting of Consultation of Ministers of Foreign Affairs* (Washington, D.C.: Pan American Union, 1960).

10. Pan American Union, Inter-American Juridical Committee, *Study of the Juridical Relationship between Respect for Human Rights and the Exercise of Democracy* (Washington, D.C.: Pan American Union, 1960), p. 18.

11. For complete text of proceedings, see Inter-American Association for Democracy and Freedom, *Report of the Second Inter-American Conference for Democracy and Freedom* (New York, 1961), or Spanish version, Asociación Inter-Americana Pro-Democracia y Libertad, *Memoria* (Caracas, 1960). See also "Comunidad Interamericana sin dictaduras," *Combate* [Costa Rica], II (julio y agosto, 1960), p. 8.

12. *The Department of State Bulletin*, XLIII (August 8, 1960), pp. 224–25.

13. Pan American Union, Council, Committee of Investigation, *Report Submitted by the Committee of the Council, Acting Provisionally as Organ of Consultation in the Case Presented by Venezuela, to comply with the Provisions of the Third Paragraph of the Resolution of July 8, 1960* (Washington, D.C.: Pan American Union, 1960).

14. Pertinent to the following discussion are Pan American Union, *Sexta Reunión de Consulta de Ministros de Relaciones Exteriores, San José, Costa Rica, 1960: Documents* [sic] (1960), and Pan American Union,

Inter-American Treaty of Reciprocal Assistance, Applications, I (1964), pp. 3–57.

15. Jerome Slater, *The OAS and United States Foreign Policy* (Columbus: Ohio State University Press, 1967), pp. 188–89.

16. John C. Dreier, *The Organization of American States and the Hemisphere Crisis* (New York: Harper & Row, 1962), p. 98.

17. Slater, *The OAS and United States Foreign Policy*, pp. 191–92.

18. Pan American Union, *Sixth Meeting of Consultation of Ministers of Foreign Affairs Serving as Organ of Consultation in Application of the Inter-American Treaty of Reciprocal Assistance, San José, Costa Rica, August 16–21, 1960: Final Act* (Washington, D.C.: Pan American Union, 1960), pp. 5–6.

19. *The Department of State Bulletin*, XLIII (September 12, 1960), p. 412, and (October 3, 1960), pp. 542–43; *New York Times*, January 19, 1961.

20. Pan American Union, *Special Committee to Carry Out the Mandate Received by the Council Pursuant to Resolution I of the Sixth Meeting of Consultation of Ministers of Foreign Affairs, First Report of the Special Committee* . . . (1960).

21. *Ibid.*, pp. 4–5.

22. *Congressional Record*, CVI, p. 18150.

23. William Manger, *Pan America in Crisis: The Future of the OAS* (Washington, D.C.: Public Affairs Press, 1961), p. 69. For a discussion which supports the legality of the resolution against Trujillo, see Isidro Fabela, "La sexta y séptima conferencias de cancilleras ante el derecho positivo internacional," *Cuadernos Americanos*, CXIII (noviembre-diciembre, 1960), pp. 9–27.

24. *Congressional Quarterly*, January 27, 1961, p. 121.

25. *Department of State Bulletin*, XLIII (September 12, 1960), pp. 412–13.

26. *Ibid.*, pp. 413–14.

27. *Congressional Quarterly*, XVI (1960), pp. 214–16.

28. *Department of State Bulletin*, XLIII (October 24, 1960), pp. 640–1.

29. Senate Committee on Commerce, *Freedom of Communications*, pt. I, "The Speeches of John F. Kennedy," 86th Cong., 2d Sess., 1961.

30. P.L. 87-15 (March 31, 1961).

31. *Congressional Record*, CVII, p. 4421.

32. Douglas Cater and Walter Pincus, "Our Sugar Diplomacy," *Reporter* (April 13, 1961), pp. 24–28.

33. *The New York Times,* December 20, 1963.

34. These facts were disclosed in diplomatic documents obtained by *The New York Times* in Santo Domingo after Trujillo's death and subsequent interviews at the White House, reported on July 22, 1962.

35. *Ibid.,* December 5, 1963 and January 11, 1964.

36. Howard J. Wiarda, *Dictatorship and Development: The Methods of Control in Trujillo's Dominican Republic* (Gainesville: University of Florida Press, 1969), pp. 164–67.

37. *The Department of State Bulletin,* XLIII (August 29, 1960), p. 312.

38. *The New York Times,* February 10 and April 6, 1960.

39. The unpublished, untitled, mimeographed report (three pages) dated June 16 was released June 24.

40. UN Doc. S/4481 and S/4491; Inis S. Claude, Jr., "The OAS, the UN, and the United States," *International Conciliation,* No. 547 (March, 1964), pp. 48–49; and Manuel Canyes, *The Organization of American States and the United Nations* (Washington, D.C.: Pan American Union, 1960), pp. 56–59.

41. Robert D. Crassweller, *Trujillo: The Life and Times of a Caribbean Dictator* (New York: Macmillan, 1966), p. 425.

42. Jerome Slater, "The United States, the Organization of American States, and the Dominican Republic, 1961–1963," *International Organization,* XVIII (Spring, 1964), pp. 284–86.

43. J. Lloyd Mecham, *The United States and Inter-American Security, 1889–1960* (Austin: University of Texas Press, 1961), p. 423.

CHAPTER VI

1. Fear of communism, for example, was expressed in *National Review* and *U.S. News and World Report;* the latter contained an article titled "Oust a Dictator, Get a Red?" in the November 13, 1961, issue. Robert J. Alexander said at the time that the United States might "in some measure make up for the tremendous damage to democratic prospects in the Dominican Republic caused by our support of the Generalissimo for 30 long years." "After Trujillo What?" *The New Leader,* XLIV (June 12, 1961), p. 4.

2. Pan American Union, Subcommittee to the Special Committee, *Report Submitted by the Subcommittee to the Special Committee to Carry Out the Mandate Received by the Council Pursuant to Resolution I of the Sixth Meeting of Consultation of Ministers of Foreign Affairs* (Washington, D.C., 1961).

3. Pan American Union, Subcommittee of the Special Committee, *Second Report of the Subcommittee Submitted to the Special Committee to Carry Out the Mandate Received by the Council Pursuant to Resolution I of the Sixth Meeting of Consultation of Ministers of Foreign Affairs* (Washington, D.C., 1961).

4. *The Department of State Bulletin,* XLV (September 18, 1961), pp. 500–01.

5. Pan American Union, Comisión Interamericana de Derechos Humanos, *Informaciones sobre el respeto de los derechos humanos en la República Dominicana* (Washington, D.C., 1961).

6. Pan American Union, Comisión Interamericana de Derechos Humanos, *Informaciones sobre la situación de los derechos humanos en la República Dominicana* (Washington, D.C., 1962), pp. 34–40.

7. *Department of State Bulletin,* XLV (September 11, 1961), p. 447.

8. *Ibid.* (September 25, 1961), p. 523.

9. *Ibid.* (December 4, 1961), pp. 929–32.

10. *The New York Times,* November 19, 1961.

11. *The Department of State Bulletin,* XLV (December 4, 1961), p. 931.

12. *The New York Times,* November 19 and 20, 1961.

13. *The Department of State Bulletin,* XLV (December 18, 1961), p. 1003; (December 25, 1961), pp. 1054–55; XLVI (January 1, 1962), pp. 34–35. At this time began the removal of virtually all statues of the slain dictator throughout the country. The name of the capital city was returned to its original (until 1936) of Santo Domingo. Trujillo's body was removed from cold storage aboard the ex-presidential yacht in Santo Domingo and shipped by chartered aircraft to Ramfis in Paris for burial in early December.

14. Pan American Union, Subcommittee of the Special Committee, *Third Report Submitted by the Subcommittee to the Special Committee to Carry Out the Mandate Received by the Council Pursuant to Resolution I of the Sixt* [sic] *Meeting of Consultation of Ministers of Foreign Affairs* (Washington, D.C., 1961), pp. 9–12.

15. *The New York Times,* January 19, 1962.

16. In addition to numerous literary works, Bosch authored *Trujillo: causas de una tiranía sin ejemplo* (Caracas: Librería "Las Novedades," 1959).

17. Rowland Evans, Jr., "First Steps in Dominican Democracy," *Reporter,* XXVIII (January 3, 1963), p. 21.

18. For a complete list of participants and observers plus a charac-

terization of representative democracy, self-determination, and non-intervention, see Unión Panamericana, *Primer simposio sobre democracia representativa, Santo Domingo, República Dominicana, 17-22 de diciembre de 1962: informe final* (Washington, D.C., 1962).

19. Henry Wells, "The OAS and the Dominican Elections," *Orbis*, VII (Spring, 1963), pp. 150-63; and Nathan A. Haverstock, "Return to Democracy," *Americas*, XV (March, 1963), pp. 15-16. A number of observers were pessimistic about the Dominican elections because of the democratic inexperience of the Dominican people. Tad Szulc felt that "after the long years of Trujillo, the people do not really seem to care about politics." "Trujillo's Legacy: A Democratic Vacuum," *The New York Times Magazine* (September 2, 1962), p. 40. Theodore P. Wright feared that supervised free elections "would only open a Pandora's box of factional strife." "The United States and Latin American Dictatorship: The Case of the Dominican Republic," *Journal of International Affairs*, XIV (1960), p. 157.

20. One of the more hopeful accounts of Bosch's success was Tad Szulc, "After Trujillo, A Reformer with a Mission," *The New York Times Magazine* (September 8, 1963), p. 30.

21. *The New York Times*, April 28, 1963; *Washington Post*, April 29, 1963.

22. George Sherman, "Nonintervention: A Shield for 'Papa Doc,'" *Reporter*, XXVIII (June 20, 1963), p. 28.

23. *Washington Post*, April 29, 1963.

24. Pan American Union, *Inter-American Treaty of Reciprocal Assistance, Applications* (Washington, D.C., 1964), II, pp. 159-77.

25. The mission was composed of the ambassadors to the OAS from Bolivia, Chile, Ecuador, Colombia, and El Salvador. The United States declined to serve on the commission in order to avoid accusations of conflict of interest. *Washington Post*, April 30, 1963.

26. Howard J. Wiarda, "The Politics of Civil-Military Relations in the Dominican Republic," *Journal of Inter-American Studies*, VII (October, 1965), p. 480.

27. Department of State, *Treaty and Other International Acts Series*, no. 4936 (1962).

28. House Committee on Foreign Affairs, *Foreign Assistance Act of 1963*, Hearings, 83d Cong., 1st Sess. (1963), p. 865.

29. *Ibid.*, p. 861. For the best discussion of the development of civic action doctrine, see Willard F. Barber and C. Neale Ronning, *Internal*

Security and Military Power: Counterinsurgency and Civic Action (Columbus: Ohio State University Press, 1966), chap. 3. The U.S. Army claims credit for the genesis of civic action which it formally advocated in 1960. Department of the Army, Civic Action Branch, *Military Civic Action* (n.p.: USA, n.d.), pp. 2–5. See also Michael J. Francis, "Military Aid to Latin America in the U.S. Congress," *Journal of Inter-American Studies,* VI (July, 1964), pp. 389–404.

30. Wiarda, "The Politics of Civil-Military Relations in the Dominican Republic," p. 477.

31. John Bartlow Martin, *Overtaken by Events* (Garden City, New York: Doubleday & Co., 1966), p. 122.

32. Department of State, *United States Treaties and Other International Agreements,* XV, pp. 701–02.

33. Martin, *Overtaken by Events,* p. 358.

34. This was the gist of Jack Hood Vaughan's testimony before the Senate Foreign Relations Committee at the time he was the Peace Corps Director; *Washington Post,* February 10, 1966. For an explanation of why the U.S. threat to cut off aid lacked credibility, see Abraham F. Lowenthal, "Foreign Aid as a Political Instrument: The Case of the Dominican Republic," in John D. Montgomery and Arthur Smithies (eds.), *Public Policy* (Cambridge: Harvard University Press, 1965), XIV, p. 152.

35. Center for Research in Social Systems, American University, *Area Handbook for the Dominican Republic* (Washington, D.C.: Government Printing Office, 1967), chap. 25.

36. For detailed accounts of the background to Reid's overthrow and the civil war, see Abraham F. Lowenthal, *The Dominican Crisis of 1965: A Study of United States Foreign Policy,* paper presented to the Seminar on the Dominican Republic, Center for International Affairs, Harvard University, February 2, 1967; and Slater, *Intervention and Negotiation: The U.S. and the Dominican Revolution* (New York: Harper & Row, 1970).

37. Martin, *Overtaken by Events,* p. 648.

38. *Ibid.,* pp. 653–54, 658, 705.

39. *The Department of State Bulletin,* LII (May 17, 1965), p. 738.

40. *Ibid.,* p. 742.

41. *The New York Times,* May 3, 1965.

42. The total Latin American contribution was around 14 per cent. By July 3, the national contingents in the Peace Force were the follow-

ing: Brazil, 1,115 soldiers, marines, and officers; Costa Rica, 20 policemen; El Salvador, 3 officers; Honduras, 250 army troops; Nicaragua, 164 army troops; Paraguay, 183 army troops; United States, 10,900 troops. *The OAS Chronicle,* I (August, 1965), p. 5.

43. *Ibid.* (October, 1965), p. 19.

44. *Ibid.,* pp. 21–22.

45. Pan American Union, *Informe del Secretario General de la Organización de los Estados Americanos en relación con la situación dominicana (desde el 29 de abril de 1965 hasta la instalación del gobierno provisional)* (Washington, D.C., 1965), pp. 29–31.

46. Howard J. Wiarda, *The Context of United States Policy Toward the Dominican Republic: Background to the Revolution of 1965,* Paper presented to the Seminar on the Dominican Republic, Center for International Affairs, Harvard University, December 8, 1966. Harold A. Hovey, *United States Military Assistance: A Study of Policies and Practices* (New York: Frederick A. Praeger, 1965), p. 54.

CHAPTER VII

1. Senate Committee on Foreign Relations, *Mutual Security Act of 1958,* Hearings, 85th Cong., 2d Sess., 1958.

2. This same analysis is presented in a different historical context by Theodore Wright, "Free Elections in the Latin American Policy of the United States," *Political Science Quarterly,* LXXIV (March, 1959), p. 93.

3. Gordon Connell-Smith, *The Inter-American System* (London: Oxford University Press, 1966), pp. 341–42.

4. Jerome Slater, *The OAS and United States Foreign Policy* (Columbus: Ohio State University Press, 1967), p. 260. The author also examines the major arguments for and against collective intervention as a means to promote democracy (pp. 284–86).

BIBLIOGRAPHY

I. BIBLIOGRAPHIES

Albanell MacColl, Norah, et al. (comps.). *Cuba, Dominican Republic, Haiti and Puerto Rico: A Selected Bibliography on the Caribbean Area Including Only Islands Which Are Members of the Organization of American States.* Gainesville: School of Inter-American Studies, University of Florida, 1956.

Bayitch, Stojan A. *Latin America: A Bibliographical Guide to Economy, History, Law, Politics, and Society.* Coral Gables, Fla.: University of Miami Press, 1961.

———. *Latin America and the Caribbean: A Bibliographical Guide.* Coral Gables, Fla.: University of Miami Press, 1966.

Comitas, Lambros. *Caribbeana 1900–1965: A Topical Bibliography.* Seattle: University of Washington Press, 1968.

Einaudi, Luigi, and Goldhamer, Herbert. *An Annotated Bibliography of Latin American Military Journals.* Santa Monica, Cal.: Rand Corp., 1965.

Florén Lozano, Luis. *Bibliografía de la bibliografía dominicana.* Ciudad Trujillo, R.D.: Roques Román, 1948.

———. (comp.). *Bibliografía bibliotecológica dominicana, 1930–mayo 1952.* Ciudad Trujillo: Ed. Librería Dominicana, 1952.

Foreign Policy Association. *Handbook on Latin America.* New York: Foreign Policy Association, 1966.

Gropp, Arthur E. (comp.). *A Bibliography of Latin American Bibliographies.* Metuchen, N.J.: Scarecrow Press, 1968.

Hebblethwaite, Frank P. "A Bibliographical Survey of Pan Americanism," *Inter-American Review of Bibliography,* XV (October–December, 1965), 324–34.

Hitt, Deborah S. and Wilson, Larman C. *A Selected Bibliography of the*

Dominican Republic: A Century After the Restoration of Independence.
Washington, D.C.: Center for Research in Social Systems, American
University, 1968.

Humphreys, Robin A. *Latin American History: A Guide to the Literature
in English.* London: Oxford University Press, 1958.

Jones, Cecil Knight. *A Bibliography of Latin American Bibliographies.* 2nd
ed. Washington, D.C.: Government Printing Office, 1942.

Library Association, London. *Latin America: An Introduction to Modern
Books in English Concerning the Countries of Latin America.* 2nd ed.
London: Library Association, 1966.

Library of Congress. *A Guide to the Official Publications of the Other American Republics: VIII. Dominican Republic.* Comp. by John de Noia. Washington, D.C., 1947.

―――. Hispanic Foundation. *Handbook of Latin American Studies: A
Selective and Annotated Guide to Recent Publications on Anthropology, Art,
Economics, Education, Geography, Government and International Relations,
History, Language, Law, Literature, Music, Philosophy, and Sociology.*
Gainesville, Fla.: University of Florida Press, 1948―――.

National Archives. *List of Records of the Bureau of Insular Affairs Relating
to the Dominican Customs Receivership, 1905–1940.* Comp. by Kenneth
Munden. Washington, D.C., 1943.

―――. *Materials in the National Archives Relating to the Dominican Republic.* Comp. by Seymour J. Pomrenze. Washington, D.C., 1948.

Pan American Union, Inter-American Committee on Bibliography.
Inter-American Review of Bibliography. Washington, D.C.: Pan American
Union, 1951―――.

Sable, Martin H. (comp.). *A Guide to Latin American Studies.* 2 vols. Los
Angeles: Center of Latin American Studies, University of California,
1967.

Trask, David F., et al. (comp. & ed.). *A Bibliography of United States–
Latin American Relations Since 1810.* Lincoln: University of Nebraska
Press, 1968.

U.S. Department of the Army. *Latin America: Hemispheric Partner – A
Bibliographic Survey.* Washington, D.C.: n.p., 1964.

―――. *Latin America and the Caribbean: Analytical Survey of Literature.*
Washington, D.C.: Government Printing Office, 1969.

Wiarda, Howard J. *Materials for the Study of Politics and Government in
the Dominican Republic, 1930–1966.* Santiago, R.D.: Universidad
Católica Madre y Maestra, 1968.

Wilgus, A. Curtis (comp.). *Doors to Latin America*. North Miami Beach, Fla.: Inter-American Bibliographical and Library Association, 1954——.

II. U.S. PUBLIC DOCUMENTS

NOTE: All United States Government publications are published in Washington, D.C., by the Government Printing Office in the year indicated in parentheses.

A. U.S. Congress, House of Representatives

Legislation Relating to Amounts of Sugar Which May Be Purchased in Dominican Republic. Doc. No. 451, 86th Cong., 2nd Sess. (1960).

Committee on Agriculture. *Extension of Sugar Act of 1948, As Amended*. Hearings, 86th Cong., 2nd Sess. (1960).

——. *A Study of the Dominican Republic Agriculture and Sugar Industry*. Committee Print, 84th Cong., 1st Sess. (1955).

Committee on Appropriations. *Mutual Security Appropriations for 1952*, Hearings, 82nd Cong., 1st Sess. (1951); . . . *for 1953*, 82nd Cong., 2nd Sess. (1952); . . . *for 1954*, 83rd Cong., 1st Sess. (1953); . . . *for 1955*, 83rd Cong., 2nd Sess. (1954); . . . *for 1956*, 84th Cong., 1st Sess. (1955); . . . *for 1957*, 84th Cong., 2nd Sess. (1956); . . . *for 1958*, 85th Cong., 1st Sess. (1957); . . . *for 1959*, 85th Cong., 2nd Sess. (1958); . . . *for 1960*, 86th Cong., 1st Sess. (1959); . . . *for 1961*, 86th Cong., 2nd Sess. (1960).

Committee on Foreign Affairs. *Act for International Development*. Hearings, 81st Cong., 1st and 2nd Sess. (1950).

——. *Foreign Assistance Act of 1962*. Hearings, 82nd Cong., 2nd Sess. (1962).

——. *Inter-American Military Cooperation Act*. Hearings, 79th Cong., 2nd Sess. (1946); and 80th Cong., 1st Sess. (1947).

——. *Mutual Security Act Extension*. Hearings, 82nd Cong., 2nd Sess. (1952); and 83rd Cong., 1st Sess. (1953).

——. *Mutual Security Act of 1954*, Hearings, 83rd Cong., 2nd Sess. (1954); . . . *of 1955*, 84th Cong., 1st Sess. (1955); . . . *of 1956*, 84th Cong., 2nd Sess. (1956); . . . *of 1957*, 85th Cong., 1st Sess. (1957); . . . *of 1958*, 85th Cong., 2nd Sess. (1958); . . . *of 1959*, 86th Cong., 1st Sess. (1959); . . . *of 1960;* 86th Cong., 2nd Sess. (1960).

——. *Report on United States Relations with Latin America*. Report No. 354, 86th Cong., 1st Sess. (1959).

————. *A Review of the Relations of the United States and the Other American Republics.* Hearings, 85th Cong., 2nd Sess. (1958).

————. *Special Study Mission to Latin America on Technical Cooperation.* Report, 83rd Cong., 2nd Sess. (1954).

————. *Twenty-Ninth Report to Congress on Lend-Lease Operations.* Message from the President, Doc. No. 436, 81st Cong., 2nd Sess. (1950).

Committee on Government Operations. *United States Technical Assistance to Latin America.* 14th Intermediate Report, Report No. 1985 (1956).

————. *United States Technical Assistance and Related Activities in Latin America.* Hearings, 84th Cong., 1st Sess. (1955).

B. U.S. Congress, Senate

Committee on Agriculture and Forestry. *A Review of United States Government Operations in Latin America.* Report of Senator Allen J. Ellender, Doc. No. 13, 86th Cong., 1st Sess. (1959), esp. pp. 483–98.

Committee on Appropriations. *Inter-American Social and Economic Cooperation Program.* Hearings, 87th Cong., 1st Sess. (1961).

————. *Mutual Security Appropriations for 1952,* Hearings, 82nd Cong., 1st Sess. (1951); [None for 1953]; . . . *for 1954,* 83rd Cong., 1st Sess. (1953); . . . *for 1,955,* 83rd Cong., 2nd Sess. (1954); . . . *for 1956,* 84th Cong., 1st Sess. (1955); . . . *for 1957,* 84th Cong., 2nd Sess. (1956); . . . *for 1958,* 85th Cong., 1st Sess. (1957); . . . *for 1959,* 85th Cong., 2nd Sess. (1958); . . . *for 1960,* 86th Cong., 1st Sess. (1959); . . . *for 1961,* 86th Cong., 2nd Sess. (1960).

Committee on Commerce. *Freedom of Communications,* Pt. I, "The Speeches of Senator John F. Kennedy, Presidential Campaign of 1960." S. Res. 305, 86th Cong., 1st Sess. (1961).

Committee on Foreign Relations. *Foreign Assistance Act of 1962.* Hearings, 87th Cong., 2nd Sess. (1962).

————. *Mutual Security Act of 1951.* Hearings [with Committee on Armed Services] 82nd Cong., 1st Sess. (1951); . . . *of 1952,* 82nd Cong., 2nd Sess. (1952); . . . *of 1953,* 83rd Cong., 1st Sess. (1953); . . . *of 1954,* 83rd Cong., 2nd Sess. (1954); . . . *of 1955,* 84th Cong., 1st Sess. (1955); . . . *of 1956,* 84th Cong., 2nd Sess. (1956); . . . *of 1957,* 85th Cong., 1st Sess. (1957); . . . *of 1958,* 85th Cong., 2nd

Sess. (1958); . . . *of 1959*, 86th Cong., 1st Sess. (1959); . . . *of 1960*, 86th Cong., 2nd Sess. (1960).

————. *Study Mission in the Caribbean Area, December 1957*. Report of Senator George D. Aiken, 85th Cong., 2nd Sess. (1958).

————. *Study Mission in the Caribbean and Northern South America, November 1959*. Report of Senator Homer E. Capehart, 86th Cong., 2nd Sess. (1960).

————. *Technical Assistance Program*. Hearings, 84th Cong., 1st Sess. (1955).

————. *United States Latin American Relations*. Compilation of Studies, Doc. No. 125, 86th Cong., 2nd Sess. (1960).

Committee on the Judiciary. *Communist Problems in Latin America*. Report by Senator Olin D. Johnston, 85th Cong., 1st Sess. (1957).

————. *Communist Threat to United States Through the Caribbean*. Hearings, 86th Cong., 2nd Sess. (1960).

Select Committee on Haiti and Dominican Republic. *Inquiry into Occupation and Administration of Haiti and Dominican Republic*. Hearings, 67th Cong., 1st Sess., Pts. 5–7 (1921–1922).

Special Committee to Study the Foreign Aid Program. *Foreign Aid Program*. Compilation of Studies and Surveys, Doc. No. 52, 85th Cong., 1st Sess. (1957).

C. U.S. Department of State

The Department of State Bulletin. Weekly, Vol. I, No. 1 (1939) through Vol. VLVI, No. 1175 (1962). News reports, press conferences, declarations, statements, speeches, documents, and articles.

Papers Relating to the Foreign Relations of the United States, editions for 1929, 1930, and 1931; subsequently published under the title *Foreign Relations of the United States: Diplomatic Papers* [nothing on the Dominican Republic in editions for 1932 or 1934], editions for 1933, 1935 through 1943.

Press Releases. Weekly, Vols. 1–20, Nos. 1–508 (October 5, 1929–June 24, 1939).

Executive Agreement Series, No. 274. "Agreement . . . Relating to Waiver in Respect of Tariff Preferences Accorded Haiti by the Dominican Republic Under Treaty of Commerce Between the Dominican Republic and Haiti," signed at Ciudad Trujillo, November 14, 1942.

No. 297, "Agreement Regarding the Exchange of Official Publications," signed at Ciudad Trujillo, December 9 and 10, 1942.

No. 312, "Naval Mission Agreement," signed at Washington, January 25, 1943.

No. 346, "Health and Sanitation Program Agreement," signed at Ciudad Trujillo, June 19 and July 7, 1943.

No. 350, "Agreement for Purchase by the United States of Exportable Surpluses of Dominican Rice, Corn, and Peanut Meal," signed at Ciudad Trujillo, June 10, 1943.

No. 404, "Agreement for Purchase of Dominican Food Surpluses," signed at Ciudad Trujillo, December 17, 1943, and February 11, 1944.

Treaty Series, No. 965. "Convention Modifying the Convention of December 27, 1924, Regarding the Collection and Application of the Customs Revenues of the Dominican Republic," signed at Washington, September 24, 1940.

Treaties and Other International Acts Series, No. 1530, "Cooperative Education Agreement," signed at Ciudad Trujillo, October 13, 1945.

No. 1955, "Air Transport Services Agreement," signed at Ciudad Trujillo, July 19, 1949.

No. 2143, "Aviation, Flights of Military Aircraft, Agreement," signed at Ciudad Trujillo, July 19, 1949.

No. 2172, "Technical Cooperation Agreement," signed at Ciudad Trujillo, February 20, 1951.

No. 2226, "Agreement for a Cooperative Agriculture Program Pursuant to the General Agreement for Technical Cooperation of February 20, 1951."

No. 2244, "Vocational Education, Cooperative Program in the Dominican Republic," signed at Ciudad Trujillo, March 16, 1951.

No. 2365, "Finance, Collection and Application of Customs Revenues of the Dominican Republic, Termination of Convention, signed September 24, 1940," signed at Washington, August 9, 1951.

No. 2375, "Education, Cooperative Program in Dominican Republic Additional Financial Contributions," signed at Ciudad Trujillo, September 10 and 19, 1951.

No. 2425, "Extending Longrange Proving Ground for Testing of Guided Missiles," signed at Ciudad Trujillo, November 26, 1951.

No. 2513, "Technical Cooperation, Agricultural Program," signed at Ciudad Trujillo, January 7 and 22, 1952.

No. 2544, "Education, Cooperative Program in Dominican Republic, Additional Financial Contributions," signed at Ciudad Trujillo, February 12 and April 4, 1952.

No. 2630, "Technical Cooperation, Assurance Under Mutual Security Act of 1951," signed at Ciudad Trujillo, December 12, 1951, and January 5, 1952.

No. 2777, "Mutual Defense Assistance Agreement," signed at Washington, March 6, 1953.

No. 2994, "Education, Broadening Scope of Cooperative Program, Additional Financial Contributions," signed at Ciudad Trujillo, February 19 and March 19, 1954.

No. 3263, "Mutual Defense Assistance, Disposition of Surplus Equipment and Materials," signed at Ciudad Trujillo, March 23 and April 22, 1955.

No. 3358, "Education, Cooperative Program in Dominican Republic, Extending Agreement of March 16, 1951," signed at Ciudad Trujillo, April 19 and May 5, 1955.

No. 3420, "Technical Cooperation, Program of Agriculture . . ." signed at Ciudad Trujillo, June 22 and 30, 1955.

No. 3699, "Weather Stations, Cooperative Program in Dominican Republic," signed at Ciudad Trujillo, July 25 and August 11, 1956.

No. 3703, "Naval Mission to Dominican Republic," signed at Ciudad Trujillo, December 7, 1956.

No. 3711, "Atomic Energy Cooperation for Civil Uses," signed at Washington, June 15, 1956.

No. 3780, "Navigation, Establishment of Loran Transmitting Stations," signed at Washington, March 19, 1957.

No. 4529, "Education, Cooperative Program in Dominican Republic Modifying and Extending the Agreement of March 16, 1951," signed at Ciudad Trujillo, June 2 and 7, 1960.

No. 4936, "Economic, Technical, and Related Assistance," signed at Santo Domingo, January 11, 1962.

Inter-American Series, No. 41. "Keeping Peace in the Caribbean Area," Pub. 3918, 1950.

————. *No. 79. Inter-American Efforts to Relieve Tensions in the Western Hemisphere, 1959–1960,* Pub. 7409, 1960.

International Organization and Conference Series, II. American Republics 6, "Peace in the Americas," Pub. 3964, 1950.

United States-Latin American Relations. Report to the President by Milton S. Eisenhower. Pub. 5290, 1953.

United States-Latin American Relations. Report to the President by Milton S. Eisenhower. Pub. 6764, 1959.

D. Other U.S. Government

Agency for International Development. *U.S. Overseas Loans and Grants and Assistance from International Organizations, Obligations and Loan Authorizations, July 1, 1945–June 30, 1965* (1966).

Department of Agriculture, Agricultural Stabilization and Conservation Service, Sugar Division. *Sugar Statistics and Related Data Compiled in the Administration of the U.S. Sugar Acts.* I. Washington, D.C.: Government Printing Office, 1961.

Department of Commerce, Office of Business Economics. *Foreign Aid by the United States Government, 1940–1951.* Supplement to *Survey of Current Business* (1952).

Department of the Navy, Bureau of Medicine and Surgery. *Naval Medical Bulletin,* "Report on Relief Work in Santo Domingo Disaster," by Lucius W. Johnson, Vol. 29 (January, 1939).

Department of War, Bureau of Insular Affairs, General Receiver of Dominican Customs. *Report of the Dominican Customs Receivership Under the American Dominican Convention of 1924, Together with Summary of Commerce.* 24th through 33rd fiscal periods, calendar years 1930–1940 (1931–1941).

International Cooperation Administration, Country Series. *Dominican Republic Fact Sheet* (July, 1955).

President of the United States, Emergency Management Office, Coordinator of Inter-American Affairs. *Caribbean Larder* (1943).

Rockefeller, Nelson A. *Quality of Life in the Americas: Report of a U.S. Presidential Mission for the Western Hemisphere.* Reprinted by Agency for International Development, n.p., n.d. [1969].

Tariff Commission. *Economic Controls and Commercial Policy in the Dominican Republic* (1946).

————. *Mining and Manufacturing Industries in the Dominican Republic* (1948).

U.S. Congress. *Congressional Record: Proceedings and Debates of Congress.* Vol. LXXII (71st Cong., 1st Sess., 1929–1930) through Vol. CIX (88th Cong., 1st Sess., 1963).

Weather Bureau. *Monthly Weather Review*, "Santo Domingo Hurricane of September 1–5, 1930," by F. Eugene Hartwell, Vol. 58 (December 4, 1930) and "Caribbean Hurricane of October 19–26, 1935," by W. F. McDonald, Vol. 63 (January 15, 1936).

III. OTHER PUBLIC DOCUMENTS

A. Dominican Government

Address of Hon. William T. Pheiffer, Ambassador of the United States of America to the Dominican Republic, at the Luncheon Meeting of the Miami Beach Rotary Club on March 6, 1956. Ciudad Trujillo: Imp. Dominicana, 1956.

Acre Medina, Juan. *An Open Letter to the Editors of "Life": re the Galindez-Murphy Case.* New York: Dominican Republic Information Center, 1957.

Canje de las ratificaciones del protocolo final del acuerdo fronterizo dominicano-haitiano. Ciudad Trujillo: 1936.

Comisión Para el estudio del informe de la Brookings Institution sobre "La colonización de refugiados." *Capacidad de la República Dominicana para Absorber Refugiados,* 1946.

Consulate of the Dominican Republic. *Bulletin of Information on Dominican-Haitian Border Incidents.* New York: September, 1941.

————. *Trujillo Forgives His Enemies.* n.p., n.d.

Consulate General of the Dominican Republic in New York. *The Dominican Republic,* I (June, 1934).

————. *Dominican Republic: A Bulletin of the Dominican Embassy.* Nos. 1–174.

Dirección General de Estadística. *Comercio Exterior de la República Dominicana.* Ciudad Trujillo: 1953.

Dunn, W. E., Special Emergency Agent. *Dominican Republic, Report of the Special Emergency Agent for the Period October 23, 1931 to December 31, 1932* (n.p., n.d.).

Ellender, Allen J. *La ley azucarera de EU y el azúcar dominicano.* Ciudad Trujillo: Editora del Caribe, 1960.

Embassy of the Dominican Republic in Washington, D.C. *A Look at the Dominican Republic.* Vol. I (1956) through Vol. IV (1959).

————. *Here Is Our Answer: A Summary of the Comments of the Government of the Dominican Republic on the June 6, 1960, Report of the Inter-American Peace Committee,* 1960.

Gaceta Oficial, September 22, 1941. [Contains Spanish text of trade agreement and additional protocol between Haiti and the Dominican Republic signed at Port-au-Prince on August 26, 1941.]

Legation of the Dominican Republic in Washington, D.C. *Presidente* [sic] *Trujillo Molina Declines to be a Candidate for Reelection, Important Message to the Dominican People, January 8, 1938.*

Memorandum a los representantes diplomáticos en Washington de los Estados en América, Estados Unidos de México, Cuba y Haití, relativo a las medidas que puedan adoptarse para evitar rozamientos entre la República Dominicana y la de Haití con motivo de la solicitud de mediación hecha por el gobierno haitiano en el dia 12 de noviembre, 1937. Ciudad Trujillo: Imp. Listín Diario, n.d.

Memoria de relaciones exteriores de 1936 presentada al Excelentísimo señor presidente de la República, generalísimo doctor Rafael Leonidas Trujillo y Molina, Benefactor de la Patria, por el Secretario de estado de relaciones exteriores el 27 de febrero de 1937. Ciudad Trujillo: Imp. García, n.d.

La nueva patria dominicano. Suplemento. La reconstrucción por el Generalísimo Doctor Rafael L. Trujillo Molina de la ciudad de Santo Domingo de Guzmán. Santo Domingo: 1935.

Ornes, Germán E. *The Other Side of the Coin.* Washington, D.C.: Embassy of the Dominican Republic, 1958.

Pérez Leyba, Salvador A. *El Generalísimo Trujillo Molina, la Convención dominicana-americana, y la política de "Buen Vecino."* Ciudad Trujillo, R.D.: Imp. Listín Diario, 1940.

Secretaría de Estado de Relaciones Exteriores. *Boletín.* Nos. 63, 64. Ciudad Trujillo: 1949.

Secretaria de lo Interior. *Libro blanco del comunismo en la República Dominicana.* Ciudad Trujillo: Editora del Caribe, 1956.

Secretariado Técnico, Oficina de Planificación. *Bases para el desarrollo nacional, análisis de los problemas y perspectivas de la economía dominicana, diciembre, 1965.*

Stefanich, Blas. *Comunismo sin máscara.* 7th ed.; Ciudad Trujillo, R.D.: 1957.

Trujillo, Molina, Rafael Leonidas. *The basic policies of a regime.* Ciudad Trujillo: Editora del Caribe, 1960.

———. *Discursos, mensajes y proclamas.* 8 vols.; Santiago, R.D.: El Diario, 1946–1948.

———. *The Evolution of Democracy in Santo Domingo.* 2nd ed.; Ciudad Trujillo: Editora del Caribe, 1955.

————. *Fundamentos y política de un régimen.* Ciudad Trujillo: Editora del Caribe, 1960.

————. *Message Addressed to His Countrymen on the Tenth Anniversary of Assuming the Political Direction of the Dominican People.* Ciudad Trujillo: Imp. Listín Diario, 1940.

————. *Position of the Dominican Republic.* Ciudad Trujillo: Editorial La Nación, 1945.

————. *President Trujillo Molina Declines to be a Candidate for Re-election,* 1938.

————. *Reajuste de la deuda external.* Ciudad Trujillo: El Diario, 1937.

B. Pan American Union

Annals of the Organization of American States. Vol. 1 (1949) through Vol. 9 (1957).

Bulletin of the Pan American Union. Vol. 64 (1930) through Vol. 82 (1948).

Fifth Meeting of Consultation of Ministers of Foreign Affairs, Santiago, Chile, August 12–18, 1959: Final Act. 1960.

Sixth Meeting of Consultation of Ministers of Foreign Affairs Serving as Organ of Consultation in Application of the Inter-American Treaty of Reciprocal Assistance, San Jose, Costa Rica, August 16–21, 1960: Final Act. 1960.

Comision Interamericana de Derechos Humanos. *Antecedentes sobre derechos humanos y democracia representativa.* Preparados por la Secretaria de la Comision. 1961.

————. *Human Rights in the American States. Study Prepared in Accordance with Resolution XXVII of the Tenth Inter-American Conference.* 1960.

————. *Informaciones sobre el respeto de los derechos humanos en la República Dominicana.* 1961.

————. *Informe sobre la situación de los derechos humanos en la República Dominicana.* 1962.

————. *Primer simposio sobre democracia representativa, Santo Domingo, República Dominicana, 17–22 de diciembre de 1962.* 1962.

Acuña de Chacón, Angela. *Study of Political, Economic, and Social Conditions of the Countries of Latin America that May Influence Human Rights.* 1961.

Council, Committee of Investigation. *Report Submitted by the Council, Acting Provisionally as Organ of Consultation in the Case Presented by Venezuela. . . .* 1960.

————. Special Committee. *First Report of the Special Committee to Carry Out the Mandate Received by the Council Pursuant to Resolution I of the Sixth Meeting of Consultation of Ministers of Foreign Affairs.* Dec. 21, 1960.

————. ————. Subcommittee to the Special Committee. *Report Submitted by the Special Committee* . . . July 2, 1961.

————. ————. ————. *Second Report of the Subcommittee Submitted to the Special Committee* . . . Nov. 10, 1961.

————. ————. ————. *Third Report Submitted by the Subcommittee to the Special Committee* . . . Dec. 20, 1961.

Department of Legal Affairs. *Aplicaciones del Tratado Interamericano de Asistencia Recíproca, 1948–1960.* 3rd ed., 1960.

————. *Aplicaciones del Tratado Interamericano de Asistencia Recíproca: Suplemento, 1960–1961.* 1962.

Executive Committee on Post War Problems. *The Basic Principles of the Inter-American System.* 1943.

Inter-American Judicial Committee. *Instrument Relating to Violations of the Principle of Non-Intervention. Draft and Report Prepared in Accordance with Resolutions VII of the Fifth Meeting of Consultation of Ministers of Foreign Affairs.* 1959.

————. *Opinion on the Legal Aspects of the Draft Declaration on Nonintervention Presented by the Delegation of Mexico. Prepared in Accordance with Resolution V of the Fifth Meeting of Consultation of Ministers of Foreign Affairs.* 1961.

————. *Strengthening and Effective Exercise of Democracy. Report Prepared in Accordance with Resolution VII of the Fourth Meeting of Consultation of Ministers of Foreign Affairs.* 1959.

————. *Study of the Proposal of Ecuador Concerning the Inter-American Peace Committee. Prepared in Accordance with Resolution VI of the Fifth Meeting of Consultation of Ministers of Foreign Affairs.* 1960.

————. *Study of the Juridical Relationship between Respect for Human Rights and the Exercise of Democracy. Prepared in Accordance with Resolution III of the Fifth Meeting of Consultation of Ministers of Foreign Affairs and Resolution XXI of the Fourth Meeting of the Inter-American Council of Jurists.* 1960.

————. *Study on Political Offenses. Prepared in Accordance with Resolution III of the Fourth Meeting of the Inter-American Council of Jurists.* 1960.

Inter-American Peace Committee. *The Report of the Inter-American*

Peace Committee on the Case Presented by the Government of Venezuela. 1960.

———. *Report of the Inter-American Peace Committee to the Fifth Meeting of Consultation of Ministers of Foreign Affairs.* 1959.

———. *Report of the Inter-American Peace Committee to the Seventh Meeting of Consultation of Ministers of Foreign Affairs.* 1960.

———. *Second Report of the Inter-American Peace Committee Submitted to the Tenth Inter-American Conference* (1954).

———. *Special Report on the Relationship between Violations of Human Rights or the Nonexercise of Representative Democracy and the Political Tensions that Affect the Peace of the Hemisphere.* 1960.

Investigating Team of the Organ of Consultation. *Documents Submitted to the Council of the Organization of American States Acting Provisionally as the Organ of Consultation at the Meeting of March 13, 1950.* 1950.

C. Other Public Documents

Costa Rica. Dirección General de Estadística y Censos. Ministerio de Economía y Hacienda. *Sexta y Sétima* [sic] *Conferencias de Consulta de los Cancilleres Americanos: Discursos.* San José, 1960.

League of Nations. *Treaty Series.* CLXXXVII, No. 4336. "Agreement Regarding Frontier Questions and the Settlement of All Disputes Resulting From the Events Which Have Occurred During the Last Months of the Year 1937 Near the Frontier Between . . . [the Dominican Republic and Haiti]." 1938.

Uruguay. Ministerio de Relaciones Exteriores [Dr. Eduardo Rodríguez Larreta]. *Paralelismo entre la democracia y la paz. Protección internacional de los derechos del hombre. Acción colectiva en defensa de esos principios.* Montevideo: Sección Prensa, Informaciones y Publicaciones, 1946.

Venezuela. *El atentado contra el señor presidente de la república de Venezuela. Rómulo Betancourt.* Caracas: Grabados Nacionales, 1960.

IV. BOOKS, MONOGRAPHS AND PAMPHLETS

Addison, T. G. *Reorganization of the Financial Administration of the Dominican Republic.* Washington, D.C.: Brookings Institution, 1931.

Almoina, José. *Yo fuí secretario de Trujillo.* Buenos Aires: Editora Distribuidora del Plata, 1950.

"The Americas: The Challenge of Change," *Journal of International Affairs*, XIV (1960).

Arciniegas, Germán. *The Caribbean: Sea of the New World*. New York: H. W. Wilson Co., 1946.

Ariza, Sander. *Trujillo: The Man and His Country*. New York: Tremaine, 1939.

Bailey, Norman A. (ed.). *Latin America: Politics, Economics, and Hemispheric Security*. New York: Frederick A. Praeger, 1965.

————. *Latin America in World Politics*. New York: Walker & Co., 1967.

Bailey, Thomas A. *A Diplomatic History of the American People*. 6th ed. New York: Appleton-Century-Crofts, Inc., 1958.

Balaguer, Joaquín (ed.). *Discursos; panegíricos, política y educación, política internacional*. Madrid: Ediciones Acies, 1957.

———— (ed.). *El Pensamiento vivo de Trujillo*. Ciudad Trujillo, R.D.: Impresora Dominicana, 1955.

————. *La realidad dominicana semblanza de un país y de un régimen*. Buenos Aires: Imprenta Ferrari Hermanos, 1947.

————. *El tratado Trujillo-Hull y la liberación financiera de la República Dominicana*. Bogotá: Consorcio Editorial, 1941.

Baquero, Gastón. *Cuban-Dominican Relations*. Ciudad Trujillo, R.D.: Diario de la Marina, 1956.

Barber, Willard F. and Ronning, C. Neale. *Internal Security and Military Power: Counterinsurgency and Civic Action*. Columbus: Ohio State University Press, 1966.

Bazil, Oswaldo. *Una conferencia. La influencia de la política del presidente Trujillo en el desenvolvimiento del progreso y la cultura dominicanos*. Ciudad Trujillo, R.D.: Listín Diario, 1938.

Beals, Carleton. *The Coming Struggle for Latin America*. Philadelphia, New York, London, Toronto: J. P. Lippincott Co., 1938.

————. *Rio Grande to Cape Horn*. New York: Literary Classics, Inc., distributed by Houghton Mifflin Co., Boston, 1943.

————. Bryce Oliver, Herschel Brichell and Samuel Guy Inman. *What the South Americans Think of Us*. New York: Robert M. McBride & Co., 1945.

Bemis, Samuel Flagg. *A Diplomatic History of the United States*. New York: Holt, Rinehart & Winston, 1955.

————. *The Latin American Policy of the United States: An Historical Interpretation*. New York: Harcourt, Brace & Co., 1943.

Benton, William. *The Voice of Latin America*. New York: Harper & Brothers, 1961.

Besault, Lawrence de. *President Trujillo, His Work and the Dominican Republic.* 3rd ed. Santiago, Dominican Republic: Ed. "El Diario," 1941.

Blakeslee, George H. (ed.). *Mexico and the Caribbean: Clark University Addresses.* New York: G. E. Stechert, 1920.

Blanchard, Paul. *Democracy and Empire in the Caribbean.* New York: Macmillan Co., 1947.

Bonet, Father Antonio. *La verdad sobre la era de Trujillo: Refutación de "La Era" de Galíndez.* Managua, Nic.: n.p., 1957.

Bonilla Atiles, José Antonio. *Discursos y conferencias enjuiciando la política del presidente Trujillo, 1940–1946.* Ciudad Trujillo, R.D.: Ed. Veritas, 1946.

———. *Un ensayo sobre la implantación de la democracia en la República Dominicana.* Santurce, Puerto Rico: Publicaciones de Vanguardia Revolucionaria Dominicana, 1960.

Bonilla Atiles, Pedro Pablo. *Un ensayo sobre la implantación de la democracia en la República Dominicana.* Santurce, Puerto Rico: Publicaciones de Vanguardia Revolucionaria Dominicana, 1960.

Bosch, Juan. *Crisis de la democracia de la América en la República Dominicana.* México, D.F.: Centro de Estudios y Documentación, 1964.

———. *Trujillo: causas de una tiranía sin ejemplo.* 2nd ed. Caracas: Librería "Las Novedades," 1961.

———. *The Unfinished Experiment: Democracy in the Dominican Republic.* New York: Frederick A. Praeger, 1965. Trans. of *Crisis . . .*

Briggs, Ellis O. *Farewell to Foggy Bottom: The Recollections of a Career Diplomat.* New York: David McKay Co., 1964.

Brookings Institution. *Refugee Settlement in the Dominican Republic, A Survey Conducted Under the Auspices of the Brookings Institution.* 1942. A critical survey. For Trujillo's response, see part III, A.

Brown, William Adams, Jr., and Opie, Redvers. *American Foreign Assistance.* Washington, D.C.: The Brookings Institution, 1953.

Calcott, Wilfrid Hardy. *The Caribbean Policy of the United States, 1890–1920.* Baltimore: Johns Hopkins Press, 1942.

———. *The Western Hemisphere: Its Influence on United States Policies to the End of World War II.* Austin: University of Texas Press, 1968.

Carey, John (ed.). *The Dominican Republic Crisis, 1965: Background Paper and Proceedings of the Ninth Hammarskjold Forum.* Dobbs Ferry, N.Y.: Oceana Pubs., 1967.

Cestero Burgos, Tulio. *Filosofía de un régimen.* Ciudad Trujillo, R.D.: Montalvo, 1951.

Chang-Rodríguez, Eugenio (ed.). *The Lingering Crisis: A Case Study of the Dominican Republic*. New York: Las Américas Publishing Co., 1969.

Cobban, Alfred. *Dictatorship: Its History and Theory*. New York: Charles Scribner's Sons, 1939.

Compres Pérez, Rafael. *La República Dominicana y España: una misma religión, una misma cultura, y un destino común: mensajes y discursos*. Madrid, 1959.

Conn, Stetson, and Byron Fairchild. *United States Army in World War II; The Western Hemisphere: The Framework of Hemisphere Defense*. Office of the Chief of Military History, Department of the Army. Washington, D.C.: Government Printing Office, 1960.

Connell-Smith, Gordon. *The Inter-American System*. New York: Oxford University Press, 1966.

Corominas, Enrique V. *In the Caribbean Political Areas*. Trans. from Spanish by L. Charles Foresti. Cambridge, Mass.: University Press, 1954.

Crassweller, Robert D. *Trujillo: The Life and Times of a Caribbean Dictator*. New York: Macmillan Co., 1966.

Cruz, Francisco Antonio. *Genesis, evolución y agonía del partido comunisto dominicano*. Ciudad Trujillo: Imprenta J. C. Pol., 1947.

Cruz y Berges, Frank. *Trujillo, gobierno y pueblo dominicano frente al comunismo internacional*. Ciudad Trujillo, R.D.: Editora Babeque, 1957.

Cuevas Cancino, Francisco. *Del Congreso de Panamá a la Conferencia de Caracas, 1826–1954*. 2 vols. Caracas: Editorial "Rogon," 1955.

Daniels, Walter M. (ed.). *Latin America in the Cold War*. New York: Frederick A. Praeger, 1952.

Dávila, Carlos. *We of the Americas*. New York: Ziff-Davis, 1949.

Davis, Harold E. (ed.). *Government and Politics in Latin America*. New York: Ronald Press Co., 1958.

DeConde, Alexander. *Herbert Hoover's Latin-American Policy*. Palo Alto, Cal.: Stanford University Press, 1951.

Dominican Revolutionary Party. *Trujillo: A Nazi*. Mayagüez, Puerto Rico, 1944.

Dorsa, Inc. *Concerning Refugee Settlement in the Dominican Republic*. February 15, 1940.

Dozer, Donald M. *Are We Good Neighbors? Three Decades of Inter-American Relations, 1930–1960*. Gainesville: University of Florida Press, 1959.

―――. *Latin America: An Interpretive History*. New York: McGraw-Hill Book Co., 1962.

Draper, Theodore. *The Dominican Revolt: A Case Study in American Policy.* New York: Commentary, 1968.

Dreier, John C. *The Organization of American States and the Hemisphere Crisis.* New York: Harper & Row, 1962.

Duggan, Laurence. *The Americas: The Search for Hemisphere Security.* New York: Henry Holt & Co., 1949.

Eisenhower, Milton S. *The Wine Is Bitter: The United States and Latin America.* New York: Doubleday & Co., 1963.

Ellsworth, Harry A. *One Hundred and Eighty Landings of United States Marines, 1800–1934.* Washington, D.C.: U.S. Navy, Historical Section, 1934.

Ernst, Morris L. *Report and Opinion in the Matter of Galindez.* New York: Sydney S. Barron & Co., 1958.

Espaillat, Arturo R. *Trujillo: The Last Caesar.* Chicago: Henry Regnery Co., 1963.

Estep, Raymond. *The Latin American Nations Today: A Study of Political Developments Since World War II.* Montgomery: Documentary Research Division, Air University, 1964.

———. *United States Military Aid to Latin America.* Montgomery: Documentary Research Division, Air University, 1966.

Fabela, Isidro. *Buena y mala vecinidad.* Mexico, D.F.: América Nueva, 1958.

Fagg, John Edwin. *Cuba, Haiti and the Dominican Republic.* Englewood Cliffs, N.J.: Prentice-Hall, 1965.

———. *Latin America: A General History.* New York: Macmillan Co., 1963.

Feis, Herbert. *The Diplomacy of the Dollar: First Era, 1919–1932.* Baltimore: Johns Hopkins Press, 1950.

Felkel, Günter. *Menschen im Hurrikan; Trujillo und die Dominikanische Republik.* Berlin: Buchverlag der Morgen, 1962.

Fenwick, Charles G. *The Inter-American Regional System.* New York: Declan X. McMullen Co., 1949.

———. *The Organization of American States; The Inter-American Regional System.* Washington, D.C.: by author, 1963.

Francisco Ornes, Pericles. *La tragedia dominicana: análisis de la tiranía de Trujillo.* Santiago de Chile: Federación de estudiantes de Chile, 1946.

La Frontera de la República Dominicana con Haití. Ciudad Trujillo, R.D.: Ed. La Nación, 1946.

Galíndez Suárez, Jesús de. *La Era de Trujillo. Un Estudio casuístico de dictadura hispano-americana.* Santiago: Editorial del Pacífico, 1956. His dissertation at Columbia University without the documentation.

————. *Trujillo el benefactor; reportaje sobre Santo Domingo.* Buenos Aires: n.p., 1956.

Gantenbein, James W. (ed.). *The Evolution of Our Latin-American Policy: A Documentary Record.* New York: Columbia University Press, 1950.

García-Godoy, Emilio. *Al margen de un aide-mémoire.* Ciudad Trujillo, R.D.: Editora del Caribe, n.d.

Georgetown University, Center for Strategic Studies. *Dominican Action, 1965: Intervention or Cooperation?* Washington, D.C., 1966.

Gil, Fontana. *Trujillo y su obra, 1930–1952.* La Romana, R.D.: Romana, 1954.

Girona, Francisco. *Las fechorías del bandolero Trujillo; estudio crítico de la vida y milagros del tirano de Santo Domingo.* San Juan, P.R.: Editorial Muñecos, 1937.

Glick, M. *The Administration of Technical Assistance: Growth in the Americas.* Chicago: University of Chicago Press, 1957.

Goldwert, Marvin. *The Constabulary in the Dominican Republic and Nicaragua: Progeny and Legacy of United States Intervention.* Gainesville: University of Florida Press, 1962.

Gonzáles Herrera, Julio. *Trujillo, genio político.* Ciudad Trujillo, R.D.: Ed. del Caribe, 1956.

Graber, Doris A. *Crisis Diplomacy: A History of U.S. Intervention Policies and Practices.* Washington, D.C.: Public Affairs Press, 1959.

Greenbie, Sydney. *Three Island Nations: Cuba, Haiti, Dominican Republic.* New York: Row, Peterson & Co., 1942.

Guerrero, Manuel M. *Sociología y política en la República Dominicana.* Ciudad Trujillo, R.D.: Imp. "La Opinión," 1941.

Hanke, Lewis. *Mexico and the Caribbean.* Princeton, N.J.: Van Nostrand Co., 1959.

Harding, Bertita. *The Land Columbus Loved: The Dominican Republic.* New York: Coward-McCann, 1949.

Heinl, Robert D., Jr. *Soldiers of the Sea: The United States Marine Corps, 1775–1962.* Annapolis, Md.: U.S. Naval Institute, 1962.

Henríquez, Noel. *La verdad sobre Trujillo: Capítulos que se le olvidaron a Galíndez.* Habana: Imprenta Económica en General, S.A., 1959.

Henríquez Ureña, Max. *Los Yanquis en Santo Domingo.* Madrid: 1929.

Herrera, César A. *Las finanzas de la República Dominicana.* Ciudad Trujillo, R.D.: Imp. Dominicana, 1955.

Herring, Hubert. *A History of Latin America from the Beginnings to the Present.* 3rd ed. New York: Alfred A. Knopf, 1968.

Hicks, Albert C. *Blood in the Streets: The Life and Rule of Trujillo.* New York: Creative Age Press, 1946.

Hill, Howard Copeland. *Roosevelt and the Caribbean.* Chicago: University of Chicago Press, 1927.

Hoepelman, Antonio and Senior, Juan A. (eds.). *Documentos históricos que refieren a la implantación de un Gobierno Militar Americano en la República Dominicana.* Santo Domingo: 1922.

Hovey, Harold A. *United States Military Assistance: A Study of Policies and Practices.* New York: Frederick A. Praeger, 1965.

Huntington, Samuel P. *Political Order in Changing Societies.* New Haven: Yale University Press, 1968.

Inman, Samuel G. *Inter-American Conferences, 1826-1954: History and Problems.* Ed. by H. E. Davis. Washington, D.C.: The University Press, 1965.

Inter-American Association for Democracy and Freedom. *Report of the Second Inter-American Conference for Democracy and Freedom.* New York: 1961.

International Research Associates, Inc. *A Survey of Latin American Public Opinion.* New York: Time, Inc., 1958.

James, Daniel. *Detrás de la cortina de azúcar.* México: Organización Regional Interamericana de Trabajadores, 1956.

Jane, Cecil. *Liberty and Despotism in Latin America.* London: Clarendon Press, 1929.

Jimenes-Grullón, Juan Isidro. *La República Dominicana: Una ficción-análisis de la evolución histórica y de la presencia actual del coloniaje y el colonialismo en Santo Domingo.* Mérida, Venezuela: Talleres Gráficos Universitarios, 1965.

————. *Una gestapo en América: vida tortura, agonía y muerte de presos políticos bajo la tiranía de Trujillo.* Habana: Editorial Lex, 1946.

————. *La propaganda de Trujillo al desnudo.* Habana: Unión democrática antinazista dominicana, 1943.

————. *La República Dominicana (Análisis de su pasado y su presente) precedido por "Un pueblo en un libro," palabras iniciales de Juan Bosch.* 2nd ed. Habana: Arellano y cía, 1940.

Johnson, John J. *The Military and Society in Latin America.* Palo Alto, Cal.: Stanford University Press, 1964.

Johnson, P. V. *Our Neighbors, the Dominicans.* Winona Lake, Ind.: Free Methodist Publishing House, 1942.

Jones, Chester F. *The Caribbean Since 1900*. New York: Prentice-Hall, 1936.

———. *The United States and the Caribbean*. Chicago: University of Chicago Press, 1929.

Knight, Melvin M. *The Americans in Santo Domingo*. ["Studies in American Imperialism" (American Fund for Public Service Studies in American Investments Abroad)]. New York: Vanguard Press, 1928.

Krehm, William. *Democracia y tiranías en el Caribe. Prólogo y notas de Vincente Sáenz*. México, D.F.: Unión Democrática Centroamericana, 1949.

Laguerre, Enrique. *The Labyrinth*. Trans. by William Rose. New York: Las Américas Publishing Co., 1960.

Lamarche, Carlos M. *La democracia en función de éxito. La democracia frente al comunismo*. Ciudad Trujillo: Editora del Caribe, 1951.

Landestoy, Carmita, *Yo también acuso! Raphael Leonidas Trujillo Molina, tirano de la República Dominicana, la actual y más cruel inhumana tiranía de América*. New York: Azteca Press, 1946.

Lieuwen, Edwin. *Arms and Politics in Latin America*. New York: Praeger, for the Council on Foreign Relations, 1960.

———. *Generals vs. Presidents: Neo-Militarism in Latin America*. New York: Frederick A. Praeger, 1964.

———. *The United States and the Challenge to Security in Latin America*. Columbus: Ohio State University Press, 1966.

———. *United States Policy in Latin America: A Short History*. New York: Frederick A. Praeger, 1965.

Loftus, Joseph E. *Latin American Defense Expenditures, 1938–1965*. Santa Monica, Cal.: Rand Corp., 1968.

Logan, Rayford. *Haiti and the Dominican Republic*. New York: Oxford University Press, 1968.

López, Nicolás F. *Algo sobre la República Dominicana*. Quito, Ec.: Editorial Colón, 1948.

Madariaga, Salvador de. *Latin America Between the Eagle and the Bear*. New York: Frederick A. Praeger, 1962.

Manger, William. *Pan America in Crisis: The Future of the OAS*. Washington, D.C.: Public Affairs Press, 1961.

Marrero Aristy, Ramón. *Trujillo: Síntesis de su vida y de su obra*. 2nd ed. Ciudad Trujillo: Imp. Dominicana, 1953.

Martin, John Bartlow. *Overtaken by Events*. Garden City, N.Y.: Doubleday & Co., 1966.

Matthews, Herbert L. (ed.). *The United States and Latin America*. 3rd ed. New York: The American Assembly, Columbia University, 1963.

May, Ernest R. *Imperial Democracy: The Emergence of America as a Great Power*. New York: Harcourt, Brace & World, 1961.

Mecham, J. Lloyd. *A Survey of United States-Latin American Relations*. Boston: Houghton Mifflin Co., 1965.

————. *The United States and Inter-American Security, 1889–1960*. Austin: University of Texas Press, 1961.

Mejia, Luis F. *De Lilís a Trujillo: historia contemporánea de la República Dominicana*. Caracas: Editorial Elite, 1944.

Metcalf, Clyde H. *History of the United States Marine Corps*. New York: G. P. Putnam & Sons, 1939.

Miolán, Angel. *La Revolución Social Frente a la Tiranía de Trujillo*. México: n.p., 1938.

Mitchell, Harold Paton. *Contemporary Politics and Economics in the Caribbean*. Athens: Ohio University Press, 1968.

Mizelle, William R. (ed.). *The Quality(?) of Life in the Americas: An OAS Association Round-Table of Assistant Secretaries of State for Inter-American Affairs*. Washington, D.C.: The Hemisphere and OAS Association, 1969.

Monclús, Miguel Angel. *El caudillismo en la República Dominicana*. 3rd ed. Ciudad Trujillo: Editora del Caribe, 1962.

Munro, Dana G. *Intervention and Dollar Diplomacy in the Caribbean, 1900–1921*. Princeton, N.J.: Princeton University Press, 1964.

————. *The Latin American Republics: A History*. 3rd ed. New York: Appleton-Century-Crofts, 1960.

————. *The United States and the Caribbean Area*. Boston: World Peace Foundation, 1934.

Murray-Jacoby, H. *The Diplomacy of President Trujillo*. New York: n.p., 1943.

Nanita, Abelardo R. *Trujillo de cuerpo entero*. 2nd ed. rev. Santiago, R.D.: Ed. El Diario, 1939.

National Planning Association. *Technical Cooperation in Latin America*. Washington, D.C.: 1956.

Nearing, Scott, and Freeman, Joseph. *Dollar Diplomacy: A Study in American Imperialism*. New York: B. W. Huebsch and the Viking Press, 1925.

Needler, Martin C. *Latin American Politics in Perspective*. Princeton, N.J.: Van Nostrand Co., 1963.

Nehemkis, Peter. *Latin America: Myth and Reality.* New York: Alfred A. Knopf, 1964.

Nemours, Alfred. *Les présidents Lescot et Trujillo.* Port-au-Prince, Haiti: n.p., 1942.

Neumann, William L., Jr. *Recognition of Governments in the Americas.* Washington, D.C.: Foundation for Public Affairs, Pamphlet No. 3, 1947.

Nixon, Richard M. *Six Crises.* New York: Doubleday & Co., 1962.

Ornes Coiscu, Germán E. *Trujillo, Brownell, and Braden.* Ciudad Trujillo, R.D.: n.p., 1953.

——. *Trujillo, Little Caesar of the Caribbean.* New York: Thomas Nelson & Sons, 1958.

——. *A Self-Portrait.* Ciudad Trujillo: Dominican Press Society, 1958.

Osorio Lizarazo, José A. *El bacilo de Marx.* Ciudad Trujillo: Ed. La Nación, 1959.

——. *Birth and Growth of Anti-Trujillism in America.* Madrid: Gráficas Rey, 1958.

——. *Germen y Proceso del Antitrujillismo en America.* Santiago de Chile: Imprenta Colombia, 1956.

Pagán Perdomo, Dato. *Por que lucha el pueblo dominicano: análisis del fenómeno dictatorial en América Latina.* Caracas: Imprenta Caribe, 1959.

Palmer, Thomas W., Jr. *Search for a Latin American Policy.* Gainesville: University of Florida Press, 1957.

Partido Revolucionario Dominicano. *Un error de Washington: la resurrección del imperialismo militar norteamericano en el Caribe.* La Habana, 1949.

Patin, Enrique. *Observaciones acerca de nuestra psicología popular.* Ciudad Trujillo, R.D.: Editora Montalva, 1950.

Pavia Franco, Alberto. *Two Letters to Mr. Charles O. Porter.* México: n.p., 1960.

Peña Batlle, Manuel A. *Contribución a una campaña. Cuatro discursos políticos.* Santiago, R.D.: Ed. El Diario, 1942.

——. *Historia de la Cuestión fronteriza dominicano-haitiana.* Vol. I. Ciudad Trujillo: Ed. L. Sánchez Andújar, 1946.

——. *Política de Trujillo.* Ciudad Trujillo, R.D.: Impresora Dominicana, 1954.

Penson, José F. *El partido dominicano.* Ciudad Trujillo: Imp. Arte y Cine, 1957.

Pepper B., José Vicente. *La gran emboscada.* Ciudad Trujillo: Montalvo, 1948.

Perkins, Dexter. *The Evolution of American Foreign Policy.* New York: Oxford University Press, 1948.

———. *A History of the Monroe Doctrine.* New revision. Boston: Little, Brown and Co., 1963.

———. *The United States and the Caribbean.* Cambridge, Mass.: Harvard University Press, 1947.

———. *The United States and Latin America.* Baton Rouge: Louisiana State University Press, 1961.

Pflaum, Irving Peter. *Arena of Decision: Latin America in Crisis.* Englewood Cliffs, N.J.: Prentice-Hall, 1964.

Pike, Frederick B. (ed.). *Freedom and Reform in Latin America.* Notre Dame: University of Notre Dame Press, 1959.

Plaza Lasso, Galo. *Problems of Democracy in Latin America.* Chapel Hill: University of North Carolina Press, 1955.

Porter, Charles O. and Alexander, Robert J. *The Struggle for Democracy in Latin America.* New York: Macmillan Co., 1961.

Quintanilla, Luis S. *A Latin American Speaks.* New York: Macmillan Co., 1943.

———. *Panamericanism and Democracy.* Boston: Boston University Press, 1952.

Resumil Aragunde, Manuel. *El estado como agente activo de la industrialización de la República Dominicana.* Ciudad Trujillo: Tip. Faro de Vigo, 1959.

Rickards, Colin. *Caribbean Power.* London: Dennis Dobson, 1963.

Río, Angel del (ed.). *Responsible Freedom in the Americas.* New York: Doubleday & Co., 1955.

Rippy, J. Fred. *The Caribbean Danger Zone.* New York: G. P. Putnam's Sons, 1940.

———. *Globe and Hemisphere; Latin America's Place in the Postwar Foreign Relations of the United States.* Chicago: Henry Regnery, 1958.

———. *Latin America, a Modern History.* Ann Arbor: University of Michigan Press, 1958.

Roberts, T. D., et al. *Area Handbook for the Dominican Republic.* Washington: Government Printing Office, 1966.

Rodman, Selden. *Quisqueya: A History of the Dominican Republic.* Seattle: University of Washington Press, 1964.

Rodríguez Demorizi, Emilio. *Trujillo y Cordell Hull: un ejemplo de política panamericanista.* Ciudad Trujillo: Editora del Caribe, 1956.

Ronning, C. Neale. *Law and Politics in Inter-American Diplomacy.* New York: John Wiley & Sons, 1963.

Sánchez Cabral, Eduardo. *De la clandestinidad.* Santo Domingo, R.D.: n.p., 1962.

Sands, William Franklin and Lalley, Joseph M. *Our Jungle Diplomacy.* Chapel Hill: University of North Carolina Press, 1944.

Schoenrich, Otto. *Santo Domingo: A Country With A Future.* New York: Macmillan Co., 1918.

Slater, Jerome. *The OAS and United States Foreign Policy.* Columbus: Ohio State University Press, 1967.

————. *Intervention and Negotiation: The United States and the Dominican Revolution.* New York: Harper & Row, 1970.

————. *A Re-evaluation of Collective Security: The OAS in Action.* Columbus: Ohio State University Press, 1965.

Steel, Ronald. *Pax Americana.* New York: Viking Press, 1967.

Stuart, Graham H. *Latin America and the United States.* 5th ed. New York: Appleton-Century-Crofts, 1955.

Szulc, Tad. "New Trends in Latin America," *Headline Series,* No. 140 (March/April, 1961).

————. *Twilight of the Tyrants.* New York: Henry Holt & Co., 1959.

————. *The Winds of Revolution: Latin America Today—and Tomorrow.* New York: Frederick A. Praeger, 1963.

Taylor, Philip B., Jr. *Hemispheric Security Reconsidered.* New Orleans: Middle America Research Institute, 1957.

Tejeda Díaz, Teodoro. *Yo Investigué la Muerte de Trujillo.* Barcelona, España: Plaza and James, S.A., 1964.

Thomas, Ann Van Wynen, and Thomas, A. J., Jr. *Non-Intervention: The Law and Its Import in the Americas.* Dallas: Southern Methodist University Press, 1956.

————. *The Organization of American States.* Dallas: Southern Methodist University Press, 1963.

Tomlinson, Edward. *Battle for the Hemisphere: Democracy Versus Totalitarianism in the Other Hemisphere.* New York: Charles Scribner's Sons, 1947.

Unión democrática antinazista dominicana. *Trujillo es un nazi (pruebas documentales).* Habana, 1943.

————. *América contra Trujillo.* Habana, 1940.

"U.S. Foreign Policy and the Caribbean Situation," *Congressional Digest,* XXXIX (November, 1960).

Uribe Vargas, Diego. *Panamericanismo democrático. Bases para una transformación del Sistema continental.* Bogotá: Ediciones Nuevo Signo, 1958.

Vega y Pagán, Ernesto. *Historia de las Fuerzas Armadas.* 2 vols. Ciudad Trujillo: Impresora Dominicana, 1955.

Verges Vidal, Pedro Luciano. *Trujillo, prócer anticomunista.* Ciudad Trujillo: Editora del Caribe, 1958.

Villoldo, Pedro. *Latin American Resentment.* New York: Vantage Press, 1959.

Walker, Stanley. *Journey Toward the Sunlight: A Story of the Dominican Republic and Its People.* New York: The Caribbean Library, 1947.

Wallich, Henry C. and Triffin, Robert. *Monetary and Banking Legislation of the Dominican Republic, 1947.* New York: Federal Reserve Bank of New York, 1953.

Welles, Sumner. *Naboth's Vineyard: The Dominican Republic, 1848–1924.* 2 vols., New York: Payson & Clarke, Ltd., 1928.

———. *Where Are We Heading?* New York: Harper & Brothers, 1946.

Whitaker, Arthur P. *Nationalism in Latin America, Past and Present.* Gainesville: University of Florida Press, 1962.

———. *The Western Hemisphere Idea: Its Rise and Fall.* Ithaca, N.Y.: Cornell University Press, 1954.

White, John W. *The Land Columbus Loved.* Ciudad Trujillo, R.D.: Editorial Montalvo, 1945.

Wiarda, Howard J. *Dictatorship and Development: The Methods of Control in Trujillo's Dominican Republic.* Gainesville: University of Florida Press, 1969.

——— (ed.). *Dominican Republic Election Factbook, June 1, 1966.* Washington, D.C.: Operations and Policy Research, Inc., 1966.

———. *The Dominican Republic: Nation in Transition.* New York: Frederick A. Praeger, 1969.

Wilgus, A. Curtis (ed.). *The Caribbean:* . . . Vol. I (1951———). [Papers of the annual conference on the Caribbean held at the University of Florida] Gainesville: University of Florida Press, 1952———.

———. *The Caribbean: Contemporary International Relations.* Gainesville: University of Florida Press, 1957.

———. *The Caribbean: Its Hemispheric Role.* Gainesville: University of Florida Press, 1967.

Wolf, Charles, Jr. *United States Policy and the Third World: Problems and Analysis.* Boston: Little, Brown & Co., 1967.

Wood, Bryce. *The Making of the Good Neighbor Policy.* New York: Columbia University Press, 1961.

Wythe, George. *The United States and Inter-American Relations.* Gainesville: University of Florida Press, 1964.

Yepes, J. M. *Del Congreso de Panamá de la Conferencia de Caracas. 1826–1954.* 2 vols. Caracas: Cromotip, 1955.

V. ARTICLES, JOURNALS AND INDIVIDUAL CHAPTERS

Alba, Victor. "Communism and Nationalism in Latin America," *Problems of Communism,* VII (September/October, 1958), 24–31.

———. "República Dominicana: La herencia del 'Benefactor,'" *Cuadernos* [Paris]. II, Núm. 63 (agosto, 1962), 67–72.

———. "The Status of Militarism in Latin America," in John J. Johnson (ed.). *The Role of the Military in Underdeveloped Countries.* Princeton, N.J.: Princeton University Press, 1962.

Alex, William. "Are We Really Good Neighbors?", *The Pan American,* V (March, 1945), 32–33.

Alexander, Robert J. "After Trujillo What?", *The New Leader,* XLIV (June 12, 1961), 3–4.

———. *Communism in Latin America.* New Brunswick, N.J.: Rutgers University Press, 1957.

———. "Dictatorship in the Caribbean," *Canadian Forum* (May, 1948).

———. "New Directions: The United States and Latin America," *Current History,* XLII (February, 1962), 65–70.

———. "The Trujillo Tyranny: The Dominican Dictatorship in Crisis," *The Socialist Call,* XXV (March, 1957), 12–14.

———. "Unions in Latin America and Caribbean Area," in Jack Schuyler (ed.), *International Labor Directory.* New York: Frederick A. Praeger, 1955.

"The Americas: The Challenge of Change," *Journal of International Affairs,* XIV (1960), entire issue.

Arande, Curt Konrad. "Should the U.S. Arm Latin America?", *United Nations World Magazine,* III (October, 1949), 27–31.

Baldwin, David A. "Foreign Aid, Intervention, and Influence," *World Politics,* XXL (April, 1969), pp. 425–47.

Ball, M. Margaret. "Issue for the Americas: Non-Intervention v. Human Rights and the Preservation of Democratic Institutions," *International Organization,* XV (Winter, 1961), 21–37.

Barcia Trelles, Camilio. "Malestar político en el Caribe y Centroamérica: El gran achaque el nuevo mundo," *Política Internacional* [Madrid], Núm. 43 (mayo–junio, 1959), 53–91.

Baughman, C. C. "United States Occupation of the Dominican Republic," *U.S. Naval Institute Proceedings,* December, 1925, pp. 2306–27.

in 1939 the Dominican Republic established an annual "Trujillo Peace Prize" of $50,000, designed "to rival" the Nobel Prize.[29]

3. EARLY CRITICS OF NONINTERVENTION

As a policy matter nonintervention carried with it the necessity of dealing with dictators like Trujillo. For almost three decades the United States defended itself against the criticism that nonintervention in Dominican affairs constituted support of a vicious dictator. Some critics felt that in the 1930's the United States should have pressured Trujillo to reform his government. A few years prior the United States had been criticized for intervening in the Dominican Republic, but now nonintervention was being attacked on the grounds that it permitted the continued existence of Trujillo. Therefore a policy of noninterference was "as bad as our former one of ultra-intervention." [30]

During the early 1930's Trujillo was quietly consolidating his power, and the real nature of his regime had not yet manifested itself. Furthermore, the United States, in response to increasing Latin and North American opposition to its intervention in other American states, was moving toward accepting the principle of nonintervention as a basis for policy. The United States pledged adherence to nonintervention, with some reservations, at the Montevideo conference in 1933; the principle's acceptance was reiterated with no reservations at the Buenos Aires conference in 1936. Thus the United States had no legal basis to interfere with Trujillo — politically, economically or militarily — despite any objections to his governmental policies or practices. The nonintervention principle was the *sine qua non* for inter-American cooperation.

In the late 1930's, with the principle of nonintervention established as the cornerstone of the inter-American system, the United States became increasingly concerned over both the threat of war in Europe and security in the hemisphere. The idea of improving inter-American cooperation for defense purposes thus became a major concern. During World War II the Dominican Republic was of great strategic importance to the United States because of its geographic position as the gateway to the Caribbean and its proximity to the Panama Canal. The United States felt it hardly could denounce Trujillo as a dictator when he was essential to the war effort. Political or ideological principle was of less consideration than the principle of survival in a time of grave national peril.

Nevertheless, attention came to be focused on the ideological orientation of Trujillo and the attitude of the United States toward the dictatorship, especially with the rise of the totalitarian threat around the world in the late 1930's and the expansion of hostilities in World War II. As expressed in a great deal of its wartime declarations and propaganda, the goal of the United States was to destroy dictatorial regimes in the name of democ-

Trujillo reviews Marines upon his arrival at Union Station, Washington, D.C., July 6, 1939. *United Press International Photo*

Beals, Carleton. "Caesar of the Caribbean," *Current History,* XLVIII (January, 1938), 31–34.

———. "Fountain of Light," *The Nation,* CLXXXII (January 14, 1956), 25–27.

Betancourt, Rómulo. "Comunidad Interamericana sin dictaduras," *Combate* [Costa Rica], II (julio y agosto, 1960), 7–9.

Bosch, Juan. "Trujillo: Problema de América," *Combate,* I (marzo-abril, 1959), 9–13.

Braden, Spruille. "In Latin America, Let's Stop Buying Dictators," *Look,* XV (September 25, 1951), 80–86.

Brown, Philip Mason. "Armed Occupation of Santo Domingo," *American Journal of International Law,* XI (April, 1917), pp. 394–99.

Brown, Wenzell. "The Terrifying Story of New York's League of Threatened Men," *Look* (May 29, 1956), 103–104, 106.

Burton, Wilbur. "Dictators for Neighbors," *Current History,* XLVII (1937), 63–68.

Cater, Douglass and Pincus, Walter. "Our Sugar Diplomacy," *The Reporter* (April 13, 1961), 24–28.

———. "The Foreign Legion of U.S. Public Relations," *The Reporter* (December 22, 1960), pp. 15–22.

Chapman, Charles E. "The United States and the Dominican Republic," *Hispanic American Historical Review* (February, 1928), pp. 84–91.

Clements, R. J. "Events that Judge Us," *The New Republic,* CXXXV (July 2, 1956), 9–12.

Compton, George C. "What About Intervention?", *Américas,* XI (November, 1959), 3–6.

Connell-Smith, Gordon. "The OAS and Santo Domingo," *The World Today,* XXI (June, 1965), pp. 229–36.

Cook, Fred J. "Who Killed Jesus de Galindez?", *Fact,* III (March–April, 1966), 42–59.

"Costly Whitewash of Black Charges," *Life* (June 9, 1958), 105–106.

"The Crisis in the Dominican Republic," *Bulletin of the International Commission of Jurists,* No. 11 (December, 1960), 23–27.

Crow, John A. "Men of Destiny" (Ch. XXXVIII) and "Ariel and Caliban" (Ch. III), *The Epic of Latin America.* Garden City, New York: Doubleday and Co., Inc., 1952.

Davis, Harold E. "Democracy in Latin America," *World Affairs,* CVII (June, 1944), 111–118.

Davis, Norman H. "Wanted: A Consistent Latin American Policy," *Foreign Affairs,* IX (July, 1931), pp. 547–568.

Delgado, Jaime. "El mundo político del Caribe (1930–1959)," *Revista de Estudios Políticos* [Madrid], CVIII (noviembre–diciembre, 1959), 147–178.

Díaz Doin, Guillermo. "La Organización de Estados Americanos y la no intervención," *Cuadernos Americanos* [Mexico], XIX (mayo–junio, 1960), 73–88.

Draper, Theodore. "Trujillo's Dynasty: . . . [I and II]," *The Reporter,* V (November 27, 1951), 20–26, and (December 11, 1951), 17–27.

Evans, Rowland, Jr. "First Steps in Dominican Democracy," *The Reporter* (January 3, 1963), pp. 21–23.

Fabela, Isidro. "La Sexta y Séptima Conferencias de Cancilleras ante el derecho positivo internacional," *Cuadernos Americanos,* CXIII (noviembre-diciembre, 1960), pp. 9–27.

Facio, Gonzalo. "Impulso democrático al sistema interamericano," *Combate* [Costa Rica], II (mayo–junio, 1960), 48–56.

Fenwick, Charles G. "Intervention: Individual and Collective," *American Journal of International Law,* XXXIX (October, 1945), 645–663.

———. "Has the Spector of Intervention Been Laid in Latin America," *American Journal of International Law,* L (July, 1956), 636–639.

———. "Intervention and the Inter-American Rule of Law," *American Journal of International Law,* LIII (October, 1959), pp. 873–76.

Figueres, José. "Mandato de las Naciones Unidas en la República Dominicana," *Combate* [Costa Rica], I (septiembre–octubre, 1958), pp. 67–70.

———. "North Americans, Share Your Democracy with Us!" *Reader's Digest,* LXXIX (August, 1961), 45–51.

———. "The Problems of Democracy in America," *Journal of International Affairs,* IX (May, 1955), 11–23.

Fitzgibbon, Russell H. "Dictatorship and Democracy in Latin America," *International Affairs* [London], XXXVI (January, 1960), 48–57.

———. "How Democratic is Latin America?", *Inter-American Economic Affairs,* IX (Spring, 1956), 65–77.

———. "A Statistical Evaluation of Latin American Democracy," *The Western Political Quarterly,* IX (September, 1956), 607–619.

———. "What Price Latin American Armies?", *The Virginian Quarterly Review,* XXXVI (Autumn, 1960), 517–532.

Fournier, Fernando. "Trujillo: Dictador Tropical y Folklórico," *Combate* [Costa Rica], IV (noviembre–diciembre, 1962), 27–31.

Francis, Michael J. "Military Aid to Latin America in the U.S. Congress," *Journal of Inter-American Studies*, VI (July, 1964), 389–404.

Furniss, Edgar S., Jr. "American Wartime Objectives in Latin America," *World Politics*, II (April, 1950), 373–88.

————. "The Inter-American System and Recent Caribbean Disputes," *International Organization*, IV (November, 1950), 593–94.

Galíndez, Jesús de. "Anti-American Sentiment in Latin America," *Journal of International Affairs*, IX (May, 1955), 24–32.

————. "Un reportaje sobre Santo Domingo," *Cuadernos Americanos* [Mexico], LXXX (marzo–abril, 1955), 37–56.

————. "Vaivenes en la política hispano-americana de los Estados Unidos," *Cuadernos Americanos* [Mexico], LXXXVII (mayo-junio, 1956), 7–16.

Gall, Norman. "How Trujillo Died," *The New Republic*, CXLVIII (April 13, 1963), 19–20.

Germani, Gino and Silvert, Kalman. "Politics, Social Structure and Military Intervention in Latin America," *European Journal of Sociology*, II (1961), pp. 62–81.

Goff, Fred and Locker, Michael. "The Violence of Domination: U.S. Power and the Dominican Republic," in Horowitz, Irving L., Josué de Castro, and John Gerassi (eds.). *Latin American Radicalism: A Documentary Report on Left and Nationalist Movements*. New York: Vintage, 1969, pp. 249–91.

Graber, Doris A. "United States Intervention in Latin America," *Year Book of World Affairs, 1962*. New York: Frederick A. Praeger, 1962, 23–50.

De Graff, Edward. "The Strange Legacy of 'El Benefactor,'" *The Reporter* (July 6, 1961), 3–31.

Gruening, Ernest. "Dictatorship in Santo Domingo: A Joint Concern," *The Nation*, CXXXVIII (May 23, 1934), 583–85.

Grullón, Ramón. "Antecedentes y perspectivas del momento político dominicano," *Cuadernos Americanos* [Mexico], CXX (enero–febrero, 1962), 221–52.

Hallgarten, George W. F. "Present Latin American Dictatorships" (Part IV, Ch. 1), *Why Dictators? The Causes and Forms of Tyrannical Rule Since 600 B.C.* New York: Macmillan Co., 1954.

Hamil, Hugh M., Jr. (ed.). *Dictatorship in Spanish America*. New York: Alfred A. Knopf, 1966.

Hanke, Lewis. "Friendship Now with Latin America," *The Virginia Quarterly Review*, XXII (Autumn, 1946), 498–518.

Hardy, Osgood. "Rafael Leonidas Trujillo Molina: The United States

Post-War Attitude Toward the Dictatorships," *The Pacific Historical Review*, XV (December, 1946), 409–16.

Haring, Clarence Henry. "Latin American Dictatorships and the United States," *Proceedings of the Massachusetts Historical Society*, LXX (October, 1950–May, 1953).

Haverstock, Nathan A. "Return to Democracy," *Américas*, XV (March, 1963), pp. 15–16.

Haya de la Torre, Víctor Raúl. "An Inter-American Democratic Front," *Free World*, IV (November, 1942), 150–152.

―――. "Intervención e imperialismo," *Cuadernos Americanos* [Mexico], X (julio–agosto, 1943), 7–12.

―――. "Toward a Real Inter-Americanism," *Mexican Life*, XVIII (October, 1942), 17, 50–51.

Herring, Hubert. "Scandal of the Caribbean: The Dominican Republic," *Current History*, XXXVIII (March, 1960), 140–43 and 164.

―――. "The Dominican Republic (Chap. 27)," in *A History of Latin America from the Beginnings to the Present*. 3d ed.; New York: Alfred A. Knopf, 1968.

Herzog, Jesús Silva. "Reflexiones sobre las dictaduras," *Cuadernos Americanos*, XI (julio–agosto, 1952), pp. 57–63.

Hickey, John. "Blackmail, Mendicancy and Intervention: Latin America's Conception of the Good-Neighbor Policy?", *Inter-American Economic Affairs*, XII (Summer, 1958), 43–82.

Holmes, Olive. "Dominican Dispute Tests Inter-American System," *Foreign Policy Bulletin*, XXIX (February 17, 1950).

"How One Man Rule Works on Doorstep of United States," *U.S. News and World Report*, June 15, 1956, 76–80.

Humphreys, Robin A. "Democracy and Dictatorship," Asher N. Christensen (ed.). *Evolution of Latin American Government: A Book of Readings*. New York: Henry Holt & Co., 1951.

―――. "Democracy and Dictatorship," and "Hemisphere Relations," *The Evolution of Modern Latin America*. New York: Oxford University Press, 1946.

―――. "Latin America: The Caudillo Tradition," in Michael Howard (ed.). *Soldiers and Governments*. London: Eyre & Spottiswoode, 1957.

Inman, Samuel Guy. "The Hard Road to Democracy," and "Dictators and Bankers," *Latin America: Its Place in World Life*. Chicago and New York: Willett, Clark & Co., 1937.

James, Daniel. "Castro, Trujillo, and Turmoil," *Saturday Evening Post*, CCXXXIX (January 16, 1960), 63ff.

Jimenes-Grullón, Juan Isidro. "Trujillo: More Croesus than Caesar," *The Nation*, CLXXXIX (December 26, 1959), 485–86.

Johnson, John J. "Foreign Factors in Dictatorship in Latin America," *Pacific Historical Review*, XX (May, 1951), 127–41.

Juárez, Joseph R. "United States Withdrawal from Santo Domingo," *Hispanic American Historical Review*, XLII (May, 1962), pp. 152–90.

Kantor, Harry. "The Dominican Republic: Politics after Totalitarianism," Chap. 15 of his *Patterns of Politics and Political Systems in Latin America*. Chicago: Rand McNally, 1969.

Kelsey, Carl. "The American Intervention in Haiti and the Dominican Republic," *The Annals of the American Academy of Political and Social Science*, C (1922), 109–202.

Kent, George. "God and Trujillo: The Dominican Republic's Dictator," *Inter-American*, V (March, 1964), 14–16.

Kilmartin, Robert C. "Indoctrination in Santo Domingo," *The Marine Corps Gazette* (December, 1922), pp. 377–486.

Knebel, Fletcher. "How Trujillo Spends a Million in the United States," *Look Magazine*, August 20, 1957, pp. 61–63.

Lane, Rufus H. "Civil Government in Santo Domingo in the Early Days of the Military Occupation," *The Marine Corps Gazette* (June, 1922), pp. 127–46.

"Latin America's Dictators," *The Economist*, December 31, 1949, 1474–76.

"Latin American Dictatorships and the U.S.," *Foreign Policy Reports*, December 1, 1949.

Lipset, Seymour M. "Some Social Requisites of Democracy: Economic Development and Political Legitimacy," *The American Political Science Review*, LIII (March 1959), 76–77, 96.

Logan, Rayford W. "Dominican Republic: Struggle for Tomorrow," *The Nation*, CXCIV (December 16, 1961), 488–90.

Lowenthal, Abraham F. "The Dominican Republic: The Politics of Chaos," in Arpad von Lazar and Robert R. Kaufman (eds.). *Reform and Revolution: Readings in Latin American Politics*. Boston: Allyn and Bacon, 1969, pp. 34–58.

———. "Foreign Aid as a Political Instrument: The Case of the Dominican Republic," in John D. Montgomery and Arthur Smithies (eds.). *Public Policy*. XIV. Cambridge, Mass.: Harvard University Press, 1965, pp. 141–60.

———. "Limits of American Power: The Lesson of the Dominican Republic," *Harper's Magazine*, CCXLIX (June, 1964), pp. 87–89, 94–95.

————. "The United States and the Dominican Republic to 1965: Background to Intervention," *Caribbean Studies,* X (July, 1970), pp. 30-55.

McAlister, Lyle N. "Civil-Military Relations in Latin America," *Journal of Inter-American Studies,* III (July, 1961), 341-50.

————. "Recent Research and Writings on the Role of the Military in Latin America," *Latin American Research Review,* II (Fall, 1966), 5-36.

Manger, William. "The Inter-American Regional System: The Dilemma of Contradictions: Multilateralism; Collective Intervention and Unilateral Nonintervention," *World Affairs,* CXXIV (Fall, 1961), 83-86.

Mann, Thomas C. "Democracy vs. Dictators in Latin America—How Can We Help?", *Department of State Pub. 7729,* Inter-American Series 90, released September, 1964.

Masur, Gerhard. "Democracy in Eclipse," *The Virginia Quarterly Review,* XXVI (Summer, 1950), 336-352.

Matthews, Herbert L. "The U.S. and Latin America," *Headline Series,* No. 100 (July–August, 1953), 3-50.

Mecham, J. Lloyd. "Caribbean Turbulence (1949–1960)," *The United States and Inter-American Security, 1889-1960.* Austin: University of Texas Press, 1961.

————. "Democracy and Dictatorship in Latin America," *Southwestern Social Science Quarterly,* XLI (December, 1960), 294-303.

————. "The General Caribbean Policies of the United States" (Chap. 10) and "Relations with the Island Republics of the Caribbean" (Chap. 11), *A Survey of United States–Latin American Relations.* Boston: Houghton Mifflin Co., 1965.

Millington, Thomas. "U.S. Diplomacy and the Dominican Crisis," *SAIS Review,* VII (Summer, 1963), pp. 25-30.

Morrison, de Lessups L. *Latin American Mission.* New York: Simon & Schuster, 1964.

Munro, Dana Gardner. "The Caribbean Region," and "Latin America and the United States," *The Latin American Republics, A History.* 3rd ed.; New York: Appleton-Century-Crofts, Inc., 1960.

Murkland, Harry B. "The Complicated Caribbean," *Current History,* XVIII (January, 1950), 8-11.

Ogelsby, J. C. M. "Haiti and the Dominican Republic," in Burnett, Ben C. and Johnson, Kenneth F. *Political Forces in Latin America: Dimensions of the Quest for Stability.* Belmont, Calif.: Wadsworth Publishing Co., 1968, 145-70.

Olch, Isiah. "A Résumé of National Interests in the Caribbean Area," *U.S. Naval Institute Proceedings,* LXVI (February, 1940), 165-76.

Oliver, Covey. "Foreign and Human Relations with Latin America," *Foreign Affairs,* XLVII (April, 1969), 520–31.

Ornes Coiscu, Germán E. and McCarter, John. "Trujillo: Little Caesar on Our Front Porch," *Harper's,* CCXIII (December, 1956), 67–72.

"Oust a Dictator, Get a Red?", *U.S. News and World Report,* November 13, 1961.

Peck, Jones. "Our Struggle Against Trujillo," *Liberation,* II (December, 1957), 5–8.

Pierson, W. W. (ed.). "Pathology of Democracy in Latin America: A Symposium," *The American Political Science Review.* XLIV (March, 1950), 100–49.

Pike, Frederick B. "Can We Slow Our Loss of Latin America?", *Inter-American Economic Affairs.* XV (Summer, 1961), 3–29.

Porter, Charles O. "The Butcher of the Caribbean," *Coronet,* XLII (April, 1957), 50–67.

———. "Ernst and Galindez," *The New Leader,* XLI (July 7–14, 1958), 3–8.

Powell, John Duncan. "Military Assistance and Militarism in Latin America," *Western Political Quarterly,* XVIII (June, 1965), 382–92.

Pulley, Raymond H. "The United States and the Trujillo Dictatorship, 1933–1940: The High Price of Caribbean Stability," *Caribbean Studies,* V (October, 1965), 22–31.

"The Question of United States Economic Aid for Latin America," *Congressional Digest,* XL (February, 1961), 34–64.

Rambo, A. Terry. "The Dominican Republic," in Needler, Martin C. (ed.). *Political Systems of Latin America.* Princeton, N.J.: Van Nostrand Co., 1964, 165–80.

Reynolds, Quentin. "Murder in the Tropics," *Colliers,* January 27, 1938.

Rippy, J. Fred. "Dictatorship in Latin America," in Guy Stanton Ford (ed.). *Dictatorship in the Modern World.* Minneapolis: The University of Minnesota Press, 1935 and 1939, 178–214.

———. "Foreign Aid and the Problem of Nonintervention," *Globe and Hemisphere.* Chicago: Henry Regnery Co., 1958, 203–25.

———. "Foreign Aid and the Problem of Non-Intervention," *Inter-American Economic Affairs.* II (Winter, 1957), 23–47.

———. "The Initiation of the Customs Receivership in the Dominican Republic," *Hispanic American Historical Review,* XVII (November, 1934), 419–57.

———. "Sugar in Inter-American Relations," *Inter-American Economic Affairs,* IX (Spring, 1956), 50–64.

————. "The Western-Hemisphere Concept: Permanent or Fleeting?", *Inter-American Economic Affairs*, X (Spring, 1957), 3–21.

Rodríguez Larreta, Eduardo. "The Call of the Hour: Respect for the Dignity of Man," *Vital Speeches*, XIII (March 15, 1947), 324–26.

————. "El derecho a la intervención colectiva," *Combate* [Costa Rica], II (julio y agosto, 1959), 23–27.

Rodríguez Plata, Horacio. "Quién es el dictador de Santo Domingo?", *Review America*, IV (October, 1945), 115–32.

Ronning, C. Neale. "Intervention, International Law, and the Inter-American System," *Journal of Inter-American Studies*, III (April, 1961), 249–71.

Sayre, John Nevin. "Shall We Arm Our Neighbors?", *The Christian Century* (October 29, 1947), 1297–98.

Schlesinger, Arthur M., Jr. "Good Fences Make Good Neighbors," *Fortune Magazine*, XXXVI (August, 1946), 131–35, and 161–71.

Schoenrich, Otto. "The Present American Intervention in Santo Domingo and Haiti," in George H. Blakeslee (ed.), *Mexico and the Caribbean: Clark University Addresses*. New York: G. E. Stechert, 1920, 206–23.

Sherman, George. "Nonintervention: A Shield for 'Papa Doc,'" *The Reporter*, XXXVIII (June 20, 1963), 27–29.

Silva Herzog, Jesus. "Reflecciones sobre las dictaduras," *Cuadernos Americanos* [Mexico], XLIV (julio–agosto, 1952), 57–63.

Sinks, Alfred H. "Trujillo, Caribbean Dictator," *The American Mercury*, LII (October, 1940), 164–71.

Slater, Jerome. "The Decline of the OAS," *International Journal*, XXIV (Summer, 1969), pp. 497–506.

————. "The United States, the Organization of American States, and The Dominican Republic, 1961–1963," *International Organization*, XVIII (Spring, 1964), 268–91.

Steinberg, David. "Dominican Republic: 28 Years of Stability," reprinted from *The New York Herald* in "A Look at the Dominican Republic," III (June, 1958), 12–14.

"The Story of a Dark International Conspiracy," *Life* (February 25, 1957), 24–31.

Stuart, Graham H. "American Imperialism in Haiti and the Dominican Republic," *Latin America and the United States*. 5th ed. New York: Appleton-Century-Crofts, 1955.

Suslow, Leo A. "Democracy in Latin America–U.S. Plan," *Social Science*, XXVI (January, 1951), 5–14.

Syrkin, Marie. "Rebirth in San Domingo?", *Jewish Frontier*, VIII (February, 1941), 9–13.

Szulc, Tad. "After Trujillo, A Reformer With a Mission," *The New York Times Magazine* (September 8, 1963), pp. 30, 114.

————. "The Haitian–Dominican Republic Controversy of 1963 and the OAS," *Orbis*, XII (Spring, 1968), pp. 294–313.

————. "Secret Trujillo Papers Disclose Intense Sugar Lobbying in U.S.," *The New York Times*, July 3, 1962, 1, 5.

————. "Trujillo's Legacy: A Democratic Vacuum," *The New York Times Magazine*, September 2, 1962, 9, 40–41.

————. "Uneasy Year 29 of the Trujillo Era," *The New York Times Magazine*, August 2, 1959, 9ff.

"Swarthy Autocrat," *The Literary Digest*, CXXII (July 4, 1936), 13–14.

Tensee, Joe. "A Canadian Writer Reports on the Dominican Republic: Finds Trujillo Is Military Anti-Communist, Finds Dominican People Proud and Prosperous," *The Washington Post*, March 10, 1961, B2. (Reprinted from February 18, 1961, issue of TAB [Toronto]).

Thomson, C. A. "Dictatorship in the Dominican Republic," *Foreign Policy Reports*, XII (April 15, 1936), 30–40.

Thorning, J. B. "The Dominican Republic: Twenty-five Years of Peace and Prosperity," *World Affairs*, CXVIII (Summer, 1955), 45–47.

Thorpe, George C. "American Achievements in Santo Domingo, Haiti, and the Virgin Islands," in George H. Blakeslee (ed.), *Mexico and the Caribbean: Clark University Addresses*. New York: G. E. Stechert, 1920, 224–47.

Tomasek, Robert D. "Defense of the Western Hemisphere: A Need for Re-examination of United States Policy," *Midwest Journal of Political Science*, III (November, 1959), 374–401.

Troncoso Sánchez, Pedro. "Posiciones de principio en la historia política dominicana," *Journal of Inter-American Studies*, IX (April, 1967), 184–94.

"Trujillo Builds for War," *U.S. News & World Report*, February 3, 1950, 19.

Trujillo, Flor de Oro [as told to Laura Bergquist]. "My Tormented Life as Trujillo's Daughter," *Look* (June 15, 1965), 44ff.; and "My Life as Trujillo's Prisoner," *Look* (June 29, 1965), 52ff.

Trujillo Molina, Rafael Leonidas. "Los principos de no intervención y la solidaridad panamericana," *Revista de las Fuerzas Armadas* [Santo Domingo], X (enero, 1959), 53–54.

"United States Foreign Policy and the Caribbean Situation," *Congressional Digest*, XXXIX (November, 1960), entire issue.

Varney, Harold Lord. "What Is Behind the Galindez Case?", *The American Mercury*, LXXXIV (June, 1957), 34–42.

Villard, Oswald Garrison. "Men and Issues—Santo Domingo 1937," *The Nation*, CXLIV (March 3, 1937), 323–24.

Welles, Sumner. "Intervention and Interventions," *Foreign Affairs*, XXVI (October, 1947), 116–33.

Wells, Henry. "The OAS and the Dominican Elections," *Orbis*, VII (Spring, 1963), pp. 150–63.

Whitaker, Arthur P. "Development of American Regionalism; The Organization of American States: Keeping the Peace in the Americas," *International Conciliation*, No. 469 (March, 1951), pp. 153–57.

————. "Inter-American Intervention," *Current History*, X (March, 1946), 206–11.

————. "Problems of Representative Democracy in Latin America," *Social Science*, XXVIII (October, 1953), 211–15.

Wiarda, Howard J. "The Changing Political Orientation of the Catholic Church in the Dominican Republic," *Journal of Church and Society*, VII (Spring, 1965), pp. 238–54.

————. "The Development of the Labor Movement in the Dominican Republic," *Inter-American Economic Affairs*, XX (Summer, 1966), 41–63.

————. "Dictatorship and Development: The Trujillo Regime and Its Implications," *The Southwestern Social Science Quarterly*, XLVIII (March, 1968), 548–57.

————. "The Dominican Republic: Dictatorship, Development, and Disintegration," Chap. 10 in Martin Needler (ed.), *Political Systems of Latin America*. 2nd ed. New York: Van Nostrand Reinhold, 1970.

————. "The Dominican Revolution in Perspective: A Research Note," *Polity*, I (Fall, 1968), pp. 114–24.

————. "From Fragmentation to Disintegration: The Social and Political Aspects of the Dominican Revolution," *América Latina*, X (abril–junio, 1967), pp. 55–71.

————. "The Politics of Civil-Military Relations in the Dominican Republic," *Journal of Inter-American Studies*, VII (October, 1965), 465–84.

————. "Trujilloism Without Trujillo," *The New Republic*, CLI (September 19, 1964), 5–6.

Wilcox, Francis O. "The Monroe Doctrine and World War Two," *American Political Science Review*, XXVI (June, 1942), 433–53.

Williams, Benjamin H. "The Coming of Economic Sanctions into American Practice," *American Journal of International Law,* XXXVII (July, 1943), 386–96.

Wilson, Larman C. "The Dominican Policy of the United States: The Illusions of Economic Development and Elections," *World Affairs,* CXXVIII (July–August–September, 1965), 93–101.

———. "The Monroe Doctrine, Cold War Anachronism: Cuba and the Dominican Republic," *Journal of Politics,* XXVIII (May, 1966), 322–46.

Wolf, Thomas. "The Caribbean Khan," *The Washington Post,* November 27, 28, 29, 30 and December 1, 1960.

Wright, Theodore P., Jr. "Free Elections in the Latin American Policy of the United States," *Political Science Quarterly,* LXXIV (March, 1959), pp. 89–112.

———. "The United States and Latin American Dictatorship: The Case of the Dominican Republic," *Journal of International Affairs,* XIV (1960), 152–57.

Wyckoff, Theodore. "The Role of the Military in Contemporary Latin American Politics," *Western Political Quarterly,* XIII (September, 1960), pp. 747–62.

Ziegler, Jean. "Santo Domingo: Feudo de Trujillo," *Cuadernos* [Paris], No. 46 (enero–febrero, 1961), 98–102.

VI. NEWS SOURCES

Council on Foreign Relations. *The United States in World Affairs.* Annual. New York: Harper & Row, 1930–1963.

The New York Times. Daily. September, 1929, through August, 1964.

The Washington Post. Daily. January, 1961, through June, 1962.

VII. UNPUBLISHED MATERIALS

Atkins, George P. *The United States and the Dominican Republic During the Era of Trujillo.* Ph.D. dissertation, American University, 1966.

Bacon, Robert C. *United States Policy Toward Latin American Dictators.* Ph.D. dissertation, University of Southern California, 1959.

Curry, Earl R. *The United States and the Dominican Republic, 1924–1933: Dilemma in the Caribbean.* Ph.D. dissertation, University of Minnesota, 1965.

Foreign Policy Research Institute, University of Pennsylvania. "Summary of Major Economic and Financial Developments in the Dominican Republic in the Post-World War II Period and Their Importance for Political Development," *Caribbean Development and American Security: Case Studies* (Interim Report 1966–67). II. Philadelphia: Foreign Policy Research Institute, 1967.

Francis, Michael J. *Attitudes of the United States Government Toward Collective Military Arrangements with Latin America, 1945–1960.* Ph.D. dissertation, University of Virginia, 1963.

Geisler, Richard Arnold. *Measures for Military Collaboration Between the United States and Latin America: The Record, 1826–1951.* Ph.D. dissertation, New York University, 1955.

González, Luis M. *The Economic History of the Dominican Republic from 1916 Through 1956.* M.A. thesis, University of Miami, 1956.

Horst, O. H. *The Legacy of Trujillo in Santo Domingo.* Paper presented at the Fifty-seventh Annual Meeting of the Association of American Geographers, Miami Beach, Florida, April 22–26, 1962.

Lamp, Harold R. *The United States Role in Dominican Republic Transition Toward Democracy: 1960–1961.* M.A. thesis, Georgetown University, 1964.

Lowenthal, Abraham F. *The Dominican Crisis of 1965: A Study of United States Foreign Policy.* Paper presented to the Seminar on the Dominican Republic, Center for International Affairs, Harvard University, February 2, 1967.

———. *Lessons of the Dominican Crisis* (Final Memo for the Seminar on the Dominican Republic, Center for International Affairs, Harvard University, January, 1968).

MacMichael, David C. *The United States and the Dominican Republic, 1877–1940: A Cycle in Caribbean Diplomacy.* Ph.D. dissertation, University of Oregon, 1966.

———. *High Tide of Empire: The American Occupation of the Dominican Republic, 1916–1924.* M.A. thesis, University of Oregon, 1961.

Rys, John Frank. *Tension and Conflicts in Cuba, Haiti, and the Dominican Republic Between 1945 and 1959.* Ph.D. dissertation, American University, 1966.

Slater, Jerome. *The OAS and Political Change in Latin America.* Paper presented to the Seminar on the Dominican Republic, Center for International Affairs, Harvard University, March 30, 1967.

——— *The Role of the Organization of American States in United States Foreign Policy, 1947–1963.* Ph.D. dissertation, Princeton University, 1965.

Themo, Elaine Marie. *The Processes and Structures in the Development of Nationalism: A Case Study of the Dominican Republic.* Ph.D. dissertation, American University, 1969.

Wiarda, Howard J. *The Aftermath of the Trujillo Dictatorship: The Emergence of a Pluralistic Political System in the Dominican Republic.* Ph.D. dissertation, University of Florida, 1965.

―――. *The Context of United States Policy Toward the Dominican Republic: Background to the Revolution of 1965.* Paper presented to the Seminar on the Dominican Republic, Center for International Affairs, Harvard University, December 8, 1966.

―――. *Trujillo's Dominican Republic: A Case Study in the Methods of Control.* M.A. thesis, University of Florida, 1962.

―――. *Trujillo's Dominican Republic: The Legacy of Dictatorship.* Paper presented at the annual meeting of the southwestern Political Science Association, Dallas, Texas, March 23, 1967.

Wilson, Larman C. *The Principle of Non-Intervention in Recent Inter-American Relations: The Challenge of Anti-Democratic Regimes.* Ph.D. dissertation, University of Maryland, 1964.

―――. *United States Military Assistance to the Dominican Republic, 1916–1967.* Paper presented to the Seminar on the Dominican Republic, Center for International Affairs, Harvard University, April 20, 1967.

Winters, John A. *Eisenhower—"Good Partner" of Latin American Dictators: A Critical Study of United States Hemispheric Defense Policy.* Ph.D. dissertation, University of Chicago, 1963.

VIII. INTERVIEWS AND CORRESPONDENCE

Col. Bevan G. Cass, USMC, Marine Corps Basic School, Quantico, Virginia, on February 23, 1967. Former Military Attaché in the Dominican Republic.

Dominican Air Force and Army Military Attachés, Washington, D.C., on September 19, 1967.

Ambassador Thomas C. Mann, Washington, D.C., on April 18, 1968. Former Assistant Secretary of State for Inter-American Affairs.

Col. Edward Simmons, USMC, National War College, Washington, D.C., on February 21, 1967. Former Military Attaché in the Dominican Republic.

Ambassador Ellis O. Briggs; his letter dated April 29, 1968. Well-known foreign service officer, now retired.

INDEX

232

arms (cont.)

embargo imposition, 20, 112,
113; revolutionary activity and,
39, 63, 175n48; United States
sales of, 5–6, 12, 80–81, 83, 84–
85, 86, 88, 90, 91, 94, 179n17
arrests, 107
Ascension Island, 85
assembly, right of, 83, 107
Atlantic Missile Range, 85, 88
atomic energy, 179n20
authoritarianism, 24, 25, 40, 126,
151; of occupation forces, 31–
33; political change and, 148–
50, 160, 161, 164

Balaguer, Joaquín, 43, 121, 127,
142; election of 1966 and, 147–
48, 154–55; sanctions and, 128–
29, 130, 131–32
bandits, 32
banking, 51, 71, 76, 135, 138
Batista, Fulgencio, 90, 93, 103
bauxite, 80
Bay of Samaná, 81
Beals, Carleton, quoted, 59
Bemis, Samuel Flagg, quoted,
166n10
Bennett, William Tapley, 141
Betancourt, Rómulo, 106–107; assassination attempt upon, 20–
21, 90, 108–10, 112, 115, 123,
128, 130, 155–56, 158–59
"Blue Book," 13
Bolivia, 68, 187n25
bonds: default, 29, 48, 49, 171n4;
receivership termination, 50–
52, 172n12
Bonnelly, Rafael F., 132, 133, 147

Bosch, Juan, 64, 138, 145, 147;
election of 1962 and, 134–35,
140; overthrow of, 136–37, 141,
142, 154
Braden, Spruille, 12–13, 158;
quoted, 83
Brazil, 64, 79, 80, 81, 97, 145; on
Dominican sanctions, 113–14;
military coups in, 16, 24
Briggs, Ellis O.: cited, 82–83,
174nn34, 37; quoted, 60–61
Brooks, Overton, quoted, 87
Buenos Aires Conference, 54
Bundy, McGeorge, 145
Bunker, Ellsworth, 145–46
Burdette, Franklin L., 122
Butler, George H., 61

Caamaño, Francisco, 142, 145
Canada, 96
capability analysis, 4, 8
Cape Francis Viejo, 179n20
Caracas, Venezuela, 110
Caribbean area, vii, viii, 5, 19, 47,
62–69, 107; United States secu-
rity and, 6, 11, 28–29, 58, 79–
80, 82, 151–52, 165n4. See also
specific nations
Caribbean Legion, 62–63, 64,
92
Cassini, Igor, 120–21
Cassini, Oleg, 120
Castro, Fidel, 90, 93, 116, 119,
137, 147, 153; Trujillo and, 103,
111, 114, 123, 160
Cater, Douglas, 77
Cayo Confites, Cuba, 64, 92
censorship, 53–54, 83, 107, 130
Chile, 4, 81, 104, 187n25

ABOUT THE AUTHORS

G. Pope Atkins is a graduate of the University of Texas and holds the M.A. and Ph.D. degrees from The American University. He is a member of the political science faculty at the U.S. Naval Academy, specializing in comparative and international politics with particular interest in Latin-American and inter-American relations. He has lived in Argentina and Ecuador, visited a number of other Latin-American countries, and has taught at The American University and the University of Ecuador.

Larman C. Wilson received his B.A. degree from Nebraska State College, and the M.A. and Ph.D. degrees from the University of Maryland. He has visited eleven Latin-American countries, done field research in the Dominican Republic, and has taught at the University of Virginia, the University of Maryland, and the U.S. Naval Academy. He is presently on the faculty of the School of International Service at The American University. Dr. Wilson contributed a chapter to *The Lingering Crisis: A Case Study of the Dominican Republic* (1970) and has published articles in a number of American and Latin-American journals.

The text of this book was set in Baskerville Linofilm and printed by offset on P & S Special LL manu-factured by P. H. Glatfelter Co., Spring Grove, Pa. Composed, printed and bound by Quinn & Boden Company, Inc., Rahway, N.J. Indexed by Roberta Blaché